DEAD ON DELIVERY

DEAD ON DELIVERY

INSIDE THE DRUG WARS, STRAIGHT FROM THE STREET

ROBERT M. STUTMAN
and RICHARD ESPOSITO

WARNER BOOKS

A Time Warner Company

Lyrics from "Lido Shuffle" by Boz Scaggs and David Paich, © 1976 Boz Scaggs Music/ Hudmar Publishing Co., Inc., and "Copper," © 1979 Chapin Music are reprinted by permission.

Warner Books, Inc., 1271 Avenue of the Americas, New York, NY 10020

Ⓦ A Time Warner Company

Printed in the United States of America
First printing: June 1992
10 9 8 7 6 5 4 3 2 1

Library of Congress Cataloging-in-Publication Data

Stutman, Robert M.
    Dead on delivery / by Robert M. Stutman and Richard Esposito.
      p.   cm.
    ISBN 0-446-51558-2
    1. Stutman, Robert M. 2. Narcotic enforcement agents—United States—
Biography. 3. Narcotics, Control of—United States—History—20th century.
4. United States. Drug Enforcement Administration—History. I. Esposito,
Richard. II. Title.
HV7911.S83A3 1992
363.4'5'0973—dc20   91-50402
                                         CIP

Book design: H. Roberts

To my wife, Lee, who stood by me and raised our family during my twenty-five years in DEA, my children, Brian and Kim, and to the men and women of the DEA, who sacrifice their lives to an almost impossible mission.
—R.S.

In memory of my grandparents
and for my loving family.
—R.E.

ACKNOWLEDGMENTS

First and foremost, a thank you to Lee Stutman and Debbie Millman, without whose patience and love this book would not have been possible. We are forever grateful. Next, Brian and Kim Stutman, two fine young people who proved excellent critics of their father and his co-author.

A healthy thank you is also due Michele Parente, our researcher, who toiled with us for two years and spared us from committing many errors. Similar thanks are due the *New York Newsday* librarians, who are always thoughtful and resourceful, and Renee Lolya, whose research helped immensely in the final days.

Countless others unstintingly contributed their time and knowledge to this book. For that gift we thank all whom we list here and any we have reluctantly omitted in an effort to speed the reader along. You've sat through speeches and testimonials, we know you'll understand. Among those without whom this book could not have been written:

Our friends in law enforcement: the police officers, detectives, DEA agents, FBI agents, federal and local prosecutors, judges, clerks and secretaries, notably Ilene Weinshall of the DEA, who gave their files and their memories for us to reconstruct as the tales in this book.

The current and former public information officers of the Drug Enforcement Administration, especially Robert Strang.

The current and former public information officers of the New York City Police Department, especially Alice T. McGillion.

New York's police reporters, whose own grueling rounds did not keep them from looking out for anything that might add to a friend's book, especially Phillip Messing of the *New York Post* and John Miller of Channel 4.

Robert Drury and Mike McAlary, who were there at the start and encouraged the writers to keep going.

Dominic Croci and R. Brinkley Smithers, for their love and affection.

Our transcriber, Mary Lamont, for the thousands of pages of conversation she recorded.

The editors at *New York Newsday*, especially Donald Forst, for their time and patience.

David Black, our agent and loyal supporter.

Michael Muskal, a fine editor, who did just that, each night for two years, and painstakingly ensured that the good in this book became better and the bad became tolerable enough to show a publisher.

Larry Kirshbaum, the president of Warner Books, who took the manuscript and shaped it into a finished book. In the process he demonstrated that in the world of modern publishing a few good editors remain.

Thank you.

—R.S. & R.E.

CONTENTS

Some identities have been changed or omitted to protect people from harm or recrimination. This is true of informants, drug abusers and one or two others. In several instances, where a pending or future criminal case might be jeopardized, an investigative technique or specific fact has been withheld. These cases are few but to list them would only attract dangerous attention.

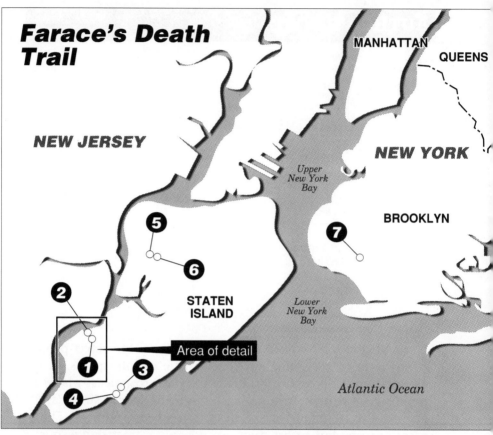

Farace's Death Trail

MANHATTAN

QUEENS

NEW JERSEY

NEW YORK

Upper New York Bay

⑤

⑥

⑦

BROOKLYN

②

STATEN ISLAND

Lower New York Bay

Area of detail

① **③**

④

Atlantic Ocean

1. The Bloomingdale Road Overpass: Here, Special Agent Hatcher met Gus Farace for five minutes on the evening of Feb. 28, 1989. They drove off in seprate cars at high speed. One hour later, Hatcher, behind the wheel of his car, was found at the meeting spot shot to death.

2. The nearby Arthur Kill Correctional Facility where Farace had served out his sentence for sexual assault and manslaughter against a homosexual man he abducted in Greenwich Village and beat to death on a Staten Island beach. At 10:01 p.m. on the night of Farace's five-minute meeting with Hatcher a guard at the prison heard the shots that killed Hatcher.

3. Gus Farace's house where on the morning of Hatcher's murder he strapped on the .357 magnum revolver later used to kill the DEA agent. (32 Melville St.)

4. Dominick Farace's father's house, just around the corner from Gus Farace's. (36 Marscher Pl.)

5. Gangster Gerry Chilli's house. He had befriended Farace in jail, and was also a suspect in the drug case Hatcher was developing. Hours after the search, agents and police knocked on the door. Chilli's daughter, Margeret (Babe) Scarpa, answered. Neither Farace nor her father was at home. (61 Sommer Ave.)

6. The apartment of Barbara Sarnelli. Farace, armed with an automatic rifle, hid here and looked out the window as agents searched Chilli's house across the street. During the nine-month hunt for Farace, which involved hundreds of door-to door searches on Staten Island, he remained safely hidden here for several weeks. (56 Sommer Ave.)

7. Nine months after the murder of Hatcher, Farace is killed on this Brooklyn street by a team of mob-sanctioned hitmen including one of his close associates. (1803 81st St. at 18th Ave.)

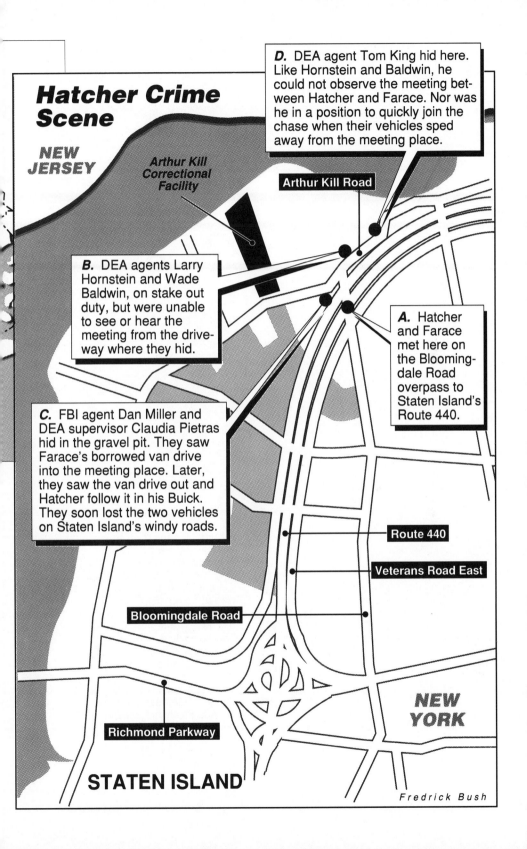

Hatcher Crime Scene

NEW JERSEY

Arthur Kill Correctional Facility

Arthur Kill Road

D. DEA agent Tom King hid here. Like Hornstein and Baldwin, he could not observe the meeting between Hatcher and Farace. Nor was he in a position to quickly join the chase when their vehicles sped away from the meeting place.

B. DEA agents Larry Hornstein and Wade Baldwin, on stake out duty, but were unable to see or hear the meeting from the driveway where they hid.

A. Hatcher and Farace met here on the Bloomingdale Road overpass to Staten Island's Route 440.

C. FBI agent Dan Miller and DEA supervisor Claudia Pietras hid in the gravel pit. They saw Farace's borrowed van drive into the meeting place. Later, they saw the van drive out and Hatcher follow it in his Buick. They soon lost the two vehicles on Staten Island's windy roads.

Route 440

Veterans Road East

Bloomingdale Road

Richmond Parkway

NEW YORK

STATEN ISLAND

Fredrick Bush

ONE

The Rules Had Changed

Everett Emerson Hatcher

Everett Hatcher, a gentle bear of a man, went to work that morning with every reason to believe he would return to his neat ranch house in Boonton, New Jersey, in time for dinner.

He arrived in Manhattan early, parked his car at 26 Federal Plaza and rode the elevator to the twenty-fourth floor where the FBI-DEA Organized Crime Drug Enforcement Task Force had offices. Hatcher had served on the task force long enough to grow weary of the petty interagency frictions. An African-American agent of the Drug Enforcement Administration, he had also begun to resent working out of the FBI's mainly white New York headquarters. But Hatcher, normally assigned to tracking Pakistani heroin traffickers or infiltrating black-run drug organizations uptown, had been drafted as the undercover agent on this case against Italian-American mobsters.

He looked forward to the end when he could be rid of the FBI and go back to working with agents he liked at the DEA's own offices in midtown. But the pace of this case made Hatcher feel that homecoming would never arrive.

By 9:30 A.M., when another DEA agent ran into him in the hall, Hatcher had the day's work well organized and had already briefed his boss, Dan Miller, the FBI agent in charge of the case. He was about to telephone the first target of the investigation, a drug dealer named Costabile "Gus" Farace, to try and arrange a meeting for later in the day.

After Miller decided there was enough evidence, agents would arrest Farace and convince him to inform on drug dealing by higher-level organized crime figures. A reduced prison sentence would be the incentive for Farace to break a lifelong code and become a rat. The top target was Bonanno crime family capo Gerry Chilli. It was his name, CHILLI, GERARD, that was typed on the index to the FBI folders for case C189Z007.

The case required Hatcher to pose as a drug-hungry, gun-dealing, rogue army colonel, a role that played off his real rank of lieutenant colonel in the Army Reserve and took advantage of his accomplishments as a marksman, one-time captain of Germany's military police and heavy weapons expert. His best days were a round of clandestine meetings with the murderous Farace, prison cell huddles with unreliable informants and regular meetings with calculating defense attorneys and prison officials. Wherever Hatcher went, a team of backup agents lurked quietly in the shadows, keeping their tether invisible while attempting to mind Hatcher from harm.

He had met with Farace twice. On February 8, he had tested the waters by talking about future drug purchases and weapons sales and Farace had appeared receptive. On February 10, the agent had purchased a little over an eighth of an ounce of cocaine. As Farace handed over the drugs, Hatcher explained that he was buying the relatively small amount to test for purity. Future purchases, he suggested, would be in the kilogram or better category. The foundation for Farace's eventual arrest had been laid. Hatcher carefully recorded the successful purchase and the incriminating conversation for the case files. The investigation was a complex enough challenge to hold the DEA agent's attention. But to Hatcher's way of thinking, the chances of success were limited by the poor way the case was being run. His boss, Miller, seemed to lack interest in the details that could make or break the effort. He appeared content to let matters such as setting up meetings or obtaining proper equipment take their own sweet time. Miller's laid-back style and Hatcher's aggressive one mixed poorly. Best days seemed few and far between.

Hatcher had complained of this to his closest friends and to someone he held infinitely closer, his wife, Mary Jane. To make matters worse, since mid-month, Farace, for some reason, had been reluctant to set up another meeting.

Now Hatcher postponed the 10 A.M. call to Farace, got up, found FBI agent Miller, and let go once more with his frustrations. This time the bout with Miller was loud enough to be heard by agents outside in the halls. How much more time and money are we going to waste on this guy? Hatcher wanted to know. He had already spent $2,500 of the government's money to buy four and a half ounces of cocaine from Farace. Now Farace kept postponing meetings. Why let Farace string us along further? We already have enough evidence to arrest him. The dope wasn't even good quality. We overpaid for it. He's low-level. Let's take him.

Even though it was his life on the line, the Harlem-born investigator found his opinions were unwanted. We'll let the investigation take its course, Miller said. Meet Farace again and try to make another buy before we arrest him.

Returning to his office at about 10:30 A.M. that morning of February 28, 1989, Hatcher knew that his day had again turned unpleasant. After leaving a message for Farace to call back, Hatcher decided to telephone home.

"I'm having a very bad day," he said. "And I have to go out on something."

"Don't go out," Mary Jane said. "Your heart is not in it."

"This is taking too long, I'm getting jerked around," Hatcher explained. Although Hatcher felt that his target was on the verge of saying yes to a meeting, he also felt something very wrong was in the offing.

"Then come home, be here as fast as you can," Mary Jane said. She had first met Everett when she was sixteen, during a summer when he worked as a lifeguard in Far Rockaway, Queens. The public beach where he worked, one of a handful of nonwhite lifeguards in the entire city, was just two houses down from her home and a stretch of private beach in front where she worked at the first-aid station. Regularly the freckle-faced young woman would hop the fence that separated public from private to visit Everett. Her Everett. They were married on May 31, 1969.

For twenty years they had borne joyfully the weight of marriage as well as the added difficulties, including the stings of the jealous and the prejudiced, that come when a white woman marries a black man. You would have thought that in law enforcement, blind prejudice would have given way to the recognition that Mary Jane, a cop's daughter, saw in her husband the same heroism and integrity she had worshipped in her father. She had not married a black man or a white man; she had married a cop she completely understood. She was especially worried by that morning's call. They had been married a long time and both she and her husband understood his job's inherent dangers. He rarely needed to call home to reassure either himself or her. The telephone call meant something was wrong. Mary Jane heard the speaker in her husband's office come on. She heard the call waiting to be answered.

"I'll be home around ten," he said, disconnecting. "There's my call. That's Gus." Hatcher asked the dealer to pick a time and a place for their long-postponed meeting. He had a buyer coming to town so he would need merchandise. Farace agreed to discuss the price of the future purchase in person. He picked his home turf, Staten Island, for the meeting. Despite Hatcher's request, he refused to meet before 9 P.M. There was no way Hatcher would be home by 10.

Costabile "Gus" Farace hung up the telephone and rubbed his misshapen left forearm. Despite years of bodybuilding it would never look quite right. He could never replace the muscle that had been torn away in a car crash. The missing tissue kept his hand from ever completely unclenching. This had earned him the nickname "the Claw." As he rubbed the arm, he pondered whether it had been wise for him to agree to another meeting with the man he knew only as "the Colonel." During the seventeen days between his most recent meeting with Hatcher on February 10 and this one, Farace had been mulling over the possibility that his customer was actually a government informant or federal agent. The suspicions were triggered by his sources in Staten Island's Arthur Kill prison where the introduction between Farace and the agent had been made. An inmate still serving time in Arthur Kill had sent word out that William "Rebel" Liberty, the inmate who introduced Farace to the Colonel, was "bad." The information was passed to Farace through his associate Petey Licata, who called Gus's house and left a message with his wife, Toni:

"Go find Gus or his cousin Dominick, Toni, tell them something is wrong with Liberty. If they are doing anything with Liberty, stop it. If they haven't started, don't bother to."

Gus Farace ducked Hatcher's urgent request for another meeting to negotiate the price of a larger drug purchase. If Liberty was bad, street slang meaning he was an informant, and he had performed the introduction to Hatcher, what, Farace wondered, did that make the Colonel? An agent? Another informer? In either case, the Colonel could be trouble, thought Gus, who had no intention of returning to prison.

"If the Colonel is bad," Gus told his cousin Dominick, "I'll do what I gotta do. Nobody is putting me back in fucking jail. Don't worry, I'll take care of it." Gus considered signing a death warrant for Hatcher. He just wished he knew whether the Colonel was an agent or an informant like Liberty.

If the Colonel was an agent, Gus knew he was in trouble because he had already sold him drugs. If the Colonel was just an informant, Gus reasoned, maybe he should kill him anyway because without him, maybe there would be no case.

At about 3 P.M. on February 28, as Hatcher prepared to meet Farace, Gus's cousin and drug-dealing associate, Dominick Farace, dropped his distinctive black Corvette at his father's house and waited to be picked up in a tan-colored van owned by Ralph Pollio, who used it in the construction business he ran from his Staten Island home. Pollio, suspected of selling drugs for the cousins, did not drive the van. It was driven by Albert Fogliani, an employee of Pollio's. Dominick and Fogliani used the van to move a television set from Dominick's father's Staten Island house, where the son had a basement apartment, to a hideaway apartment Dominick kept in New Jersey. Sometime after 5 P.M. Dominick received a telephone call there from Gus.

"Bring that thing you have over there," Gus said. Dominick removed an AR-15 semiautomatic rifle from a closet, slapped in a thirty-round banana clip, took along three smaller clips and placed everything in the van. He then drove, still accompanied by Fogliani, back to Staten Island to meet Gus.

Gus, meanwhile, slapped six Winchester rounds into the chambers of a stainless-steel snub-nosed Ruger Security Six .357 Magnum revolver and jammed the handgun into the waistband of his trousers. The rifle and handgun had been purchased from Jeff Donnelly, an associate of the cousins. The handgun rounds had been purchased in Florida by Pollio at Dominick's request. "It's for the animal," Dominick said in requesting the purchase. Pollio took that to mean Farace, who with the aid of anabolic steroids had bulked his six-foot-three-inch frame to more than 220 pounds.

On Staten Island again, Dominick and Fogliani stopped by Gus's mother's house at 61 Van Wyck Avenue. Gus came out, wearing a bulky leather jacket, and took the rifle from his cousin, then stashed it inside a mint condition 1956 Chevy that Gus kept in the yard. Gus told Fogliani they would need the van later. Fogliani drove off in it.

Dominick and Gus went inside and visited briefly with Gus Farace's wife, Toni, his mother, Mary, and Dominick's grandmother. The women had gathered to have coffee together. After a half hour, Dominick was summoned around the corner to the house of his father, Frank Farace, at 36 Marscher Place. He found his father in the kitchen talking to an old friend, Harold Donnelly, a city police officer.

It was approaching 9 P.M. Frank Farace told his friend that he had to leave for an appointment. Donnelly said in that case it was time for him to be going. Dominick's father had nowhere else to go, but was expecting wiseguy friends to stop by and did not want Donnelly to see them.

A few minutes later, Gus, still wearing the bulky jacket, arrived in his Lincoln. Dominick climbed in. Gus told him they were going to get the van and drive to New Jersey to pick up a new engine for the Chevy.

"But first we have to make one stop, I have to meet the Colonel," Gus said. They drove to Fogliani's house where Dominick picked up the keys to the van and, following his cousin, drove it back to Marscher Place and Van Wyck Avenue where Farace dropped off his Lincoln, the car he had driven to his previous meetings with the Colonel.

Once in the van, with Dominick still driving, the two men headed toward the meeting with Hatcher on Bloomingdale Road. They stopped once for Gus to buy a pack of Marlboros. They had left the AR-15 in the Chevy, but beneath his jacket Gus was carrying his Magnum.

Along the way the cousins debated whether the Colonel was a drug dealer, an informant or a cop.

"Is he good or bad, whadda you think, cuz?" Gus wondered. "Cause if he's bad, I gotta whack him."

When they arrived at the meeting they did not see the BMW the Colonel had driven the previous time. Instead a gray car was waiting.

They pulled alongside the driver's window and Gus leaned out the passenger side of the van, saw the driver was the Colonel, and told him to follow them to a diner. Hatcher too had changed vehicles tonight. No big thing.

When Mary Jane Hatcher made dinner for herself and their two sons, nine-year-old Zackery and three-year-old Joshua, she thought to leave her husband's in the microwave. She knew the way cases and meetings dragged out. She might be asleep when he finally came home.

It was already approaching dinnertime when Hatcher, Miller, Claudia Pietras, the DEA co-supervisor on the case, and the agents who would provide Hatcher's safety net met at 7 P.M. to be briefed.

Miller directed. Farace had agreed to meet Hatcher but cautiously picked as the spot a deserted overpass on the farthest reaches of Staten Island, New York City's most out-of-the-way borough. The meeting would be after dark. The combination of geography and time meant surveillance would be difficult. But, Miller stressed, there was little to worry about. Hatcher would not be exchanging drugs or money with Farace tonight, just discussing the price and quality of an upcoming shipment.

"Who's going to cover the undercover agent?" interrupted Wade Baldwin, one of the backup agents. He wanted to know who would be the agent closest to Hatcher.

"Don't worry about it," Miller said. "He's not going anywhere with a black guy." With no merchandise to pick up, Hatcher was not expected to leave the meeting spot with Farace. Miller felt there would be no need to plan for a difficult moving surveillance.

But Miller also knew, or should have known, that Farace had killed a black man. The murder took place after Farace and friends picked up the man and his companion on a Greenwich Village street, forced them into a car, and began a gang sex assault during the drive back to Staten Island. The assault continued on a beach. It did not end until Farace had beaten in the man's brains with a piece of driftwood. The second victim survived his beating to testify, sending Farace and the others to prison. In June, Farace had been released after serving seven years, the minimum sentence for manslaughter. The state had accepted his plea to the lesser charge of manslaughter rather than go through the uncertainty and expense of a murder trial.

It was in prison that Farace met Chilli, the mobster the agents now hoped he would betray. Chilli, fifty-eight, had adopted Farace, then in his late twenties. Capo or no, Chilli knew a muscular young man was a good friend to have in prison. Farace, whose cousin Greg Scarpa, Jr., was an acting capo in the Colombo crime family, knew that having ties in two mob families would work nicely for him. At the time of his release, Farace, with the blessings of both mob families, stepped into the drug trade.

As the briefing drew to a close at 8 P.M., Hatcher told his backup team, DEA agents Baldwin, Tom King and Larry Hornstein, "No money, no drugs, nothing to worry about." For once, he and Miller seemed to agree that the night's meeting

would go smoothly. Hatcher did not mention his earlier misgivings.

With seventeen years' experience as an undercover agent, and confident the meeting was routine, Hatcher locked his machine gun, DEA credentials and badge in the trunk of his car and placed his Glock semiautomatic pistol in the glove compartment rather than risk a pat-down search and the dealer's questions if a weapon was found. As his only insurance, Hatcher took along a compact voice transmitter, an often balky machine known as a T-4. Taped under his shirt, the remote microphone would allow him to whisper instructions to the backup team. Ideally, it would allow them to overhear his entire conversation with Farace. Should anything go wrong, Hatcher would be heavily dependent on a quick response from the team. But he was more concerned about the slow pace of the case than about the risk of being armed only with the poorly performing transmitter. Now that the drug dealer had agreed to meet him, Hatcher didn't want to cancel because of unreliable equipment. He wanted to get this case moving again.

The backup team departed for the meeting at 8:15 P.M. and Hatcher gave them a good start before beginning his drive to Staten Island, a precaution in case Farace was having him tailed. The dealer wasn't that careful, but the lead still gave the other agents plenty of time to set up. If Farace arrived early and the backup team was visible, Hatcher wanted to be far away and able to deny any connection to the cops.

As soon as the backups had a chance to look around, they could tell that the drug dealer had chosen well. At night, the overpass was like a clear plateau, far above and out of sight from the highway and its access ramps. Bushes and trees blocked any view from the windows of the nearest houses. Nor was there any place to hide along the narrow shoulders of the overpass. The area was deserted after dark, so any car parked on the street would risk arousing the dealer's suspicion. Surveillance would be difficult.

The backup agents, joined by the supervisors, Miller and the DEA's Pietras, reluctantly took up their distant positions at 8:45 P.M., fifteen minutes before the scheduled 9 P.M. meeting. From their hiding places none could see the actual inter-section of Bloomingdale Road and Route 440 where Farace and Hatcher would meet.

Miller and Pietras had backed their car into the closest cover, the mouth of a gravel pit along the sole approach from the south side of the overpass. Larry Hornstein and Wade Baldwin were in Hornstein's car, hidden at the top of a steep driveway that looked down on another approach, a section of rutted road that looped behind a hardware store before straightening out 500 yards north of the overpass. King was also staked out on the north side of the overpass. From his position, several hundred yards farther away than Hornstein and Baldwin, he could see only a third approach. This one ran parallel to the north side of the highway before rising and turning onto the overpass. With five agents divided into three widely spaced teams, only one group, the one stationed along the approach road the dealer actually selected, would see him arrive. As luck would have it, Farace chose the road watched by Pietras and Miller.

At 9:05 P.M., Hatcher, driving his Buick Regal sedan, pulled into the meeting spot. Farace pulled in right behind him.

"He's coming into the area with the undercover agent," Miller whispered into his portable police radio to alert the other agents.

Goddamn it, Hornstein thought, tense behind the wheel of his Mercury Cougar, the agent I'm supposed to protect is completely out of my sight.

Five minutes later, Hornstein was startled to hear another outside transmission so soon after the meeting had begun.

"Did you hear anything over the T-4?" Miller asked.

"I haven't heard shit," Hornstein replied.

"Well, I heard something to the effect that he's going to a diner or a restaurant two miles away," Miller said.

Once again, the voice transmitter had failed. Of the three cars staking out the meeting, only Miller's had received the garbled broadcast. Hornstein was not surprised; the T-4 had failed on the last meeting with Farace. Every agent knew that the machine was nowhere near as good as the government could provide. Reports indicated that the T-4 failed 50 percent of the time. For all its talk about the war on drugs, the government continued to skimp on equipment. But just now Hornstein had a more pressing worry. Hatcher was leaving and Hornstein knew it would be difficult to follow him undetected on these empty roads.

"Check the intersection," Miller said. He neglected to tell Hornstein that he and Pietras had already pulled out of the gravel pit and were three miles away, following Hatcher's Buick and Farace's van.

Hornstein flicked on the lights and wheeled his black Cougar down the steep gravel and dirt drive onto the road behind the hardware store. Then he turned in front of the store to check the intersection on his side of the overpass. He was looking for Hatcher's Buick and a dark brown Lincoln town car. Miller had also failed to relay that the dealer had not used the vehicle the agents were briefed to expect but had switched to a tan van. In any case, Hornstein saw nothing but a vacant intersection.

When Miller finally broadcast that he was behind Hatcher—who was now following the van down the south service road of the highway that ran under the overpass—it was too late for Hornstein, Baldwin and King. They couldn't speed from the opposite side of the highway to box in Hatcher and the suspects. Hatcher had only the car containing Miller and Pietras to cover his back.

The van sped through an intersection and Hatcher followed as the signal light turned from green to yellow. It turned red as Pietras approached. She paused. By the time she regained speed, Hatcher was out of sight.

"We've lost him," Miller broadcast.

What had begun as a routine meeting between Hatcher and a drug dealer had now collapsed amid a flurry of mistakes.

During the meeting Hornstein's mission was simple: Stay out of sight; listen, observe and protect the undercover agent. Many things aren't supposed to happen in an undercover operation but it seemed that all of them had taken place in this one. The backup team was out of position, the equipment had failed and the undercover agent had moved when he was expected to stay in one place. It didn't help that the meeting had been held against a backdrop of friction between Hatcher and the FBI supervisor on the case.

As Hatcher and the dealer sped through the maze of dark and unfamiliar streets, Hatcher's minders were at a serious disadvantage. The island's many deserted byways were a mystery to those who lived off its shore. Gus Farace, however, had grown up there.

He and his cousin Dominick drove briskly even though they had yet to decide which diner they would go to. They discussed their destination as they drove, never once looking back to see if they were being followed, but never exceeding the area's fifty-mile-an-hour speed limit.

In the end, they did not go to a diner at all, but to the Marina Cafe, a bar and restaurant on Mansion Avenue owned by associates of the Faraces. This change of plans and the now-total failure of Hatcher's transmitter further frustrated the backup team's attempting to track them. Not one of the agents knew the haunts of the Staten Island underworld, a knowledge they should have had readily available since it was already in the DEA's case files. They resorted to fruitless checks of the few open diners on nearby Hylan Boulevard.

Once inside the Marina Cafe, Gus called Dominick by the name "Pete" as a protective measure in case the Colonel, who was dressed in a shirt and tie, was also wearing a hidden tape recorder. They did not bother to frisk him. Pete was also the first name of the man who had told Farace that Hatcher might be bad, Petey Licata. But if Gus was looking for a revealing flicker of knowledge in Hatcher's eyes, he did not share that with his cousin Dominick.

Seated at the bar, Farace and the Colonel talked business. Dominick sometimes listened, sipped a club soda and otherwise occupied himself by watching television.

Once, looking up at the sound of his cousin's laugh, he saw Hatcher make gestures that seemed to promise Gus a shoulder-held rocket launcher. At another point he heard the two men negotiate a price of between $7,900 and $8,700 for a half kilogram of cocaine. They had two drinks each during the course of this conversation; then Gus went to the bathroom.

When he did, Hatcher turned to Dominick and pointed out the beautiful boats in the marina. Someday, he added, he would like to have a boat of his own.

Gus returned and resumed his conversation with Hatcher. After twenty-five minutes they decided it was time to leave. Rising, Gus leaned over to his cousin and said, "He's a good guy, right?" The twenty-three-page, single-spaced, legal-size document of Dominick's subsequent conversations with government interrogators does not contain his answer.

The document next notes how Gus then told the Colonel they would show him the way to the highway, and once again the gray Buick followed the tan van, this time back toward Bloomingdale Road.

Inside the van, Dominick explained, Gus continued to wrestle with the idea that the Colonel might be bad.

"He seems like a nice guy," he said at one point.

"But I don't know," he said later.

"I can't take any chances," he said later still.

Gus seemed to be talking more to himself than to Dominick. By the time Dominick drove past St. Joseph's by the Sea, a Roman Catholic church on Hylan Boulevard, Gus had made up his mind.

"Fuck it, I think I'll kill him," Gus said.

Dominick saw the church in the background as he turned his head to see his cousin's expression. The look in Gus's eyes said he wasn't kidding.

"You gotta be out of your mind," Dominick screamed. They were almost halfway back to the meeting spot. Hatcher was right behind them.

"I'll kill him at the next traffic light," Gus replied.

"You can't just kill somebody at a fucking red light in the middle of Hylan Boulevard right in the middle of a neighborhood where everybody knows you. Gus, you can't just clip somebody at a red light. Are you nuts, are you nuts, cuz?" Dominick was so agitated that he found his head was hitting the roof of the van and his palms were sweating.

"It's okay, cuz, relax. I'll take care of everything," Gus said.

They continued their drive back to the original meeting

spot without mentioning murder again. By the time they arrived, Dominick thought his cousin had changed his mind.

Dominick stopped the van in the middle of the road. Hatcher squeezed his Buick onto the right shoulder, rolled down the window and tilted his head up to talk with Gus, who was leaning out the passenger window of the van. Gus extended his left hand out the window, pointing toward the service road of the highway beneath the overpass, as if giving the Colonel directions.

Within seconds, Gus had put his other hand under the bulky leather jacket, pulled out the powerful Ruger handgun and fired three shots.

"Let's go," he shouted and Dominick stepped on the gas. As they lurched away at high speed, Gus, without bothering to lean out the window, stuck his arm back out and fired a final shot. It too struck Hatcher.

Then Gus slumped back into his seat, the Magnum still in his right hand. He kept it there, resting in his lap, as they fled the scene.

After a while, Gus suddenly began to laugh. Then he told Dominick to relax. "Ease up, cuz, everything went perfect."

A few minutes later, exhausted after an hour of unsuccessful searching, the agents on Hatcher's backup team returned to the meeting place on the chance that Hatcher had doubled back.

Hornstein and Baldwin were the first to arrive. As soon as Hornstein pulled his speeding coupe through the last curve in the dark country road he saw the gray Buick. After the frantic search it felt like he had stumbled upon an open grave. The exhausted DEA agent tried to shake off a bitter chill.

"Hatch is dead," Hornstein said softly to Baldwin, envisioning already what he would see when he stepped up to the car and peered inside. No sign of understanding registered on Baldwin's young face. He was twenty-two, ten months out of the DEA's fourteen-week training school, and already close to shock after listening for the past hour to the jumbled and angry radio transmissions among three cars of desperate agents seeking their missing companion. He had not spent enough time in the company of death to know how it could pervade a place. Hornstein had. He had been a street cop in Baltimore before joining the DEA, and he had had a street cop's experience with death: homicide, suicide, natural causes. There was no question that this one was a homicide.

The chromed nose of Hatcher's Buick was pressed hard against the edge of the halo that a lone street light cast down on the foot of the overpass, marking the end of the twisted two-lane road. A trail of warm exhaust spilled steadily from the idling car's tailpipe into the cold night. The brake lights were on.

Hornstein slammed on the brakes and threw his Cougar into park. It bucked, fighting off momentum. He jumped out to the sound of dislodged stones. The cold hit him. There was no more of the adrenaline that had pumped so hard during the search. His anger at letting Hatcher die alone had used it all up. They should never have let this meeting between Hatcher and the drug dealer go down, Hornstein thought as he sprinted the last steps to the idling Buick.

Blood still trickled from Hatcher's right eye.

Hornstein was transfixed by death. His eyes were riveted on the form slumped in its brown overcoat behind the steering wheel. Then he remembered the scrubby trees and the possibility that the killer might still be around. He saw no one. The killer had fled. Hornstein left his Smith & Wesson in its ankle holster.

When the silence exploded it was with fear and hysteria.

"Hatch is dead," Hornstein shouted.

Baldwin had followed his partner to the Buick and now he was forced to confront the enormity of death. The rest of the search party pulled up in time to see him throw up his hands and scream.

Tom King got out of his car.

"Hatch is dead," Hornstein said, fighting to return control to his voice.

"You're kidding me," King answered.

Pietras and Miller could not get out of their car. Pietras put her hands to her face and started to cry.

King called for help on an open frequency monitored by

radio buffs, drug dealers, reporters, firemen, police officers. The agent's death was public now.

Hornstein sprinted a few yards to the first house where lights burned. He banged on the door.

"Police. Emergency," he shouted. The startled woman who lived there let him in to use the phone. He dialed the DEA communications base in Manhattan and asked them to make doubly sure an ambulance and local police assistance were on the way. He warned that the killer had escaped and gave the dispatcher the few descriptive details he had. The dispatcher would now prepare the first radio bulletins of the manhunt. Hornstein was then connected to DEA operations chief Kevin Gallagher. He repeated the hasty briefing.

Official notification made, he zipped his parka and hurried back to what he now thought of as the crime scene.

"Don't touch anything," he said. "It's too late to help Hatch."

Hatcher's Regal was in the gear marked Drive. But Hatcher's left foot was pressed down on the brake pedal and the more than 200 pounds of the agent's dead weight held the car in place. Hornstein could tell from the very small amount of blood on the upholstery that Hatcher's heart had stopped pumping almost the second he was hit. The agent's mobile telephone was resting on the seat beside him. The window on the driver's side was partially rolled down. Hatcher's head was turned toward it, as though he were answering a question. He couldn't be angry with Hatcher for overconfidence; that was the way undercover agents needed to be. They took all the risks. It was the backup team that was supposed to keep the unexpected in check.

"We'll leave Hatch where he is until the homicide detectives arrive. None of us saw anything, we're going to need all the physical evidence we can get," Hornstein said. With no eyewitness to the shooting, he wanted to protect whatever traces the killer might have left behind. Fingerprints. Hair. Tire tracks. Anything that could be saved from a careless hand or foot.

The homicide detectives would be on their way soon enough. They would determine and the medical examiner would later confirm that four heavy-caliber slugs, killer rounds from a .357 Magnum, had passed through the open car window and torn life away from Everett Hatcher. They would find little in the way of physical evidence. The killer had left no fingerprints, hair or shell casings that could be used in court.

The moment of death, they would establish, occurred at 10:02 P.M. That was when the guard standing in the tower at Staten Island's Arthur Kill Correctional Facility told them he heard the pistol shots as they echoed across the salt marsh to the prison. He had turned his wrist and checked his watch.

Mary Jane Hatcher, not knowing she had been widowed, sat straight up in bed. Normally a sound sleeper, she awoke thinking that she heard her husband in the kitchen.

Within a half hour after the shots were fired, federal agents, police officials and senior investigators across the city dropped whatever they were doing and began speeding toward the scene to help piece together the homicide and organize the manhunt. Satisfied that the crime scene would be kept intact until they arrived, Hornstein knew he had fulfilled the responsibilities of the first officer on the scene. There was nothing more he could do that might later help to avenge Hatcher's death.

He again felt the cold, a bitter cold that seemed to come from inside. He ran back to the house to make the second phone call.

TWO

The Crime Scene

I slowed a little to pick up the thin plastic handset of the car telephone and listened to the voice of an exhausted Larry Hornstein.

"I'm sorry, Mr. Stutman," he said. "We lost him."

"It's okay, we can skip that. Kevin Gallagher reached me at home," I said. "Just tell me what happened, pal." Hornstein had been pulled from my personal security detail to work this case. I trusted my life to his judgment. If Everett Hatcher had been killed while Hornstein watched his back, then something had gone terribly wrong.

I found the clipboard wedged between the blue velour seats and scribbled notes from his briefing by the green light of the armored Buick Riviera's digital instruments. It took less than two minutes. "There was hardly any blood," he said. "But I knew he was dead as soon as I returned to the overpass."

I hung up, those words still ringing, and replaced the clipboard. In my twenty-four years of law enforcement, much of it in command, I had never had an agent killed. I was numb. I turned on the flashing lights and siren and stepped on the gas.

I aimed the car for the approach to the Outerbridge Crossing that separated Staten Island from the New Jersey suburbs where both Hatcher and I lived. Beneath the crossing lay the waters of the Arthur Kill. A dank estuary of New York's inner harbor, its marshy islets, despite the grit and oil of urban pollution, somehow remain a breeding ground for blue herons and egrets. Those birds survived by fleeing each time a human approached. Like politicians faced with a drug epidemic, I couldn't help thinking. The United States was no closer in 1989 to addressing the overarching question of why society seemed to need drugs; no closer to creating the police, education and treatment policies to effectively attack drugs than the nation had been when I became a narc. It was a bitter thought. I didn't know what else to think about. There wasn't much I could do until I got to the crime scene.

When I saw the distant beacons I raced the final miles, braking only to identify myself to the uniformed policeman whose blue-and-white patrol car with the bar of flashing colored lights on the roof blocked the foot of the off-ramp at Staten Island's Route 440. I asked, "How far?"

"Right over there," the policeman answered. "I'm sorry." He set his lips into a thin line and pointed out the overpass now draped with the yellow-and-fluorescent-pink tape of a crime scene. The car swerved as I braked too hard.

It was about 11:30 P.M. Homicide detectives huddled, comparing the details that already filled their first notebooks. The tough cops from the Emergency Service Unit had brought in their generators and set up powerful floodlights. It's something I'll never forget. The place was so bright that it almost looked like a stage set. Fifty feet away from where I had parked, I could see Hatcher behind the wheel. For the first time, I realized the body was still in the car where he had been killed.

I felt a cold knot in my stomach, a twist of pain that I tried to keep from showing on my face. Dozens of cops were watching me. I had anticipated the neatness of a body under a sheet on a stretcher, something finished and complete, the way it often was when I arrived at the scene of a crime. The savagery of murder hit me like a sledge. As I got closer I could see the bullet hole in his face. I could see it clearly under his right eye, beside his nose. His head was slumped back and turned toward me. As I walked to his side I could see a bullet hole right in his ear. I throttled the urge to strike out. Instead, I stood there feeling impotent and anguished, trying to appear calm as my blood raged.

The city's ranking police officials had already arrived. They had gotten out of bed or up from a late dinner and into winter overcoats to play their funereal parts. They and the homicide detectives were waiting to shepherd me through. I was amazed and grateful when I saw First Deputy Police Commissioner Dick Condon. For him to be out there with my guy shot was tremendous. This was not his cop killed.

Condon, like several top police officials, was able to cope with the frantic crowds and frontier-town violence of much of the city by keeping his home in this more tranquil borough of Staten Island. Here, much of the time, the pace of life seemed almost rural, certainly a match for any suburb within sixty miles of Manhattan. So the man who day to day ran the 36,000 officers and employees of New York's Finest had arrived before me.

In the past Condon had often said how he disliked these things. When it had been his cop slain, he had wondered aloud why every official got dressed to go—it was, after all, the detectives who would do the actual investigating. But Condon always went and stood death duty. It was expected. When there was yet another officer killed, or yet another piece of violence of such magnitude that it seemed to threaten to take seven million people in New York another step closer to living in chaos, the top officials came.

Our presence was meant to suggest the talons of official vengeance would soon claw the violator. This manhunt was to have the weight of the nation behind it. I knew when I spoke to the media I would stress that. Standing there, by my first dead agent, beside police officials who lost nearly a dozen cops a year, I quickly realized federal officials like myself saw a lot less of the callous violence that accompanied policy decisions than did our brethren in the blue uniforms who, month after month, conduct manhunt after manhunt for another killer of another cop.

Condon touched my arm.

"Anything you need, Bob." He said it softly enough to comfort, but he said it firmly and no words had been wasted. I would have whatever assistance he could provide.

"How do we stand on catching the guy?" I replied.

Steam coming from his mouth, his boyish face and sandy hair and the collar turned up on his dark winter trenchcoat, he looked like a priest as he set his jaw. Like a number of cops, Condon had a cleric in the family. "I've put all my people at your disposal," he answered. The heavy-weapons teams, crime scene experts, homicide detectives were all ready and waiting for orders.

Then I spotted Chief Francis Hall, the head of the city's narcotics police squad. He was standing far away from the crowd that had gathered inside the flapping crime scene tapes and seemed to be bearing the cold like a burdensome, but necessary, coat. Hall stood on the shoulder of the highway overpass about a hundred yards from where Hatcher was slain. His wide eyes sparkled in a face stretched tight with pain, so tight that his polished, raw-boned, bald head looked like a death mask.

"I'm burned out," Hall said. "I can't take the body count anymore." Twenty-two days earlier in the thirty-fifth year of his career, he had handed in his retirement papers after a year that seemed filled with scenes like this. If he was lucky, he would see no more dead narcotics officers or agents before he left the job.

By this time, the U.S. Attorney in charge of federal narcotics cases in the region, Charles Rose, arrived. Since the NYPD Crime Scene Unit was already there, Rose saw no need to wait for the federal evidence experts to arrive.

We went over to open Hatcher's car. He had been sitting in it for over two hours now and the faster we logged the evidence the faster we could get him out. I badly wanted to do that. Too many people were gathered here and whatever lesson they could learn from his mute body was already learned. Now I wanted to restore whatever dignity I could to his death.

We found his wallet credentials in the trunk. We removed the official picture and passed it to the search teams. They would need it in their effort to find people who had seen the agent and his killer together. The shadowy figures in the fleeing van that the backup team had seen would not amount to much in court.

"We're lucky Larry thought to preserve the evidence, Bob," Kevin Gallagher said. He had been standing next to Condon. "That was a good split-second decision. This looks like a bad one and we're going to need whatever we can get."

Also in the trunk, in a dull, black leather case that had molded to its shape, was Hatcher's badge, a gold eagle perched atop a gold globe with sunbeams radiating out to the edges. After seventeen years each detail was as easy to read in the leather as it was in the gold.

As Rose put the shield in his pocket his pale eyes softened. A cop's son, part Welsh and part Italian, the prosecutor said he hoped that one day he would take it out again, to shove it in Farace's face.

I saw Hornstein with a group of agents and homicide detectives, and behind them, Dan Miller and Claudia Pietras sitting in a car. These two agents were obviously in terrible shape, so I went to them first.

"What happened?" I asked.

"We lost him as he went through a red light," Pietras answered. She was sitting behind the wheel looking forlorn.

"Listen, nobody blames you," I said. "Surveillance is not something you can guarantee. It is an art, not a science. If it was a science we would not need agents."

The point I was trying to make was an important one. There was no doubt in my mind that they had made mistakes. There was no doubt in Hornstein's mind that he had made mistakes. If Hatcher were alive there would have been no doubt in his mind that he too had made mistakes. But he was dead, and all the blame in the world wasn't going to bring him back.

I turned to Hornstein.

"What do you need?" I asked. He limited his response to the case.

"The homicide guys were asking me for almost an hour, 'Who is the suspect? Where does he live?' But Dan was in bad shape. Finally, I had to pull open the door to his car and physically take him out to get the information. It was all in his notebook. Now that we have it, I guess we need to go hit some houses," he said.

"Fine," I replied. "I want you out with the Emergency Service cops that hit the important spots. When they do, I want someone with them who can make a good identification of the suspect."

I walked over to a group of young agents who were uncomfortably shifting their weight from one foot to the other while making certain they kept a good distance from Hatcher's car.

"I want you to go up there and take a look at it. As gruesome as it is, and believe me it is gruesome, learn a lesson that this isn't a game," I said. I felt that was the most important thing I could tell them. It was a lesson that I had just completed learning myself, one that had begun, for me, two years earlier.

Ronald Reagan, midway through his last term as president, had proposed to radically reduce federal funding of anti-drug efforts. The pronouncement came five and a half months after Reagan announced with the fervor of a television minister that he would head the national crusade against drugs. As had three presidents before and one after him, Reagan ensured the nation's anti-drug policy was dead on arrival.

The day he did so, January 20, 1987, Special Agent Raymond Stastny of the Drug Enforcement Administration was shot by a drug dealer in an Atlanta shopping mall. Stastny was a New Yorker. When his body came home to his family, as the highest-ranking DEA agent in the region, I attended the wake and burial. I stared into Stastny's coffin and thought, God, life is so fragile. Yet a president can send men out to fight and die at the same time that he removes any chance of their effort succeeding.

It was cold in Sayville, Long Island, at the Stastny family's Catholic cemetery. The funeral procession wound through one of those bleak lowland winter days that in memory grow sleetier until the sky is as gray as the winter ocean and seems to blend with the road. Standing on the frozen burial ground as Taps played over the flag-draped coffin I just kept thinking, Someone killed this kid over eight ounces of cocaine.

Hatcher had been killed over four and a half ounces of cocaine. I watched now as a few of the agents went up to his car. I noticed that a few others couldn't even take the steps. Somehow they don't really think it can happen. The younger agents, like Baldwin, still think they are immortal. Or they think that older agents, like Hatcher, sometimes get a little sloppy. They go to work sure that death is not in their cards. Now here it was in front of them. The more of them I could get to face the devastating, surreal scene, the better off I thought they'd be for the future.

Agents continued to pour in to the crime scene. They came to comfort the survivors or participate in the hunt for the killers. It's always that way with us. We all come. It gives us unity and it gives us something to do. The worst thing you can do to a law officer is leave him at home when there's a crisis. Coffee and donuts were being passed around to take the edge off the bitter cold. By now people were bullshitting. They were all cops and all of a sudden cops were together who hadn't seen each other in a while, so they stood there catching up. Hatcher all the while was sitting there dead.

Condon came over again. It was well after midnight. "Bob, we really should go over and give a statement," he said.

I have given thousands of speeches on drugs. I've held hundreds of press conferences after big arrests. I always knew how to reach the reporters and bring home the point I wanted to make, whether it was to get people thinking about why we used drugs or about why they were sold or about what effect supply and demand were having. But I had no idea what I was going to say now. I was more shaken than I had ever been in my life.

I walked to the edge of the crime scene with Condon on one side, and Robert Strang, my aide, on the other. Across the tape, I could see the faces of the reporters were as grim as the faces of my agents. For five years many of them had covered the drug beat. It was the biggest story of our time and no one expected a happy ending. I stood there and waited a few seconds for the TV lights to come on.

"Okay. At about 10 P.M. tonight a DEA special agent working undercover was found dead. Shot in the head. During the course of an undercover meeting with a Costabile Farace. He had met Farace before. Purchased cocaine from him before. During the course of the undercover negotiation the agent got separated from the surveillance team. Shortly after that they found the agent seated in the vehicle. He was shot through the head. The window was rolled down. The car was running. His foot was on the brake. The Police Department is issuing an All-Points Bulletin for Farace at this time. And basically that's it."

A question came: "Obviously you and a lot of the other agents are shaken by this," a television reporter asked. "Is there anything you can say that makes any sense out of this?"

I thought for a few seconds. I wanted to make sure that the reporters heard the anger, impotence and confusion I felt. "It's questions like that that you ask yourself on nights like this. This man is a friend of mine. He worked with me. He worked for me. He worked in my immediate office. When you see something like this and you see people walking around buying lines of coke, thinking it's a joke, I wish every one of those who bought a line of coke could be here." I could feel my mouth contort with pain. "Look at this young man who is a father and a husband. See this dead agent lying here and let them tell me it's a joke."

I walked back to my car and sat down wondering what Hatcher would look like in his coffin. He was a big man, six two, over 200 pounds. He wouldn't look small and hollow like Ray Stastny, would he?

Through the windshield, I spotted Nick Alleva, who had put in nineteen years as an agent and who, like Hatcher, was a veteran of hundreds of undercover operations. I got out to join him. He was standing in the middle of that desolate overpass and I could see his broad shoulders shaking beneath the skin of his expensive leather jacket.

When he turned, I saw the tears stream down his face. They fell from his cheeks and onto the chest hair and the half dozen gold chains that peeked out from his shirt, open even in this cold. The chains and the obvious black toupee were Alleva's signature on the street and they were the only residue of toughness amid the tears. Hatcher had been his backup on a two-year undercover investigation during which Alleva had posed as a drug dealer to infiltrate the Colombo organized crime family.

"During the case, he never left me, Bob," Alleva said. "As long as I was there, he was there. And believe me, there was nobody better to watch your back. I used to joke that going through the door I wanted him in front of me. He was a gentle bear of a man, but he carried all those guns. On a surveillance, he was the kind of guy you wanted at your back.

"You know I'm a fatalist," Alleva continued. "I figure when it's my turn, I go. But I couldn't keep from thinking when I went up and looked in the car, that there, but for the grace of God, go a lot of other guys, because in this business the violence has escalated so much that it becomes everyday. When Hatch and I first started there was never any thought of hurting an agent."

Now the rules had changed. The undercover case that led to Hatcher's death was a terrible example of what they had become in the hands of high-flying drug gangsters, brain-addled by their own wares and armed with heavy weapons. The case Alleva and Hatcher had worked together was a perfect illustration of what the rules once were.

Alleva had gone to the house of a gangster named Patty Catalano down in Florida. His pose as a drug dealer had gotten him that far. Now he hoped to find evidence linking Catalano's group to the drug trade. There, on the sun porch, the mobster poured him coffee.

"Nick, I know your real name is Nick Alleva. I know your wife's name is Rose Ann. I know you live on this street in Queens. I know you're a federal agent. Look, Nick, you know that I tried to talk you out of the dope business. You know I have nothing to do with the dope business," Catalano said.

"Patty, I know that, and I'll get up on the witness stand and say that. But there are other things that you told me that you may have to live with," Alleva recalled telling Catalano.

Then the gangster invited him out on his boat with him.

"No, Patty, I don't think I want to go out cruising on the Everglades with you. My boss wouldn't like that," Alleva told him.

At that point Catalano replied, "Hey, I could almost shoot you I feel so bad. I feel bad because now we can never be friends."

But he didn't shoot and that's the point. He accepted that Alleva had a job and that he did it.

"If he was one of these young turds, who knows," Alleva told me.

They had backed the ambulance toward Hatcher's car. Alleva and I went over to lend a hand. The uniformed police formed their cordon to prevent undignified photographs as Hatcher was carried from the car. Once he was in the orange-and-white ambulance two of the officers in their blue tunics stood on the stamped-steel rear bumper to block the rear windows with their backs. They rode as far as the highway entrance to prevent anyone from taking a photograph of Hatcher laid out under the sheet. The ambulance picked up speed and at the last minute they hopped down, the gesture of modesty and respect complete. The bobbing lights and mournful siren of the ambulance faded and Hatcher wound his way toward Manhattan and the morgue.

There would be an autopsy and no semblance of dignity when they used a power saw to cut away Everett's skull and pry out the bullets.

THREE

The Widow's Home

Most of the police officials had already left, but a few detectives stood beside Hatcher's car. They would wait until after the car was removed so they could get a final look at the murder scene. The search parties were roaming. Most of the reporters had gone back to their own beds. The crime scene, stripped of these actors, could be seen for what it was: an ugly, lonely place for a man to die.

I got into my car and headed for the highway. Behind me, I heard the heavy drumming of a diesel. I looked in my rear-view and I saw that the blue police flatbed truck had arrived and was tipping itself down to gather up Hatcher's official government vehicle. A large mute piece of evidence: OGV, Buick, Regal, Gray, New York License Plate DDN 350. The car would not likely be needed for court, but the methodical homicide detectives nonetheless would cache it in an evidence warehouse as a hedge against the remote possibility that something had been overlooked. The headlights, which had been on all night, had finally been turned off.

This was the end of a peculiar roadside service that occurred too regularly now that a cop or agent was killed every two and a half days in America. I left the place that in the minds of agents would always be Everett Hatcher's unmarked grave. I stepped on the gas and felt the grab of the tires on the smooth road that headed away from the morgue and toward Mary Jane Hatcher's New Jersey home and an anguish that I don't think we are capable of imagining.

Her husband was an athlete, a counselor to younger agents, an ideal to his sons. The man who had killed him was a professional dirtbag, a steroid-popping, muscle-bound punk whose résumé before prison included forcible sodomy and homicide. After prison, this rap sheet noted, Farace had remarried, sold drugs and become an adulterer as soon as his second wife was visibly pregnant. Now he had killed Everett Hatcher and out of respect for the law we would not publicly call him a murderer, only a suspect.

It was around 1:30 in the morning. The car radio's bulletins on Hatcher's slaying had lapsed into repetition. Ann Hayes, the agent in charge of our trauma team, had been at the house for hours I expected. Andy Wnukowski, the agent who knew Hatcher the longest, was probably with her. I telephoned the DEA dispatcher and asked him to connect me.

"Bob, I was very frightened," Ann said when she got on the phone. "I've never had to do anything like this in my life. When I got here, the house was dark so I knew that she was probably asleep. I had a uniformed officer from the police here in Boonton come up to the door with me. I never would have found the house without him. When we got there I saw that Everett had set up a basketball hoop at the foot of the drive, you know, for his sons. There was a camper too, and a canoe off in the side yard. It was awful, Bob, that really brought it home for me. I mean, that hoop standing there just told me how much Everett had left behind. We knocked and Mary Jane came to the door. She didn't ask, 'What happened?' or anything."

She didn't have to. Once Mary Jane saw the accompanying officer she knew her husband would not be coming home. She had known this police protocol since she was a girl. The grim news of death was carried in the face of the uniformed sentinel, in the stiffness of the back, in the uncomfortable hands of a policeman who had not prevented the most terrible of crimes, the death of a brother officer.

"Since she didn't ask I just decided to tell her," Ann continued. "So as soon as I got inside I said, 'Something terrible has happened to Everett.' She was sitting in a chair. I had brought Tom Rooney with me because he's an older agent and he stood beside her when she asked back, 'Is he hurt?'"

Although Mary Jane already knew, she more than anyone else was wishing that it couldn't be true.

"Then I fumbled a little and she said, 'Just tell me.'

"'He did not make it.'"

When Ann said it, Mary Jane shut her eyes tight and clenched her fist hard and said, "No, I can't believe this has happened. I talked to him this afternoon, I told him not to go out." She wanted details and Ann had none to give.

"Tell her I'll be there right away," I said.

"Please hurry, Bob. She wants to go to Everett. She is ready to walk out the door and who can blame her? She wants to be there with him."

Through the entire recounting Ann kept her voice composed in the soft, graceful Southern lilt that had not cracked after all her time in New York and would not crack now. A woman who stood just a shade over five feet, Ann had been a tough case agent. But during the past eighteen months on the trauma team she had developed a horror of the incessant sound of her beeper. Each time it went off she dropped whatever she was doing and ran to help someone deal with a crippling emotional pain: four shot agents, an agent suicide, a child who accidentally killed himself with his father's gun, an agent who allegedly murdered his wife and an agent who drove into another car while drunk, killing two of its occupants. She had handled each of those trying cases well. But this time she sounded close to exhaustion.

I told Ann I would hurry and hung up. Then I contacted the Boonton police and got directions to their station. They would escort me from there to the house. As I continued the half-hour drive I started to think about Andy Wnukowski. How must he feel, I wondered, racing to comfort the widow of his close friend while still reeling with pain over the death of his first son, Christopher?

*   *   *

It had been the Monday before Thanksgiving. Andy Wnukowski was driving home from his DEA office at New York's Kennedy Airport. It was 4:30 in the morning and he was almost too tired to breathe after sixteen hours with his anti-smuggling unit and two almost sleepless weeks at home where the younger of his two sons, the infant Robbie, was sick. His wife, Kathy, met him in the kitchen.

"Why don't you sleep down here," she suggested, thinking he would get more rest on the TV room daybed than upstairs with the fitful infant.

"Good night," Wnukowski said. "I'll see you in the morning."

He took his gun off, laid it on a bench and took his pants off. Then he collapsed onto the bed. When Christopher woke up at 7 A.M., he came down to the room, which is also the playroom, where he kept some of his toys.

"Hi Daddy," the four-year-old said.

Then Kathy looked in.

"Okay, Andy, the kids are up. Why don't you come to bed and get some decent sleep now."

Wnukowski was almost out of the room when he noticed Christopher had a sad look. "Daddy has to go upstairs," he told the child. "Daddy has to go sleep."

He forgot to take along the automatic pistol, a combat gun with no safety. Andy was not a careless man but like all my agents, he was overworked past the point of fatigue. Days, nights and weekends, everybody worked. There was no other way to keep up with the case load in a city with 90,000 drug arrests a year.

At 8:55 A.M. Kathy screamed: "Oh my God, Chris is hurt."

Wnukowski still can't feel the memory of his feet touching the floor as he raced down the stairs to the TV room.

Kathy, a nurse, was performing cardiopulmonary resuscitation on their son.

"Help me plug the hole," she said, still not knowing what had made it.

He tried for about twenty seconds.

"What happened?" he asked.

"I heard a thud and then it was quiet and I came in to look," Kathy said. She found Christopher under the television set.

Then Wnukowski noticed the gun on the floor by the television. He went over and smelled. It had been fired. Christopher had picked it up and accidentally had sent a bullet into his heart. Wnukowski jumped up to call an ambulance. Neither of them had heard the shot. Then shock began. They had been married fifteen years before they were able to have children; Andy was forty-five then, Kathy thirty-eight. Now, four years later, their first son was gone.

It was not until mid-January that Wnukowski went back to work. At first, he would not carry a gun. He could not accept it. The job, the gun, was responsible for the death of his son. By the end of February, he had just started learning to carry a gun again. The first day at the range he almost collapsed. An expert marksman when he left Vietnam and joined the DEA, Wnukowski had brought Hatcher on the DEA rifle team and they had won a silver medal in the 1976 Police Olympics. I'll never forget Wnukowski telling me, "Now, I had to go and break this record too, because I think a four-year-old is the youngest who ever accidentally killed himself with a pistol."

The last time I had seen him was at his son's wake. Wnukowski had greeted me at the entrance to the funeral parlor. "Thank you for coming, Bob, it means a great deal to me," he said. Then he cried. Afterward I walked up to view the body. To a Jew, it seems the cruelest thing, this Christian custom of the open casket. I walked up to it and I saw this little boy. He looked like an angel. Arranged all around him were his toys. His toy soldiers all stood at attention in a young boy's honor guard on the gleaming edge of the casket.

By the end of February, Wnukowski was just able to complete the drive home without pulling off the road to be sick.

As it turned out, Ann told me, at almost the same moment that the four bullets passed through the open car window and killed Hatcher, Wnukowski was in his car heading home. The route, from Kennedy Airport to Elizabeth, New Jersey, had taken him right across Staten Island, to within one exit of where his friend lay dead. The uncanny coincidence struck me too. I remembered what Andy had said of his son's death: "It only happens on television until it happens to you."

Now, according to what Ann had told me, she was relying on Wnukowski to comfort Mary Jane Hatcher.

"I want to go to my husband," Mary Jane told them. "He was alone, wasn't he?"

Ann was at a loss for words. Wnukowski tried to explain. "Alone means, doesn't really mean anything. You know, he was undercover. You can't have all the other surveillance people sitting in a car with him."

It was just after two in the morning when I pulled up. Robert Strang, who had followed in his car, pulled up right after me. The house was ablaze with light. When we came up to the door we could hear the hushed voices inside. Wnukowski had tried hard to comfort her, but Mary Jane still sounded as though she felt abandoned when she opened the door.

"Mary Jane, I'm terribly sorry," I said. "Everett was special and he didn't only work for me, he was a friend," I told her. "I feel I owe it to you to tell you exactly what happened." I really didn't know what else to say, but saying this as Hatcher's boss made the words feel like stones in my mouth. She seemed to have already put together in her mind the death scene and I saw that the details weren't really necessary.

"Everett was alone when he was shot," she said again after letting us in. "Everett lost his surveillance. Didn't he? I told him not to go on this deal. I had a bad feeling. I asked him not to go tonight." She knew that her husband was unhappy with the FBI agents and their style of working a case. Grief was turning to anger.

"There were four DEA agents and one FBI agent on surveillance," I told her. "Good, bad or indifferent this was ours. It would be very nice to point the finger at someone else but this was ours." I wasn't sure I completely believed it myself. The FBI agent was not the finest example of that agency's usually excellent investigators. He tended to be lax, from what I was told. But our team had opted to go to the meeting. Our team noticed how risky it was. It seemed to me we had made mistakes in judgment too. And now was not the time to heap recriminations onto sorrow. Her husband had died, and blaming someone, even the killer who deserved all the blame we could find, was not going to bring him back.

Mary Jane again asked to see Everett.

I called her brother into the kitchen.

"Jude, let me tell you, we'll go down there and he's going to be pulled out of a refrigerator in the morgue," I told him. "His face is a mess. They're not cleaning him up until the autopsy is done. I need you to go out and convince her."

He swallowed hard at the blunt truth. Then he went out and said, "Mary Jane, you don't want to go see him like that." That seemed to be almost enough to convince her to stay.

"He's lying out there someplace," she said.

"No," I said. "He's not, he's right here. He is watching you." I am not religious, but I felt it and I meant it. She seemed to accept it too, and appeared to resign herself to the pain that came from not being able to go out and take him into her arms and make it right. Then I forced myself to look around the living room into each of the grief-torn faces. There was Wnukowski standing near Mary Jane, with his wife, Kathy, by his side.

"How are you and Kathy, can you do this?"

"Yes," he said. "In a way, for us having to go through this is very helpful, Bob. It forces us to function and to put ourselves on the back burner."

Mary Jane was still sitting in a hard chair with Jude beside her. Tom Rooney of the trauma team and Ann were on the sofa, and finally there was Kevin Gallagher, who had arrived after me and looked as uncomfortable as I felt.

For the first time in a long time in my career the pain and grief, like a fist holding an ice pick, had completely punched through the thick callus that I had built up as protection from the constant diet of death and violence.

I left Mary Jane Hatcher's house at 5:30. The sharp smell of winter before morning was rolling down from the cemetery up the hill. Her morning would come down from the cemetery and up from the reservoir across the road until the smells mingled and passed across her lawn.

By the time I pulled into my own driveway the sky had thinned to an almost colorless winter morning and I was more tired than I had ever felt in my life. I went up to bed. I didn't feel bitter, I didn't feel unhappy. I just felt drained and ready to do something else. I fell asleep.

Less than forty-five minutes later the telephone rang. It was Steve Medwid, my partner during the early years and my neighbor now. Once your partner, always your partner.

"Hey, Bob, I just heard what happened on the radio, what can I do?"

"Do it yourself, I'm quitting," I yelled. "Now you can let me get fifteen minutes of goddamn sleep."

"Hey pal," he said. "You did the best that you could do."

FOUR

The Toll

I hung up and felt a little better. I had done the best that I could. The DEA in New York, with the help of the police department, agents of the FBI, the Alcohol, Tobacco and Firearms bureau, State Police officers, Immigration investigators and small-town police, kept a constant pressure on the drug trade. We raided, harassed, made undercover purchases, identified conspiracies and raided again. This staggering combined effort cost the drug dealers dearly.

In 1988, the New York City police recorded 90,000 drug arrests. Thousands of federal arrests were heaped on top of this tally. That year, the DEA seized from drug dealers $75 million in property in New York: 385 cars worth $4.3 million, seven boats worth $270,000, one $15,000 plane, 139 pieces of jewelry appraised at $1.785 million, 51 buildings worth $24.2 million, an uncatalogued assortment of possessions worth $18 million and $26.785 million in cash.

But even the efforts of nearly 35,000 officers, troopers and agents, the equivalent of one of the world's larger standing armies, had not been enough to reclaim the streets.

Life in the city had taken on a hellish cast. By the end of 1988, the murder count approached 2,000 and almost half these homicides were blamed on drugs. Child abuse by parents who used drugs had tripled and more than 8,500 cases were reported. Instances of child neglect rose from 41,000 to 52,000 and much of the rise was blamed on drugs. The number of babies born with drugs in their system increased from 1,325 to 5,088. Reported cases of venereal disease more than doubled, topping 4,500, and the promiscuity associated with crack joined the sharing of contaminated needles by intravenous drug users as a factor in the spread of AIDS.

No toll we could exact from drug dealers could compare with the toll they were exacting from our society.

Those of us in law enforcement knew that without help our task was hopeless. The jails could hold few of those arrested—less than 5,000 of the 90,000 arrested in New York City were sent to prison. Nationally, drug treatment was only sparsely available, there was almost no systematic anti-drug education and, electioneering protestations to the contrary, little budgetary recognition that drug abuse was more than a police problem.

In 1969 the United States spent almost $300 billion in 1989 dollars on war operations in Vietnam. At the beginning of 1989, the government authorized about $1.9 billion for drug treatment and prevention, and a bit less than $4 billion on all drug-related law enforcement operations, including intelligence gathering, interdiction, investigations, corrections, prosecution and international efforts. A little over a year later the federal government had committed troops to a Mideast war that cost at least $50 billion before the first shot was fired.

Sadder than the comparison with military spending was the idea that the thinly funded reliance on cops, federal agents and guns continued to be our primary tool to curb drug abuse. Woefully ill-funded on the law enforcement front, the drug war's treatment and education aspect was hardly funded at all.

My career had spanned several wars on drugs beginning with the marijuana wars of the early 1960s through the peak of the crack epidemic. By the beginning of 1989, I sensed that President George Bush and his then-drug czar, William Bennett, had set up a strategy that would allow them to declare a rhetorical victory owing to a lull in middle-class drug use. Then they would turn their attention to another problem.

It was a cycle I knew well. I had been through Lyndon

Johnson's war on marijuana, Richard Nixon's war on heroin, Ronald Reagan's war on cocaine and the brief respites that quickly followed each declaration of war. Just as quickly, society turned its attention away, ignoring the continuing problem.

When we declared war on marijuana, at best two million Americans smoked it. At the close of the 1980s there were twenty million marijuana smokers in the United States. When Nixon declared war on heroin in 1971 there were an estimated half million heroin users. There were still that many in 1989. Cocaine, which had a relative handful of users in the years before Reagan declared war, had 2.4 million when Bush took office.

As the decade drew to a close, almost four years after prepackaged crack, the smokable cocaine product, was crowned king of the illicit street drugs, the violence spewed by crack users, crack dealers, cocaine traders and the always volatile heroin traffickers, seemed everywhere. A temporary decline in middle-class use of one drug was not going to end it.

In South Jamaica, Queens, Lorenzo "Fat Cat" Nichols and his black gangsters used firebombs and murder to dominate a street corner crack and heroin trade worth by one estimate $100 million. On February 26, 1988, a year to the week before Hatcher's assassination, the effort to reclaim this neighborhood cost Police Officer Edward Byrne, a twenty-three-year-old rookie, his life. He was murdered by minions of the Fat Cat and his lieutenant, Howard "Pappy" Mason, while guarding a witness in a drug case. When Mason, Nichols and their associates were jailed, they were merely replaced by another clique of gangsters.

In Brooklyn, where Delroy "Uzi" Edwards earned his machine-gun-toting nickname by leading his Jamaican-born drug posse in the shootings, beatings, torture and murder necessary to control a crack, cocaine and marijuana empire that stretched to London and Washington, D.C., the arrest and conviction of his gang led only to its replacement by new drug-dealing posses.

In Woodside, Queens, by 1987, more than 120 homicides, stretching back a decade, had been linked to the Colombians of José Santa Cruz Londono's cartel. Despite the seizure of thousands of pounds of cocaine, Londono's faceless lieutenants continued to run the day-to-day affairs of his Cali, Colombia, based importation empire from barstools of Roosevelt Avenue saloons. They kept their grip on the lucrative franchise through indiscriminate violence. They machine-gunned whole families, raped babysitters, tortured children. When shortchanged in drug payments, they took hostages. If the ransom was a penny short, the hostage was returned minus a finger.

Despite numerous successful prosecutions, Italian-American would-be gangsters in Brooklyn and on Staten Island used baseball bats, ear biting and assassination to control a still-thriving marijuana and cocaine empire sanctioned by La Cosa Nostra.

In upstate New York where just ten federal agents could be spared to patrol the northern two thirds of the state, a region that includes the Great Lakes, the Niagara frontier, the Thousand Island wilderness and the vastness of the Canadian border, Sicilian and Chinese peddlers shipped their narcotics with impunity.

In Washington Heights, the upper reaches of Manhattan where crack first surfaced in 1986 as a national menace, the crack gangsters continued to sell their product openly on street corners.

DEA informants, working on commission, were kept so busy that at times the 300 registered informers outearned investigators, annually pulling down $50,000 to $75,000 in their constant quest to bring us information.

Law enforcement struggled to contain the drug dealers and their violence but we could not control the demand.

In 1986 a Manhattan crack addict had hurled his eight-year-old niece from the window of a Schomburg Plaza apartment to her death on 110th Street 330 feet below. He killed her in a fit of rage at her mother, who caught him stealing from her purse to buy drugs. That same year it was reported that the use of drugs among the city's 7,069 jail guards was becoming epidemic. Nor were the rich exempt. It was reported that 40 percent of the nation's doctors younger than forty admitted using marijuana or cocaine.

In January 1987, a sixty-five-year-old nun was slain at a

Bronx homeless shelter and police blamed a former resident who was thrown out for repeatedly taking drugs against house rules. That same month, jet-setter Jerry Hall was jailed in Barbados for marijuana possession. The thirty-year-old was arrested and charged after she picked up twenty pounds at the airport outside Bridgetown. "Give us a good write-up, mate," her husband, Mick Jagger, told one reporter as he joined Hall in court. A few weeks later a Bronx mother was charged with allowing three neighbors to rape her six-year-old in exchange for money and vials of crack. In other reports from the demand front, a nine-year-old boy was arrested at Kennedy Airport as he delivered $3 million in heroin. The child had flown in unaccompanied from Nigeria. And in September, the chairman of the Metropolitan Transportation Authority stated that one out of three applicants to drive a city bus had failed a drug test.

A Wharton School survey that year estimated that 20 percent of the nation's murders and rapes, 25 percent of its automobile theft, 40 percent of its robbery and 50 percent of its burglaries were related to drugs. Despite an increase in federal law enforcement spending from $500 million in 1981 to $2.5 billion in fiscal year 1988, efforts to reduce supply had failed abysmally and demand was greater than ever.

By January 1988, the residence of the Roman Catholic Cardinal of New York, adjoining Fifth Avenue's St. Patrick's Cathedral, had been broken into by a man carrying $5 worth of marijuana. Caught by a housekeeper, Maura O'Kelly, he told her he had just smoked crack. She later told detectives, "I was hoping whatever he was under would wear off." Later in the year, New York reported its first rise in the infant mortality rate—to 12.9 per 1,000—after a ten-year decline. Parents on drugs were blamed for part of the increase. By June, the police department was grappling to keep still-stable neighborhoods from the outlaw rule of drug dealers. Police Commissioner Benjamin Ward declared, "The city is not out of control." Not everyone was reassured.

Shortly after William Bennett was appointed drug czar in January 1989 and began his initiative to reduce, if not the problem, at the least the public perception of the problem,

New York State released a report estimating that regular users of cocaine had more than tripled, from 182,000 in 1986 to 600,000. The state's prison population was also going through the roof, approaching 45,000, surpassing the 44,000 inmates the entire federal prison system held just fifteen months earlier.

I was caught in a bind. The more vigorously we prosecuted, the more likely we would weaken the very system we love. When those guilty can't be punished, justice is cheapened. Once it might have been a cop's dilemma, but now it's the nation's. Lack of treatment, prevention and continued education can cost us another generation. A telling example of the failure of our educational system to deliver an anti-drug message took place just weeks before Hatcher's murder. An eleven-year-old boy showed up at his Bronx elementary school with 411 vials of crack. He only brought the drugs to school, he told authorities, because he failed to make a delivery and didn't want to be late for the start of class.

On this job, the war on drugs, time was always marked in statistics and initiatives, in kilograms of cocaine and heroin seized, in plans to seal our borders and take back our streets. It was time to measure whether it was worth the cost.

Over the years, the bodies of cops and agents had been heaped on this landfill of human misery that our blindness to the demand for drugs had caused. It was bound to happen. These men and women were on the front line. It did not matter that there was no one standing behind them. In 1979, DEA agents were involved in two shootings. By 1987, they were assaulted eighty times. And the favored weapon was an illegal gun. Five DEA agents were slain in the United States in 1987 and 1988.

The horrifying surge of violence, in New York and across the nation, is all too easy to document.

On May 30, 1986, city Police Officer John S. Verwoert became the first recorded casualty of the new epidemic. A member of the special anti-crack unit, he was shot in front of a Harlem tenement in the aftermath of a drug raid.

Seven months later, Officer James Delmonico, off duty and returning to his suburban home after riding a horse through the crush of New Year's Eve at Times Square, was shot when he told a teenager to put out a cigarette in a no-smoking car on a Long Island Rail Road commuter train. Crack was seized when the youth was arrested.

On January 20, 1987, Raymond Stastny was mortally wounded in Atlanta. His body was returned to New York for burial. There, three other agents had been shot in the space of three weeks.

That same month, Officer Michael Reidy was killed by a crack addict who confronted him in the vestibule of his Bronx apartment building when the officer returned home after work.

In February, Special Agent Gary Blanch of the Bureau of Alcohol, Tobacco and Firearms was shot in the jaw while attempting to serve an arrest warrant on a drug dealer in the Bronx.

In September, a drug gangster with an automatic weapon killed plainclothes New York Transit Police Officer Robert Venable.

In January 1988, all DEA agents were authorized to carry submachine guns in an effort to turn the odds in their favor. By that time, DEA records showed that 144 agents were assaulted nationwide in the past twenty-four months compared to fifty in the two years before.

In 1988, beginning with Edward Byrne, five city cops were gunned down by drug dealers. Another was accidentally killed by fellow officers shooting at a pregnant woman trying to fire a gun at the officer, who led the raid into her suspected drug den.

For 1989, the death toll among the anti-drug forces had begun with the death of Everett Hatcher.

Nobody even bothered to stop and count the wounded any more, and the wounded included everyone whose life was touched by drugs. In a particularly ugly manner, Everett's wife, Mary Jane, and their two sons had joined that group.

FIVE

Taps

The wake for Everett Hatcher was held two days later in Boonton, New Jersey. The vestibule to the parlor of the Mackey Funeral Home was in a crowded hush as mourner after mourner stood to be greeted by the recent widow of a federal agent before passing inside to pray over his remains. Mary Jane Hatcher was clear-eyed and brave as she firmly shook each hand and ushered the visitor inside.

At the far end of the parlor, Hatcher was laid out in a brown suit. His body and head had been arranged by the undertaker to artfully disguise the damage of the fatal wounds and the autopsy. A very young girl in a pretty little dress and white anklets rested her bare knees on the padded kneeler, peered over the lip of the coffin and prayed. Beside her, a gray-uniformed state trooper, his sharp-brimmed hat tucked under his arm, stood at parade rest and openly wept. When my turn came I stepped up to the coffin, bowed my head, and said a prayer for Hatcher's soul and a prayer for the living. Then I stepped back and joined the knot of agents and police officers gathered at the rear of the parlor. We spent the night speaking quietly of our dead friend.

Outside, along the path to the two-story frame house and among the parked cars and tall bare trees that lined the hillside down to the corner, another set of agents stood at widely spaced intervals. They wore black armbands of mourning on the left sleeve of their trenchcoats and another strip of black across the top of their gold shields. They were on guard to prevent intruders from wandering into the privacy of grief. There were none. The only sound was of the sentinels breathing, the only motion from the clouds of their regular exhalations into the still night air.

Following the final afternoon session at the funeral home, which took place the next day, a Friday, the media, with their tangle of television cables, tape recorders and microphones, gathered in the cold at the request of Mary Jane Hatcher.

She walked down the path to a podium that had been set up away from the doors to the funeral home, bit down hard on her grief, and began:

"Ladies and gentlemen of the press,

"As you are well aware, a good man has been taken from us. The loss that we feel is exceedingly deep and almost unbearable. Everett and I were, and are, a team. We believed in each other. We were bound together; willing to surrender our personal beings. He died for society in general and for every one of us in particular. As I stand here now, law enforcement people are scouring the country for the evil one who has committed this act. But even through the grief of our loss I must ask the question: Who are the ultimate guilty parties? Who create the market for the poison which he valiantly tried to remove from our society? Look around. As Pogo said, 'I have met the enemy and they is us.' We, middle-class, suburban users. We, casual users. We, dabblers in drugs, keep the market in drugs an ever-increasing one. Therefore, Everett Emerson Hatcher was killed by all of us nice people who in every other way are above reproach. All of you who hear me now and fit this description, all of you must accept the blame for the loss of this good, gentle man.

"Thank you."

She turned her straight back and walked away.

On Saturday morning the funeral was held. At the police barracks in Suffolk County on Long Island, one group of outriders to the procession rose before dawn and kicked to life its growling Harley-Davidsons. The officers tightened the black armbands over their black leather coats, adjusted their belts and buckles and silently mounted the big machines.

Down one hundred miles of highway they rode in a weaving single file. The flashing police lights on the grumbling bikes were set to blink blue, then white, at the pace of a dirge. The sirens that motorists might have expected when they first spotted the big bikes stayed silent. Then, as the outriders overtook them, a glimmer of sad recognition crossed each motorist's face and one by one they bowed their heads momentarily as the officers passed.

Across the metropolitan area other police officers, federal agents, sheriffs, marshals and prosecutors joined these in heading toward New Jersey where they converged at St. Christopher's Roman Catholic church in Parsippany. There, the New York City Police Department's white-gloved funeral detail, which has too much experience at this sort of ritual, arranged them in formation behind their department or unit flags to wait for the arrival of the hearse.

At 9:05 A.M., in the funeral parlor in nearby Boonton, the lid was closed on the coffin. A priest stood beside it and asked the Hatcher family, their closest friends and a crowd of dignitaries to join him in prayer, "We bow our heads and ask Our Father..."

A few minutes later these mourners became an entourage that filled one hundred cars and followed the hearse to the church where 2,000 law officers from as far away as northern Canada now stood with their collars turned up against a biting wind and threatening skies.

When the gray hearse stopped in front of the stone church, the kilted police bagpipers began their wail. As the piercing thin strains of "Amazing Grace" slipped toward the sky, 2,000 left hands slapped to the side as one, 2,000 right hands touched foreheads in salute and 2,000 sets of heels clicked together.

The coffin entered the church. Parade rest was ordered. Cigarettes were puffed as the honor guard broke up. Then those who could squeeze into the church followed Hatcher's body inside, filling first the pews and then the aisles along its cold stone walls. Those standing were the front-line agents and police officers, many of the same people who, professionally, knew Hatcher the best. Heroes like him.

Mary Jane Hatcher, a single red rose in her hand, a set of pearls over a black turtleneck, and a beige suit jacket over a black skirt, climbed the two steps to the podium to the right of the altar and spoke.

Her voice was firm and clear. "I am calling you by name, Everett," she said quoting from the Book of Isaiah. "Because you are precious in my eyes, because you are honored and I loved you. Do not be afraid." The power of her belief resonated through the church. Sniffling could be heard among the family members and law enforcement officials.

But Mary Jane did not cry.

She lifted the red rose to her nose and inhaled. She seemed to draw new strength from it, and her eyes sparkled as she said, "You walked through fire and you were not burned."

She finished the reading and stepped down, her husband's friends accompanying her to a front pew. Her face softened as she sat beside her sons, Joshua, three, and Zackery, nine.

Now she listened as one of Hatcher's best friends, former DEA agent Joe DeGenaro, spoke.

"His most potent weapon was a vodka gimlet," he said, softening the mood and drawing a laugh. That and "a well-placed tickle" as he stole an extra bite of Mary Jane's ice cream sundae. Hatcher was a man, DeGenaro recalled, who after decades of looking at life's worst had not lost the ability to love. "He could get lost in the simple pleasure of a soccer game on the front lawn with his son."

Then DEA Administrator Jack Lawn stepped to the podium where he eulogized Hatcher with pointed brevity. Quoting the speech that John F. Kennedy never got to deliver in Dallas on November 22, 1963, Lawn said, "'If we are strong, our character speaks for itself. If we are weak, words can do little.' Everett's character did speak for itself."

As he finished, six uniformed policemen stood and walked to the coffin handles, ready to lift it shoulder high. The priest stepped forward to swing the noisy thurible over it, and as he did the smell of incense rose with each arch of the burner on its heavy chain. After a few swings by the priest, the altar boy lifted the processional cross and stood behind it at the head of the center aisle. This was the signal for the mourners to rise. But before they filed out of their pews to follow the family behind it, they paused to watch as Mary Jane, still at her pew, reached out to her son Zackery and showed him how to salute. As he raised his right hand, a proud smile passed across her lips. Then the widow and her family fell in behind the coffin.

Once outside, as his father's body gently slid across twelve white-gloved hands and back into the hearse, Zackery touched his hand to his brow and with sadness on his young face said farewell.

The funeral motorcade stretched a mile and filled all three lanes of Interstate 80 as it headed to the cemetery. There, a twenty-one-gun salute crackled for Hatcher, a bugler raised his instrument to his lips and all heads were bowed as Taps was played. Mary Jane stood over the hole where her husband had been lowered, with the rose still in her hand, and the American flag that had covered his coffin tucked under her arm.

As the crowd filed away from the gravesite, in the trees just a short distance away I could see the members of Hatcher's surveillance team standing together. They were weeping openly.

I had come to New York thinking it was the place where hope could be harnessed to press the fight against drugs. I had increased the number of seizures and put more agents on the street.

I had hoped public sentiment would grow strong enough to hold the educators and makers of health and social welfare policies as accountable as agents, officers and jailers. I wanted to bring the power of their thinking to the front lines. But in the end policy had not changed. The war on drugs was not being waged very differently from the way we tried to put out the brushfire wars when I had first enlisted twenty-four years ago.

TWO

Waging War on Drugs

SIX

The Early Years

I began as a street agent. A pudgy, moonfaced Jew from the New England mill town of Providence, Rhode Island, I was something of an anomaly in the world of federal law enforcement, which was still largely an Irish-American cloister when I joined in 1965.

I didn't realize how tightly knit that society was on the winter morning when I stepped for the first time into the Washington, D.C., field office of the Federal Bureau of Narcotics, a virtually unknown agency that was grandfather to the DEA. But I soon learned.

I raced up the three flights of stairs in the Internal Revenue Service Building to the FBN's borrowed suite of offices hardly noticing the disapproving frowns from the quiet auditors. To a man, I later learned, they despised the rebellious narcotics agents and the dirty trade they plied. Had I known it then, it would have only made me run up the stairs faster.

Unlike most agents who join today, I had no idea of what narcotics enforcement meant. All I knew for certain was that I was bored with the Central Intelligence Agency where I had analyzed information on Soviet bloc countries for six months. I had taken the CIA job straight out of college, thinking that it might be exciting, but it looked like it would never amount to anything more than culling embassy papers and clipping newspaper articles. I was looking for excitement.

A breathless young man with thinning red hair, wearing a medium gray suit, I turned the knob to the wood-paneled door marked with only the gold leaf initials FBN and stepped into a shabby set of rooms. There, a half dozen preoccupied characters nonchalantly lifted heads, gave me a glance, then returned to their studied slouches. Some, I noticed, chose to sit with feet upon their desks even as they two-thumb hammered out reports on clackity manual typewriters. Each seemed to have a signature—a hat pushed back on the head, an overcoat thrown over the desk instead of on the handy coatrack, a tie tucked military fashion into the shirt or a toothpick dangling. These were not the gray-flanneled automatons of other federal bureaucracies. I could look like that, I thought happily, noticing the chromed guns holstered under their arms or in their belts, the cigarettes from the mouths, black phones at the elbows, and coffee (or, I later found out, whiskey) at their hand.

At that moment, Leroy Morrison, the special agent in charge, lifted his head and said, "So, you're the new guy?"

"Yes," I said, and I heard the typing stop as I walked over to his metal desk.

"Well, son, just what was wrong with the CIA?" Morrison looked like he already knew so I just told him the truth instead of worrying about how it would sound.

"It wasn't what I had in mind. It was an office job and a boring one at that," I said.

There wasn't much more to the interview than that. I was snotty, dumb, unaware of just how much depended on the boring job of gathering intelligence from which I had just walked away. But Morrison had looked me over and arrived at his decision: I was teachable.

I was too nervous to smile when he pulled a sheet of paper from his desk, asked the other agents to shut up, and then said, "Raise your right hand. Just repeat after me." I did.

"I, Robert Marvin Stutman, do solemnly swear to uphold

the Constitution of the United States." That was that. I had just become a narc.

It was a Tuesday morning. February 25, 1965. It was twenty-four years to the week before Everett Hatcher was killed, making for one of those imponderable coincidences that later seem to mean something although you can't pin down what. I could not know it then, but the next twenty-five years would be a career exciting enough for anyone.

My case work and lectures would take me from the alleyways of Washington to the boardrooms of dictators halfway across the globe. On my return I would sit at the polished conference tables where our nation's anti-drug policy was shaped and reshaped. I was there for the very beginning of our modern anti-drug efforts. I watched them grow, decline and grow again, but never succeed in winning the drug wars. I would see the chance of success time and again stymied by cynical policy decisions.

Toward the end of my career, I could no longer see death in the service of this country's misguided policies as an acceptable choice: a grim, unfortunate but admirable tragedy. By the time Everett Hatcher was killed those policies should have been changed. The failure to do so meant Hatcher had died in vain.

It was excitement that led me to begin this career—the excitement of the unknown. I didn't know that in each narcotics case the excitement of beginning is routinely followed by calm, plodding days of investigation that lead only to the too-quick exhilaration of a violent conclusion and then a period of letdown. By the time I discovered that sequence, my sense of excitement was replaced by one of duty.

Within half an hour of breakfast on that winter day, my identity as the son of Harry Stutman, electrical contractor, and Anna Kapnick, housewife, originally of another mill town, Paterson, New Jersey, had begun its metamorphosis from a recently married, unsure boy-man into that of a federal drug agent.

"Boys, meet Bob Stutman," Morrison said to the agents in the field office. Then he took me over to 633 Indiana Avenue, the FBN national headquarters, to meet the property clerk.

"Give him his gun," Morrison told the clerk, a man named Harry Terrain, who until the end of my career worked for the DEA.

The headquarters of the 265-agent, $5-million-a-year FBN wasn't a whole lot fancier, just a rented suite of offices on the second floor. I noticed that the entire first floor of the building was taken up by the People's Drug Store, a branch of one of Washington's largest chains. The drug store might have been just coincidence, Morrison explained on the way up, like the way a city's police headquarters always seems to wind up in a neighborhood with plenty of organized crime and cheap Italian and Chinese food. But it did make it a little easier to bear a definitely unexciting part of the job, regulatory compliance. It was our job to regularly undertake the boring task of checking a pharmacist's inventory against his record of prescriptions to ensure he wasn't slipping out a few narcotics under the counter. Not even the fear of boredom could dampen my excitement.

I had never handled a gun before I took the black revolver Terrain handed me, a long-barreled, six-shot .38-caliber Smith & Wesson, stuck it in its holster and put the whole thing onto my elastic belt.

It was too heavy for the elastic and the entire arrangement began to stretch, taking my pants with it toward my knees, ruining my dream of instantly fitting in. As I fumbled to retrieve it, I discovered that all of those guys I envied had managed to slouch over from the field office two blocks away in order to witness a new agent strapping on his gun for the first time. By now they were bent over by laughter.

"Welcome to the FBN, kid," one of them said. "Either get a new belt or buy a water pistol." I did neither, and for the rest of my career I continued to wear elastic belts. They became my signature. The agent who spoke was named Johnny Thompson, and since he had taken a liking to me, Morrison assigned him as my senior partner.

That was how training was done back then, no fourteen-week training academy and no controlled "practicals," as the simulated fieldwork is now called. Thompson would make me into an agent, passing down everything he felt I needed:

federal narcotics laws, the rudiments of office politics, the ways to protect your partner and the telltale signs of a dealer or drug user. Lessons began the moment I walked into the office and continued all day, at the desk, in the car and at the lunch counters of Washington.

When I started it was one year and three months into the presidency that Lyndon Johnson assumed when assassination shortened John F. Kennedy's administration. Johnson was set to publicly declare war on poverty at home while quietly stepping up the U.S. military involvement in Southeast Asia. I didn't know it then, but he would be the first president I served who cynically bent narcotics policy to fit his political agenda.

Although the office where I stood that first day was inside the Capital Beltway, the road that circumscribes government thought in America, I was too young and inexperienced to understand or anticipate the effect that ideas generated in this self-contained world would have on drug policy. There was no war on drugs, declared or undeclared, and I had plenty of time to decompress before I got down to business. Within a week, Thompson felt he had me well enough versed in the Marijuana Tax Act, the Harrison Narcotic Act and the federal drug conspiracy laws to take me out on the streets.

"There are a couple of things you need to know, kid," he told me. "If you're out on surveillance and somebody looks at you and you don't want him to, pick your nose, he'll always turn away. The other thing is when we get to court, never cut a fart on one of those wooden courtroom benches because it reverberates through the entire room."

Those were my rules for survival. My exhilaration was hard to avoid, so they decided I needed to learn patience— Johnny Thompson taught that by example. We spent months walking and riding the streets on a single conspiracy case without ever making an arrest. By today's standards it was a nothing case. I'd blow my stack if one of my agents wanted to do nothing for six months but a single case for half an ounce of heroin. That's a one-buy case these days and a quick bust later. But not back then. Especially if you wanted to teach someone patience.

At the end of each day we'd go back to the office and type our paperwork. Leroy Morrison would always be waiting. Short, heavyset, with a drinker's red face, he was for a time my idol, a real G-man who had started in the Bureau of Prohibition. One day I asked him how come he had never risen higher than the rank of Agent in Charge of this eight-man office. In those days the Washington field office wasn't even big enough to be independent; it reported to Baltimore.

"I got drunk during the 1948 Truman inauguration, when I was supposed to be working, and drove my car through the inaugural parade," Morrison said. "So if you're gonna fuck up, kid, don't do it in Washington."

"He means if you're a cop, kid, not if you're a politician," Thompson explained. And they were done with that day's lesson.

"It's sure not like those good old days," Morrison said.

"That's for sure," Thompson answered. "How's the place you've been looking at for retirement?"

And they were off. Day after day it was the same routine. I swore I would never sound like that. But that, of course, was a meaningless vow. Ten years later, I would get together with Steve Medwid and within fifteen minutes we'd be talking about the good old days and I'd be dreaming about the waterfront property I would own. When I finally came to New York, my house in New Jersey had a water storage tank behind it and whenever Medwid would sit out on the deck, he'd wait for the appropriate moment, turn and say, "Yeah, Bob, sure is nice that you got your dream of waterfront property." Some things never change.

After six months of me pounding the streets, Johnny Thompson decided I was ready to make my first arrest. I knew the conspiracy case was ready. While I had a gun, I still had never fired it, not even on a range. While I was itching for excitement I had no idea of how to act on a raid.

We were going to raid a house. The house of a guy named Judson Brodus Bay. He was a big son of a bitch and a well-known drug trafficker. He lived in the basement apartment. We had a search warrant. The whole office was going there. Six of us were to take the front door, two would take the back. I remember Leroy Morrison telling me before we went, "Kid, you'll know you're crazy in this business when you have a fight about who is going to get to kick in the door."

Sure enough, when we get there, a fight breaks out over who gets to kick in the door. It is still unbelievable to me since kicking in a door is the most dangerous thing you can do in this business. There could be a guy with a shotgun on the other side. And there you stand with your leg up, absolutely exposed.

Well, at least I know these guys are all crazy, I say to myself. Then they knock.

"Who is it?" Bay said.

"It's the rabbi," an agent answered. There really was a rabbi in Washington who was also a heroin addict, so Bay slipped the lock. We kicked in the door and went in, guns drawn, God knows what I aimed mine at. We got the five people in the room under control by screaming, "You move and I'll kill you." I had never seen anything like this in my life. It took about a week for my adrenaline-soaked heart to slow down. In the end Bay only had about half an ounce of heroin.

What stood out later was more than the case. It was the scabs. Bay had giant sores on his arms, scabs like half dollars all the way up to his elbows. It was the first time I'd ever seen anything like that. I said to myself, Just look at what this shit does to these people.

The other thing that stood out were his hands. When we tried to handcuff him, his hands were puffed up so big from the poison in his system that the cuffs wouldn't go on his wrists, so we had to take him out holding on to his arms. And man, I did not want to touch his arms.

I had come, by the day of that first raid, a long way for a kid who slept in his parents' house all through college. A long way down to the end of the drug trail from my parents' comfortable home. I had seen the ugly result of drug addiction. It was not hard to imagine the ill effect a growing class of addicts would have on the quality of life in our country.

There had been nothing in my childhood that pointed toward law enforcement. If you could have looked closely at the public high school student in the black leather jacket and white T-shirt who had recently graduated from Henry Barnard, the private grammar school and junior high, the word "jail," not "cop," might have come to mind.

Everybody assumed I was going to get in lots of trouble. I was a rebel. I came from a nice middle-class community, very Italian, very Jewish. While my parents were blue collar, they were comfortable. They expected their children to go to college but I chose to hang out with a tougher crowd. If there had been drugs available then, I probably would have tried them. In any case, my friends were the worst group of kids I could find.

Before I was finished with high school I had been arrested three times: twice for fights, once for puncturing a car tire on Halloween, 1959. They charged me $60 to replace the tire as a fine, something I still get angry about when I think of it, because I'm sure they ripped me off.

But if there was one job that prepared me for the scabs I saw on Judson Brodus Bay's arms it was the job I took during my last two years in college. The job was as a gravedigger in the cemetery beside Interstate 95 on the north edge of Providence. We were opening the graves to make way for more highway.

I loved that job. I was gravedigger on the North Burial Grounds. At first, I was scared to death, really scared. But after two weeks, I'd get in, hop on the old caskets, sling them and then pull the ropes to get them out. Most of the boxes we moved were rotting like old wet leaves. Then there would be the bones. We would kid around, and the old-timers, finding the only thing remaining was a skeleton with a head of hair, would hold it up by the roots and joke. These old-timers in the graveyard would put their hands in the casket, take the rings off the corpses, then eat lunch.

Gravedigger never made it onto my résumé, of course, but looking back, it certainly was a job that prepared me to become a federal drug agent.

After the raid my mind was still racing when we returned to the office. I couldn't stop telling Morrison and Johnny Thompson about my big experience.

When we hit the door, the first guy going in had a big

raincoat, I told the agents, as if their sharp eyes could possibly have missed so obvious a detail. But talking seemed the only way to calm down, so I told them how the coat swung out into a cape and I felt like I was following Batman through the door.

They smiled.

"It gets even wilder," Johnny Thompson said.

"Yeah, like the guy from Texas we hired. He didn't last very long, but he sure had a wild time," Morrison said.

I was probably the only agent in that small clique too new to have heard the story. Now it was my turn to listen as Morrison talked.

"They had staked out one of those tenements in Harlem, but when they got to the front door it was fortified so they were about to give up when this Texas guy tells the group, 'Don't worry, I'll go around the back and lasso myself something and drop in the window and hold them until you get there.'

"Hard to believe, but they went for it. Anyway, kid, he lassoed himself straight into the apartment. His feet crashed in but they caught on the blinds and he was dangling in midair, his gun wavering over a room packed with about two dozen Puerto Ricans, men, women, children, infants. All innocent, except he didn't know that.

"So he spots a woman carrying what looks like the littlest baby in her arms and says, 'Nobody move or I'll kill the kid.' Well, it turned out he had lassoed himself into the wrong apartment. And there was a stink with the lawyers and the civil liberties people so we had to let him go."

I was sweating thinking back on the threats we had made against the people in Judson Brodus Bay's apartment.

Johnny Thompson noticed my discomfort. "Don't worry, kid, you had the right apartment. But next time, if it makes you feel better, you can say, 'Federal agent. Move and I'll kill you.' Still, it better be the right apartment." This was my awakening to the public scrutiny that comes with the job of law enforcement—every action, no matter how well intended, will be questioned and second-guessed by someone: editorial writer, defense attorney, the government's own internal affairs investigator.

I quickly settled down into a routine of fourteen-hour days and I would have made them longer if I could have stayed awake. I loved it. I had begun to develop my own network of informants, the users, small-fry dealers and their associates who are the source of most narcotics information. I also developed a couple of the undercover roles that all agents learn. I was "Stucky" to the dealers on the street; a white addict and small-time pusher until it came time to make an arrest. With my soiled tie and worn sport coat, I looked for all the world like an Ivy Leaguer gone lush.

I repeated the same drill straight through the fall: contact, buy, bust; all small-time heroin dealers, all black. At the time, the only drug cases the federal government seemed willing to pursue with any regularity were against lower-level black dealers. In essence, our policy at the time was to enforce narcotics laws only within the ghetto. This myopia left us blind to drugs spreading through the rest of society. It was a mistake that I swore never to repeat. When the crack epidemic surfaced in the mid-1980s, I fought hard to get our policymakers to see that the problem extended beyond the ghetto.

But in 1965 our policy was as untried as I was, so it was understandable that drugs were still viewed as solely a problem for the ghetto. Not since the first great cocaine epidemic ended in 1906 when the Pure Food and Drug Act made cocaine illegal had the middle class been a significant clientele for cocaine or other illegal drugs. However, by 1966, marijuana had changed that. Marijuana was also how I got to meet Steve Medwid. The son of a Pittsburgh steelworker and an avid football fan, Medwid had been working in the Baltimore office when word came that there were a lot of white kids screwing around with dope. His supervisors told him, "We want you to go up to Washington. They've got a young guy up there who you'll partner up with." The friendship born of that partnership would outlast both our careers.

In the Washington office, Leroy Morrison called the two of us in. I remember it vividly because it turned out to be the day I began to learn one of the most important lessons of my early career.

"Go out," Morrison coughed, "and see if you can find some dope among those smelly fucking hippies."

We didn't look at all like Miami Vice. Medwid had his madras jacket and white socks and I wore my outfit of beige slacks, green velour shirt and black penny loafers. We looked like members of an old-fashioned vice squad. It being a Monday, Morrison looked hung over. He reminded me that day of Hank, the bloated detective played by Orson Welles in *Touch of Evil,* the one who fixed dope cases and who, when described at the scene of his death as "a good detective, all right," was eulogized by Marlene Dietrich's rejoinder: "And a lousy cop."

There was plenty of marijuana to be found. Every month Medwid and I had to stop making undercover buys on the eighteenth and use the rest of the time to catch up on our paperwork. You typed everything from a case on individual investigative forms and then gathered it together and retyped it on one long narrative form that ran fourteen to eighteen pages. We hated that. But it is a cornerstone of the DEA's case method even today. Those narratives are all retrievable from the computer and can be mined for seemingly insignificant bits of information to help make a later case anywhere in the country.

Medwid and I decided we could get the most for our efforts by targeting college campuses. From the start, the cases caught the media's attention.

"American U. Student Accused in Sale of Dope in 1st Campus Arrest Here," read the *Washington Post* page one headline on January 14, 1966. It was my first case to make the papers and I felt great.

"The arrest yesterday of an 18-year-old American University freshman from New Haven, Conn., has brought to 19 the number of persons charged with violations of the Marijuana Tax Act here over the past three months," staff writer Alfred E. Lewis wrote.

"The suspect taken into custody by agents of the Federal Bureau of Narcotics yesterday was booked as George R.

Cronk.... Narcotics agents said Cronk's was the first arrest made on an area campus. The city ranks fifth in the number of narcotics users among large cities around the country, a spokesman said, but few complaints have involved college students—a growing problem elsewhere.

"Cronk was charged specifically with selling 4.2 grains of marijuana for $10 to a Federal undercover man who was brought into the case by University officials who asked the Bureau to check out rumors of marijuana activity involving the suspect."

I practically know the story by heart. I was the undercover man. I had masqueraded as a student by using the name "Bob Evans" and purchased the pot in a dormitory room. I made the buy on October 1, our first on a college campus.

Other arrests followed and I began to see the power of the media. The reaction to the case on the college campus was so favorable that Morrison told us to drop the heroin cases and stick to marijuana. He also told us to find a way to make cases all month long, instead of using half our time for paperwork. We began to do our paperwork in the daytime, leaving our evenings to go out on the street and make our cases. The thing I remember best about it was feeling, Jesus Christ, can't I go home sometime?

We were the two men assigned to control marijuana in Washington. That was it. And it snowballed. A few of the more successful cases got prominent display in the Washington papers. In each case, Medwid and I were dubbed "agent-hippies." Some were large seizures, others like the first case, no more than a small bag of marijuana.

Then we arrested a congressman's daughter for possessing a little grass, and all of a sudden lawmakers were reading about their kids. Now they wanted marijuana stopped. Not one of them had raised the same stink when reporters in their home states had picked out the problem. But reading it in Washington, which as far as most legislators are concerned is their hometown, they wanted it stopped, and now.

That was the kernel of the lesson. Whether it was 1966 or 1987, a bag of marijuana or vial of crack sold in Washington had more power to shape national policy than drug gang firebombings in Los Angeles or New York or mass shootings in Miami. If you're a cynical drug agent you would almost think the DEA Washington office should spend its time identifying the trends spotted across the rest of the country, then staging those problems in Washington so that it doesn't take five years for policy to catch up with a problem that has already burned half the nation.

Medwid and I kept making marijuana cases and the cases kept getting attention. As a young agent, I didn't question whether these people should actually go to jail for smoking pot. The one time I started to have doubts, the person I arrested convinced me otherwise.

We were driving down to Georgetown when I spotted a girl hitchhiking. We're in a government car, so I said, "Quick, Steve, hide the radio."

Then we let her in.

"Hey, where you goin', baby?" I asked.

"Hey, man, if you take me down to Montgomery County I'll give you a bag of grass," she answered.

"Okay," I said.

She handed over the grass.

"Honey, I hate to tell you this, I'm a federal agent and you're under arrest."

Then she started to cry and I felt terrible. I mean she could have been anybody's kid and I was feeling guilty at having tricked her.

"Look, we don't care about the grass," I said. "Just tell us where you get the stuff and we'll let you go."

She picked her chin up and answered me with the hate in her eyes. "Go fuck yourself," she added, almost unnecessarily.

I put the handcuffs on.

In hindsight, I don't think any of those people should have ended up doing prison terms for using marijuana, but I don't have any regrets. What those cases did was show people for the first time that drugs had left the minority communities. Before 1966 we concentrated purely on heroin and nobody paid attention. The predominant attitude among most Americans, and certainly most agents, was, "Who cares who sells it as long as only black people are using it?" What was happening, and we didn't realize it, was we were living through history. Drugs were leaving the ghetto, so all of a sudden they were becoming understood as a truly American problem.

It would still be a few years before the newspapers would trace the trail of heroin from the poppies of Turkey to the arms of suburban, white Americans. In the meantime, marijuana was the subject of their burning editorial interest. Mainstream newspapers joined legislators in screaming for an immediate attack on the problem. Busy with the war on poverty and the war in Vietnam, the Johnson administration couldn't declare war on drugs. Instead, it decided to use the drug issue and the FBN agents to declare war on peace, on those activists opposed to the escalation of U.S. involvement in Southeast Asia. Rather than see the growing evidence of marijuana abuse as proof that drug use had taken root in the middle class, the administration decided it would try to prove that anyone opposed to Vietnam was a dope addict.

It was a shameful attempt by Lyndon Johnson. But if you had laid it out to me back then, I still might not have understood what a great disservice it was to both law enforcement and civil liberties. I was a young agent, and like young agents and cops everywhere, I was trained to do my job without looking for the larger view. In the end, seeing how law enforcement can be bent to questionable policies makes you cynical, because a federal agent, like a cop on the beat, is supposed to serve the public, not a particular administration.

Yet drug agents have always been held hostage by each administration's budgetary power. The effect has been the same as what would happen if a city police department was cut in half or doubled each time there was a new mayor. It would lead to massive confusion. And that is the state of our nation's drug enforcement efforts.

Agents called Johnson's distasteful plan to subvert drug policy Operation Bent Penny.

Anti-war activists had a massive sleep-in set for the Washington Monument. The next day they planned a parade and a march in front of the White House. They had all the necessary paperwork but the Johnson administration ordered us to find a reason to revoke the permits. One hundred FBN

agents, almost half our number at the time, were brought to
the big auditorium over at the Department of State.

"You guys spend the night in there, work undercover and
get probable cause," the senior agents were ordered to tell us,
"so that in the morning we can revoke the permit and clean
them out."

That was their only purpose. To dress it up, they told us
all this fancy stuff about how important this was to the nation.
Most of us were the kind of guys who were for the war. We
didn't have any problem with being the means to a just end.

"There's one other thing," the senior agents told us. "You
can't carry badges. Because if you get any trouble, we don't
want you carrying badges." That way they had deniability if
someone charged the government had planted cops in a peace
demonstration. That should have tipped us off that this was
wrong, but it didn't.

"So we're going to give every one of you a bent penny to
carry instead. And every cop in Washington, D.C., is going to
know that there are undercover agents in there with these
pennies bent in half.

"And make sure you're out of there by eight o'clock
because at eight the horses are coming in, lots of them, and
those horses when they charge can't tell that you're a cop."

We went in and it was unbelievable: drugs, open sex and
we legitimately got more than enough probable cause for drug
cases.

At 6 A.M., Medwid said to me, "We got to get out of here."

So we start to walk out and we run into a cop, one of
hundreds surrounding the perimeter.

"Where you guys goin'?" he asked.

"I got a bent penny," Medwid said.

"I don't give a fuck if your penny's bent or not," the cop
answered. Then he took a swing at us. Before he took another, we went back inside where we waited for the horses to
charge.

When they came at 8 A.M. it was a horror. We and the
100,000 hippies were on the same side now, the side of trying
to get out of this cordon of horses and cops alive. This
operation was on direct orders from the president, his idea,

and they managed to screw it up. Which was why, even if you didn't see anything wrong with the politics, as Morrison explained to us afterward, "You never want to get involved with a bunch of amateurs."

I realized that Morrison had sent us in there knowing that it was wrong and aware all along that it was going to get screwed up. But from his perspective, there was nothing he could do to tip us off. He didn't trust us that much. I suppose I understood, but he went from idol to mere mortal real fast in my eyes. And President Johnson became someone I knew the country could never trust.

The Bush administration found its own version of Bent Penny in the spring of 1989. Crack, the smokable form of cocaine, was finally noticed in Washington in the fifth year of an epidemic that had already ravaged New York, Miami, Detroit, Los Angeles and the lungs of suburban, rural and inner-city youths across the nation. Crack-related murders were even taking place inside the Beltway. The government moved quickly to use enforcement solely for political effect.

William Bennett, then drug czar, acting on orders from George Bush to redeclare war on drugs, ignored the national catastrophe and created a fake focus on Washington: Bennett announced the formation of a $100 million plan to fight drugs in the capital. He explained that expense by stating that before effectively fighting the drug war on a national level, America needed to examine a microcosm of law enforcement—federal, state and local—at work in the capital. It was the last thing we needed, as any federal agent or local police officer could have told Bush and Bennett.

We had already witnessed the results of a similar strategy in force in New York since Police Officer Edward Byrne's 1988 death at the hands of drug ring assassins. The plan, with its identical $100 million price tag, had only succeeded in clogging the courts, overcrowding the jails, pushing the drug problem from one neighborhood to another and increasing the number of dead and wounded local and federal agents.

Sadly, Jack Lawn, our administrator, had to scramble to pull troops from other battles to fight Bennett's war. When asked why he committed his manpower to a maneuver that had already proven unsuccessful, Lawn resorted to tact and called the decision to use his agents to police the capital, "Not a law enforcement decision.

"Bill Bennett...was looking for immediate impact and believed that immediate impact could be felt in Washington, D.C., in the microcosm," Lawn said privately. "But while it certainly has captured media attention, there has been a very negative impact on police departments around the country. Focusing the task force issue and Bennett's first swing of the bat in Washington, D.C., clearly indicates to the rest of the law enforcement community that this is a political task force, not a law enforcement task force." Shortly afterward, Jack Lawn left the DEA. The Brooklyn-born cop who cared went home to take a position as an executive for the New York Yankees.

During the Green Death era, as Medwid and I called the years of tough marijuana law enforcement, we still made an occasional heroin arrest but only when it was unavoidable. One of them, a particularly colorful case, taught me a key portion of my lesson on the media, even though it never made the papers.

We saw a black guy driving a beautiful Cadillac. He had just stopped at a place called Wing's the Thing. Its motto was, "Chicken ain't nothing but a bird, the wing's the thing."

The restaurant featured a condiment called Mumbo sauce, pretty spicy, greasy stuff. The guy had just gotten his chicken. We spotted him. He spotted us. He took off and threw the bag of heroin out on the street. And of course the bag also had the chicken grease on it. Even though it was a half ounce of heroin—at the time a hell of a case—nobody in the press was interested.

That proved the other half of a credo I would later teach my agents: "Good cases don't necessarily make good press. And good press doesn't necessarily need good cases." A white kid was going to have to die before anyone was interested in heroin. The inequity was as ugly and as simple as that.

My education in drug enforcement and the effect of politics and the media on drug enforcement continued to grow each day.

One morning shortly after this incident, Morrison was

ready to give his final lesson, one that would shape the remainder of my career. I have a bittersweet memory of the appointment. Morrison was looking worse every day as his retirement date approached. I didn't know it then, but it was one of the last times we would speak.

"Bob," he asked, "ever give a speech?"

"No," I said.

"You're giving one at the Lion's Club next week."

"Okay."

I went home in a panic to prepare. My appearance, since the beginning of my career, was my biggest insecurity and with some justification. A picture of me that appeared in one of the papers shows the buttons straining to close my double-breasted suit. I was chubby. I had also begun to comb my thinning hair across the top of my head, one of a series of desperate cosmetic attempts to attack baldness that only ended in 1984.

I was also terrified that I would have nothing to say. I read everything available. Nervously, I gave my speech. When I did, I discovered two things. I liked speaking; and the public, as represented by the fifty people at the luncheon, knew nothing about drugs.

The speech was titled "Narcotics and Marijuana Use."

It must have been a terrible speech. But by November, I was speaking everywhere, including the suburbs. I remember telling one group, "All of a sudden, white suburbia has become addicted. I would hate to think what would happen in this country if marijuana were legalized." I still believe that before we reach what may turn out to be an inevitable decision to legalize some drugs, we ought to attack the drug problem in a coherent way. We have to ask ourselves first, Why do we want a society dependent on drugs?

My speechmaking began to get noticed in the higher reaches of the government.

It was not, however, getting much favorable notice by Steve Medwid, who did not even bother to attend. His job, as he saw it, was to make cases, not blow bubbles.

At the time we partners were chewing over this latest

difference, which already included football, religion and everything else, Leroy Morrison sank into depression and retired.

I continued to make speeches.

One day, about a year later, we came to work and were told that Morrison had placed his revolver in his mouth and pulled the trigger, blowing his brains out. After the funeral Morrison's son went down to the police station, reclaimed the gun, and repeated his father's actions.

During the years ahead, I attempted to steer a zigzag course through the treacheries of Washington. But when faced with a particularly tough dilemma I would unaccountably shudder and then I would imagine that revolver's reports. "Remember, kid," the echo seemed to say. It would be difficult not to screw up in Washington.

SEVEN

The Growth Years: 1969–1971

Richard Nixon became president in 1969 when social upheaval and the war in Vietnam were at their height. It was a presidency, a climate and an event that shaped, more than anything since, the domestic and overseas policies governing the war on drugs.

Nixon wanted to combat heroin, marijuana and LSD on America's streets while simultaneously carrying the war to the opiate and cannabis producers overseas and in Mexico. It was the first attempt by an administration to fully orchestrate an anti-drug policy, and Nixon's people at the State and Justice departments were methodical in implementing it.

They began with a series of steps that evolved from Lyndon Johnson's move in April 1968 to combine two overlapping agencies, my Federal Bureau of Narcotics and the Bureau of Drug Abuse Control. But Nixon's plan had much greater scope than Johnson's merger, which aimed solely at increasing efficiency and eliminating bureaucratic infighting. Nixon's staff intended to substantially increase the nation's anti-drug forces while upgrading their haphazard training. This professional force would carry a clear anti-drug message to the nation and carry that same message overseas, where agents would assist allies to battle the drug producers.

In two short years, the Nixon administration revamped the entire mechanism for narcotics enforcement. Then, in 1971, Nixon, gearing up for reelection, declared "total war" against drugs.

It was the nation's first formal declaration of a war against drugs; Nixon, correctly sensing a growing fear of drug abuse, was able to make it, knowing his staff had already completed much of the groundwork in preparing our forces to fight it. Mired in an unpopular war winding to an end in Southeast Asia, Nixon now hoped to capitalize on domestic success against drug abuse.

To a large extent, the policy he shaped and the mechanism for fighting abuse Nixon developed has remained the core of every anti-drug campaign that followed. With little more than the perfunctory addition of treatment and prevention language to their speeches, each future administration declared war on drugs by following the Nixon blueprint: Local and federal law enforcement overseen by the Justice Department and influenced by the State Department on foreign policy issues would carry the burden of the fight against drugs.

The Nixon plan demanded the government begin an immediate scramble to find the right agents to help professionalize our methods and polish our anti-drug image. If the drug wars were to be waged for maximum media impact from the start, the gruff, hard-drinking mold from which agents like Leroy Morrison were cast would have to be broken. Shortly after the revamping started, I was chosen to develop the first federal training program for the nation's local police forces. The course would teach cops the best methods to enforce the drug laws and serve to introduce the federal government's increased interest. At the same time, I was asked to begin a lecture tour to explain the government's anti-drug message to community groups and the police agencies the course couldn't immediately reach.

I had been searching for that type of a job. For months, whenever I had had a free moment to relax, my thoughts had returned to Morrison. Looking ahead, I could see how easy it would be to take the personal emptiness that thirty straight years of case work can leave and wind up like him, if not tragically dead, certainly a broken man. One Saturday night, I had been mulling over that kind man and his tragic last lesson, when the telephone rang. I picked it up and heard a senior agent bark: "Monday, you're moving to Baltimore."

I tried to explain I needed some time with my family. As it was, my schedule left me little enough time at home. Not knowing what lay ahead, I wasn't looking forward to losing another two hours each day to the boredom of a commute.

"Never mind. We need you. Just report," the senior agent said before completing his briefing.

I was leaving behind an eight-agent office to join the regional headquarters for the Bureau of Narcotics and Dangerous Drugs, the name of the agency that resulted from the merger of the 265 agents of my Federal Bureau of Narcotics and the 335 of the Bureau of Drug Abuse Control. In 1969, the BNDD's Baltimore office was the closest thing that we had to a major field division. It was the home base for two dozen narcotics agents assigned to patrol a four-state region plus Washington. The smaller field offices, including our outfit in the District of Columbia, were under its command.

In the months before my transfer I had been sent from Washington to the Baltimore office several times to assist in developing a corruption case against one of our agents who was suspected of selling heroin. I liked the agents I had met in Baltimore and I liked the idea that I would be able to follow my corruption case to its conclusion. But even more, I liked that the new responsibilities in training and lecturing satisfied the doubts that had been nagging me for months. When I added up the cases I had made, they seemed to lead nowhere. Certainly they had failed to dent the still-growing marijuana problem.

I could already see that in a career built on case work I would each day merely add another bead to the string of ugly lives I had encountered. When that criminal rosary was completed, I would still be left to wonder if I had made life better for anyone else. I didn't think I was up to it. I craved a less abstract satisfaction and a greater sense of respect that was missing. This new job seemed a perfect way to get both.

After my wife, Lee, agreed to the transfer, my only

concern was that I was being torn away from my partner. I dialed Medwid.

"Steve, they're moving me," I said.

"You're not going alone, pal," he replied. "I got the call too. I guess they figure we make a pretty good team."

I began to smile. It now looked like I was moving on to an exciting job with the blessing of my wife and with my partnership intact. Lee and I, with Medwid, who was single at the time and felt like a part of our family, spent the rest of the weekend happily planning our futures. As Monday approached, I wished that I could pick up the telephone and call Leroy Morrison. It had been his recommendation that I make speeches against drugs that began the chain of events that had earned me and Medwid this opportunity.

One of those early speeches was to an audience of Central Intelligence Agency agents and executives at the agency's Langley, Virginia, headquarters. The CIA had its own interest in the anti-drug efforts, including, it seemed, a continued effort to pin the blame for increased abuse on those who protested the war.

I told the audience that while the pro-drug forces had high-profile spokesmen, including Timothy Leary, lecturing on the mind-expanding properties of drugs, the government had virtually no one out there combating that message—for at the time, I was the only agent making speeches.

The November 1967 speech was well received. Government agents were beginning to receive parental requests to "do something" about drugs, an onslaught that later helped galvanize the Nixon administration into action. Shortly afterward, the CIA chiefs sent a letter to my FBN superiors encouraging them to increase the number of my lectures. When Nixon was elected, the CIA followed up their letter by contacting his senior advisers to suggest my speeches could be an effective tool. Amid the flux of developing the Nixon anti-drug plan, that caused me to stand out as a spokesman and singled me out for advancement to Baltimore.

Monday morning, I plowed my government Chevrolet Corvair over to Medwid's house to begin our first trip to Baltimore and what would become a two-year road show of training, cases and speeches across Maryland, North Carolina, Virginia, West Virginia and the District of Columbia.

"You know, Bob, the next dealer we arrest had better be driving a more comfortable car," Medwid said as he struggled into the passenger seat. In those days, our agency had no budget for cars, so we drove whatever we seized.

"I know. This guy must have been dealing aspirins," I said. While Ralph Nader had yet to force the Corvair, America's first rear-engine production car, from the road with his book *Unsafe at Any Speed,* Medwid and I wished the car was gone. Its pancake-design, four-cylinder engine barely kept us in the flow of traffic. Embarrassed, we drove it past the front of Baltimore's impressive Federal Building, then quietly slipped into the basement parking garage. Compared to our old offices above the drugstore, the place looked like a palace.

But inside, there was a revolt going on.

It had been about nine months since the merger of the FBN and BDAC into the Bureau of Narcotics and Dangerous Drugs. In our backwater field office the merger had seemed theoretical and our little cadre of agents conducted business as usual, right down to the faded FBN logo on our office door.

But here at the regional headquarters, bitter infighting had erupted between agents of the two factions within the mongrel agency. Medwid and I stepped out of our Corvair and smack into turmoil.

Two federal agents were slugging it out in a barehanded fistfight in the garage. The landing of each blow was punctuated by a cheer from agents of the former Federal Bureau of Narcotics or from those agents who hailed from the Bureau of Drug Abuse Control. A clot of the warring agents had gathered around and were egging on their former agency's champion.

"What's going on?" I asked a guy I knew had been with the FBN.

"The rat-shit inspector was trying to tell our guy how to make a case," the agent said. The curse referred to BDAC's health code responsibilities, which had included checking restaurant kitchens. "Now he's getting his ass kicked."

"Welcome to friendly Baltimore." As I said it, I turned my head away from the fight to see the disbelief forming on

Steve's face. "We really want to join this?" Steve said. Then he just shook his head and we went to find our lockers. We didn't have much choice.

The point of the merger had been to stop infighting and increase efficiency. Instead, agents of each faction were continuing to settle their differences with blows. Prior to the merger we had often found ourselves doing just that out in the field as two sets of agents independently chased one set of defendants and occasionally wound up trying to arrest each other. Medwid and I had been involved in one of these embarrassing incidents. As agents of the Federal Bureau of Narcotics, we had been developing a marijuana case against a group of middle-class kids in Washington. The Bureau of Drug Abuse Control, meanwhile, had put together an LSD case against the same group.

Of course, neither set of agents was aware of what the other was doing since we never talked to each other.

Finally, one afternoon, Medwid and I decided to take down the case. We drove over to an apartment in southeast Washington that the group was using as a stash pad, and with Medwid beside me, our guns in our hands, I kicked in the door.

When it crashed down, all hell broke loose.

"You dumb sons of bitches," this one guy in the room shouts.

"Shut the fuck up, pal, and get your hands up," I said.

But he keeps screaming. "Do you know who I am? I'm a federal agent!"

Whoever he is, he's panicked. I'm worried because the situation is in danger of getting out of control. The other defendants in the room can feel the confusion.

"My name is Strickler, Jerry Strickler, I'm with BDAC," he shouts in my face.

It's the last thing he utters before Medwid steps up, gun in his right hand, and slaps him left-handed across the mouth. The half dozen defendants gasp and the room goes still as Medwid slaps him several more times, first one side, then the other. In the quiet all you could hear were the echoes of the slaps off this guy Strickler's face.

Finally Medwid stops. In an even voice, with a breath between each word, he said, "Shut your fucking mouth." He said it very calmly and Strickler shut up. "And the rest of you," he added in the same even voice: "Hands up, shut up and sit up straight."

The room was back under control. That was the way we were taught: If things get out of hand, take control fast, however you have to do it.

It turned out that there was plenty of dope and we made our case. Unfortunately, the BDAC could just as easily have made the case. Instead, one federal agent wound up slapping another around, and for several months a great deal of manpower had been wasted and effort duplicated.

By putting the merger of the FBN and BDAC under the direct control of the Attorney General, who also controlled the Justice Department's army of federal lawyers, everyone hoped to prevent these types of incidents and to ensure that drug arrests and prosecutions would be better coordinated.

But the effect of the merger was weakened and frictions among new co-workers heightened by the failure of Nixon's decision makers to pick one leader for the agency. Of course, one chief would also have meant that the head of one or the other defunct agency was out looking for work. The Justice Department punted. It decided to maintain that status quo by running the new agency with three bosses. The head of the FBN and the head of the BDAC were both kept on as the two deputies in charge of day-to-day operations. They were put under the titular direction of John Ingersoll, a new man who had never before worked in federal law enforcement. From the start, orders issued by one of the top deputies were usually countermanded by the other, often at a moment's notice. There was no way Ingersoll could control them—they just knew too much and he too little about the ins and outs of drug enforcement. By the time Nixon was reelected, Ingersoll, who was a wonderful guy, had taken the blame for the ongoing factional friction and was forced to resign.

Medwid and I handled the frustration the same way agents handle frustration today, by burying ourselves in our work.

We worked on "the Block," which was actually a two-and-a-half-block square with the headquarters of the Baltimore police at its center and an array of cheap attractions laid end to end on the streets. There, the blue-collar Slavs and Germans could take in the best corned beef in the world at Jack's, get propositioned by a $5 prostitute on any corner, walk by a strip show on every block, and if they were too rowdy, feel the thick pound of their blue-uniformed brethren's hand upon their collars and end up sleeping off the night in the basement of police headquarters.

On weekdays, Medwid and I, with our staff of two other agents, would stroll through those streets and climb to the upper floors of headquarters to prepare the narcotics enforcement lectures that we delivered to small groups until we reached each of Baltimore's 3,000 cops.

The program became the Federal Bureau of Narcotics and Dangerous Drugs national model for in-service training, and in a much-updated form it is the same school that the DEA provides for law enforcement colleagues today. It was the beginning of the professionalization of narcotics enforcement. The idea was to teach the cops how to identify illegal drugs, the users and the dealers. By carefully explaining the scientific facts of each drug, we gave the cops the tools they needed to fight drugs effectively.

During those first heady months when Medwid and I were still fumbling to develop our curriculum and get comfortable in this new role for federal narcotics agents—that of educating our colleagues—the corruption case I had begun while still stationed in Washington reached its finale.

Frank Pappas, the regional director of the BNDD, called me into his office. Very early on, Pappas had run a license plate check on a suspected drug dealer's car only to be told by the Motor Vehicle Bureau that the car was registered to the U.S. government. As the case developed, I had traveled regularly from Washington to Baltimore where I worked undercover and gathered information from drug dealers confirming that our agent was corrupt. Since I was from out of town, Pappas figured there was little chance of the agent recognizing me during any encounter. Now it was time to complete the case against him by recording him during a drug transaction.

"Bob, it's time to take down the case we began when you were in Washington," Pappas said in his earnest, quiet voice. I sensed he was as unhappy about it as I was.

"When?" I asked expectantly.

"Tonight. We're going out to buy the drugs from him. We've already got enough conversations on tape that with the buy we can bring him in," Pappas said.

That night, Joe Arpaio, who was Pappas's assistant, another senior agent and I were crammed together in the back of a van parked on a suburban side street. There we watched as the rogue agent, Charlie MacDonald, pulled up in his black government Ford. Before the merger, he had been the senior BDAC agent in charge of the Middle Atlantic States.

"It's sad," I said to Arpaio.

"Yeah," he said, and sucked on his stogie. Arpaio and the other agent were both old-fashioned Italians and they smoked those gnarled stogies with the well-earned nickname "guinea stinkers."

"You know," I said, "those things have to be worse than any drug they use to get high, I'm friggin' dizzy."

"Yeah," Arpaio said, sucking again on the foul stogie. "You'll get used to it. Or else, someday they'll figure out how to ventilate these vans."

Then a flash of motion outside caught our attention and we turned to watch MacDonald hand a package to the undercover agent he had arranged to meet. I felt a hollow sickness in my stomach. Although I knew all along that MacDonald was dirty—I had also sat on the wiretaps for weeks—I had just had my first taste of corruption. It is an ugly thing. The package contained a kilogram of heroin. I wondered if MacDonald carried his government gold shield while he sold drugs.

The undercover paid and got back into his own car with the package of heroin.

"That's it, kid, let's go home," Arpaio said. "Tomorrow Pappas can bust him." But MacDonald wasn't arrested the next day. Before the arrest could be made he managed to resign with his record still clean, protecting his pension. At some point between the buy and the arrest, he apparently got wind of the case. I always wondered if he had been allowed to retire rather than risk a public scandal, but I was never given an answer to that question. It was the open ending to what turned out to be my final case as a field agent.

The day after I witnessed the buy, Medwid joined me on the Block for a corned beef. "You know, Steve, this guy had been going around saying openly that after the merger he would head the joint office for this region. Meanwhile he's dealing heroin. I just can't believe it."

"I know, pal, and I'm sad about that too," Medwid said. "But I'm wondering, because it's a government car already, does that mean we're still stuck with the Corvair?"

We were, just as we were stuck with corruption as a fact of life. And that was the way we explained it in our lectures to police and community groups—a fact of life that narcotics agents had to live with. We stressed to the cops that each officer needed to be aware of corruption and report it because it could taint us all. We told the community groups that only a handful of agents were corrupt—no different, we explained, than the handful of bank tellers who stole. Only we were never sure we believed it, because we, like most people, believed the shield of a federal agent carried with it a higher standard. That is why the question of whether MacDonald was allowed to escape unpunished still troubles me.

While the talks to the police groups were basically a scaled-down version of the Baltimore seminars—the idea was to give uniformed officers an overview of drug identification techniques—the talks to community groups veered off in another direction.

The first hurdle, always, was to explain who we were and why we were interested in helping. In those days, federal, to just about everyone, meant FBI, and the FBI meant civil rights law, intelligence gathering, witch hunts, the works. Everybody respected the FBI's power but nobody wanted an FBI agent in their living room. They'd much rather have a narc, and for better or worse, we played on that, explaining, as we later did on our overseas tours, that we were only responsible for enforcing the federal narcotics statutes.

Then we outlined, as we did for the cops, the effects of each drug, the laws governing its use and characteristics of a user. But after that, we launched into scare tactics. Each civilian group that expectantly sat before us, the first government drug agents most had ever met, heard a litany of horror caused by drugs. Of course, the stuff we told them was exaggerated.

One night in 1970, I got caught. It happened at the University of Maryland as I stood before a group of about 400 people, including the resident advisors and faculty counselors.

"Marijuana," I began, spitting the word out at the audience. "By now many of you have tried it and you probably think you like it. But let me tell you about the long-term effects, the permanent marijuana psychosis."

The hands went up, confusing me as I had barely launched into my fire-and-brimstone sermon.

"Mr. Stutman," someone said. "Look around the room. Many of these people have tried marijuana. Some use it regularly. We are all educated enough to know there is no long-term psychosis attached to the drug."

He was right and I was mortified. I had been caught in a lie and this sermon was over. What I had been feeding the public was disinformation that just didn't jibe with the facts. By overstating the case, I, and the growing cadre of government spokesmen I had helped train, let drug culture advocates have a field day poking holes. The result was like the film *Reefer Madness* all over again—so exaggerated that the real dangers would be laughed off. From that time on I never overstated the dangers of drugs. I began to see that what the public needed was an education based on the facts, not a Grimm's fairy tale cloaked in purple haze. When I tried this in later speeches, expounding on the real harms of marijuana—fouled motor coordination, reduced testosterone levels and short-term memory loss—the audience responded better. But the lesson was painful. My speeches and other speeches like them had destroyed our credibility at a time when we needed it most.

In mid-1970, we in narcotics enforcement were at the height of our growth years. The Nixon administration had approved hiring another 600 agents, bringing us to a strength of about 1,200. While still in their infant stages, overseas operations had begun and we already had several offices operating abroad. Although drug enforcement efforts were growing rapidly, they still desperately needed to mature. We were terrible at spotting the next wave of abuse.

I also needed to mature, as I soon learned when Frank Pappas called me into his office.

He looked up serenely from across the beige desk blotter as I opened the door. Then he carefully capped the fountain pen filled with green ink that he used to criticize an agent's reports and dropped it into his shirt pocket.

"Bob, there is something you should know." Pappas said it in the sincere, straight-arrow way that he had, but the even-toned voice managed to let me know I had sinned. What made me edgy was that it gave me no clue as to the magnitude of the offense; the level voice hid any hint. In my nervousness I ran through the entire list of sins that federal agents routinely commit. Stealing time from the job? I was guilty. Taking shortcuts on reports? I was guilty of that too. Borrowing government cars for shopping? Guilty. Threatening to violate suspects' constitutional rights by killing them? Guilty and I'd kill them if they'd complained, I thought.

"You should know that you can't be one of the boys and direct the boys. You're young, but you're the training guy. You can't go out and drink with the guys and later expect to give orders to them. They might like you, but ultimately they won't respect you," Pappas finally said.

I could only nod with relief. My sin had been only one of omission in the eyes of the strict Greek Orthodox Pappas. As such, it was one I could correct.

"Thank you, Mr. Pappas. This is a lesson I'll never forget."

"It's okay, Bob. Congratulations." Pappas handed me a government form.

At age twenty-seven I had just become the youngest supervisor in the BNDD, an $18,000-a-year Government Service Grade 14. Until now, my supervisory duties had not been official.

"I guess I'm stuck with you if I want company," I told Medwid on the way home that night. I thought it was a nice way to let him know that the two of us would remain partners.

"Thanks a truckload super-Jew. Now will you quit acting like Wally Cleaver and figure out where it is we're gonna stop for a sandwich for the rest of our lives?" Our days on the Block were over.

Medwid dialed the radio looking for a sports score. When he needed both hands for the wheel, I turned it back to rock 'n' roll. I had my own scores to think about. MacDonald had turned informant, "flipped" in the language of federal agents, and his revelations made clear to me that the corruption was deeper in the BNDD than we had ever imagined. The lesson Pappas was giving me was one not only in management, but in staying clean. If you didn't know someone personally, it didn't pay to get too close. By the beginning of the 1970s, drug agents were making headlines not for catching crooks but for joining them.

Disheartening reports were cropping up everywhere. The earliest came out of New York, where by the late 1960s the entire office had been investigated. Then, in Boston, U.S. attorneys began a crackdown to sweep the BNDD office of the bad agents who had only recently joined them in the Justice Department.

In the years ahead, corruption, coupled with the disastrous disinformation campaign, would be seen as part of a pattern that tainted every good thing we did and every attempt at education. Narcotics enforcement developed a reputation as perhaps the only job worse than dredging corpses from the bottom of a harbor.

By 1971, this growing undercurrent was not yet strong enough for our detractors to tap. But it lay waiting beneath our feet as Nixon put the drug agents squarely in the public eye, declaring "total war against public enemy No. 1 in the U.S." It was to be a war on heroin and marijuana and Nixon promised that our allies overseas and in Mexico would be called on to help fight it. In December 1971, I learned that I would play a key role.

Frank Pappas, BNDD Administrator John Ingersoll and Ingersoll's training director, Perry Rivkind, called me to Washington. I drove up to the BNDD's headquarters at 1405 I Street. It was a far cry from the shabby Washington field office above the People's Drug Store where my career began almost seven years earlier, but it was still far enough outside the mainstream to be in the capital's peepshow district. Except for Benny's Rebel Room, a rock club where drugs were openly sold, the BNDD headquarters was the only non-X-rated business in this Northwest Washington neighborhood.

"Bob," I was told as the meeting got under way, "the agency is going all out in our effort to take the heroin war overseas. To the source. We think with your experience training cops here, and with the profile you've created for our agency through your speeches, you'd be perfect for part of the job."

"What part?" I asked.

"We'd like to make you director of overseas training," Rivkind answered.

"Congratulations," Pappas said, extending his hand before I could say a word.

"You take Medwid from Baltimore and design a course. We'll give the two of you whoever you need and the equipment to make it work," Ingersoll added. I would be moving back to the capital, only this time not to the Washington field office but to the headquarters office, where despite the neighborhood the agents all looked immaculate in their suits and bore a closer resemblance to congressional aides than to field men.

Nonetheless, I was thrilled, and to this day, despite his abuses I find it hard to have a bad word to say against Richard Nixon. From a cop's point of view, he was a friend—he gave us authority and manpower, the first president to do so. He was also, correctly, taking the drug war overseas to the opium-producing countries and to the intermediary nations through which opium, morphine and the heroin end product were transported to the United States.

The role that was carved out for Medwid and me required us to travel across the world training foreign officers on how to combat traffickers, in the hope of stopping the drugs before they landed in the United States. Our efforts would pave the way for establishing more than forty overseas bases for our agents. Combined with the domestic training efforts and community speeches—our first public appeals—this strategy completed the groundwork for our successful efforts in the decade to come.

As it turned out, as I left the meeting, I also saw a glimpse of the kind of foolishness that, when combined with corruption, disinformation and some reckless tactics on the part of our agents, almost destroyed all of our work in less than half that decade.

"You know, Elvis is coming today," Rivkind told me as we left the meeting where I was told of the overseas assignment.

"You're kidding, what does Elvis want here?" I asked. The entertainer's image was already so surrounded by a swirl of rumors of drug use that a visit to the anti-drug headquarters sounded more than just odd.

"A badge and BNDD credentials. But Ingersoll's a pro, he tried to refuse him," Rivkind said.

"We can't give a civilian a badge and creds, what if someday he's caught with drugs?" I asked as we walked down the hall. "What happened?"

"Nixon overruled. He said just give it to him. Elvis thinks he can help keep our youth off drugs. The White House promised Elvis would arrive quietly and things would be kept quiet."

It was clear from the minute we hit the lobby that quiet was the last thing this visit would be kept. There was Elvis, clad head to foot in a purple caped jumpsuit, with tinted shades and an entourage, climbing from a white limousine to the entrance of the BNDD. The man whose autopsy several years later revealed that he died with at least ten drugs in his system had conned Nixon into a badge. In return for this never-before-granted privilege, Elvis awarded the president a Colt .45 pistol and a promise to rid the entertainment world of commie drug users. As Elvis left the Oval Office, Nixon offered some parting advice:

"Never lose your credibility."

EIGHT

The Global Mission: 1971–1979

I returned home to Baltimore to pack. During my seven years as an agent the anti-drug apparatus had grown from a band of 265 rabble-rousers to a disciplined brigade of 1,200 agents charged with stopping a plague upon the nation. Our training methods had been polished and our speeches had introduced us to the public. Capitalizing on the knowledge that he had a group of anti-drug professionals at his command, President Nixon had thrown us into the spotlight with his declaration of war. He had given us a mandate to become narcotics cops for the world.

I knew that it meant our years as a quiet, backwater agency were over for good. With this latest mission, our anti-drug force was destined to continue to expand. At the close of 1971, the Bureau of Narcotics and Dangerous Drugs embarked on shaping a clear foreign policy against drugs that united our efforts at home with those of every country Steve Medwid and I visited. Drug traffickers, whose sophisticated distribution networks were becoming global, would be met with a global alliance.

I also knew that at twenty-eight, I had become a full-fledged administrator, with the daily concerns of shaping and executing a large part of this foreign policy. It would be a long time before I would again take part, even as a supervisor, in a drug case in the field. I felt the bittersweet transition most strongly when I returned to Baltimore's Federal Building and began to pick my possessions from the scraped metal-bottomed drawers of my desk. I knew I had a difficult task ahead but that was not what troubled me most as I lifted the indictments, speech notes, pencils, bullets and paper clips from my drawer and pushed them into boxes. It was taking on a job that would keep me away from home for three to four weeks at a time.

Our daughter, Kim, had just been born. Lee and I, with our son, Brian, had managed to maintain a semblance of family life on weekends and nights when I was not on the road lecturing. Now we faced the prospect of Lee raising two children with an absentee husband and father.

As it turned out, that described our marriage during the next seven years as I trotted from one country to the next. It's not something I'd recommend, but it certainly illustrates one of the hidden hazards in drug enforcement—getting divorced. By the end of this period, we had come very close before we fortunately worked our marriage out happily. The careers of many other agents are not all that different from mine, spending long stretches apart from their families. One result is that federal narcotics agents have a divorce rate of more than 50 percent, and most of the remaining 50 percent have been through several bouts of marriage counseling.

Who can say whether I would still think it was worth it if I had to do it all over again? But at that point I patched things up as best I could and right after New Year's excitedly headed for Washington. I left Lee behind in Randallstown, a suburb outside Baltimore where we had moved, and an unhappy Medwid behind in Baltimore to clean up our paperwork while I began planning our lecture tour.

I picked Rome, Italy, for our first training site. We already had an office there, an early attempt to combat the Italian Mafia's involvement in heroin transshipment. But Italy's reluctance to accommodate our requests to deport drug suspects and cooperate on cases had so far kept the office from making much headway. It seemed a perfect place to see if the course could become a useful tool.

It was also a choice that no one could quarrel with politically—it affected no other policy issues. In my education up to that point, I had become savvy enough in the ways of bureaucracy to know I had made a wise choice. I would have all the agency's factions, and those of the Justice and State departments, if not behind me, on the sidelines. This seemed important if the fledgling overseas program was going to succeed.

By the time Medwid arrived from Baltimore, I had pretty much worked out a two-week course that included surveillance, investigation, coordination between agencies and basic drug identification techniques. The curriculum also included briefings on sharing intelligence with the United States and the development of file systems to keep track of suspects by name, nickname, trafficking pattern and place in an organization. My own briefings by the State Department had helped me tailor the course specifically to the Italian law enforcement agencies' needs.

Medwid arrived angry.

"You dumb, conniving son of a bitch," were his first words. I had left him with so much owed paperwork—work we ducked by pleading that our lecture schedule was too demanding to spend time filing reports—that Medwid had received an official reprimand for sloppy case work.

"Don't worry, I'll make it up to you, Steve," I said. "Our first trip will be to Rome. How about it?" I told him that from what the State Department briefers had told me, a major failure of narcotics enforcement in Italy stemmed from the fact that the three Italian police agencies charged with drug enforcement refused to cooperate. Between the course and long hours of socializing every night, I told Medwid that we would have the opportunity to change that and convince them to cooperate with the United States and with each other.

We both knew how formidable this task was. Our agency's fights with others in government had for years hampered the nation's anti-drug efforts. Knowing how slowly bureaucracies change, neither of us had any confidence that we could succeed in two short weeks. But Medwid agreed to come along and give it a shot. We spent the next several weeks picking and training a support staff and a team of instructors. Medwid, in addition, prepared us for life on the road. He designed a set of metal "Blue Boxes," which contained all the things we'd need for weeks at a time: drug samples, ammunition for target training, camera equipment, microphones, batteries, bulbs, everything. He wisely figured that with our tight schedule anything we weren't carrying might be impossible to find in time.

Our planning was completed in February 1972, so we sent the instructors to Rome three weeks early while we put together an expanded curriculum for a six-week course we developed for high-ranking foreign law enforcement officials. That course would be conducted in Washington.

Then, in March, it was off to Rome.

The Italian police agencies involved were the elite carabinieri, the treasury agents and the Italian border police—their Customs Department. The agencies had never before conducted training, or even routine briefings together. From the start, we stressed that working together would allow them to build an airtight drug case against any target. Each night we went out to eat or drink and regaled our guests with our adventures fighting the drug traffickers and how our agency grew with success. During these evenings we hammered home how much fun we could all have by working together to beat the drug dealers. Then came the practical exercise, in effect, the graduation ceremony and final exam rolled into one.

We pulled together more than a hundred law officers, cars, helicopters and radios to trace a fictitious heroin shipment from the Rome airport to a hotel where mock arrests would be made. A couple of our instructors, accompanied by a couple of the Italian officers, played the parts of the narcotics smugglers. They would remove drug-laden suitcases from the baggage area and we would tail them through Rome's fierce traffic to the hotel. Along the way, they would do their best to shake us. At the hotel, if all the officers from the different agencies succeeded in working together, we would handcuff the bad guys, toss them in a car and drive off. In every detail, it would duplicate a real case.

The night before, I called Medwid in his room.

"This is never going to work," I said.

For once, he had nothing reassuring to say.

"I know," Medwid said. "So I'm doing the only thing I can do: I'm going to sleep."

A short time later I followed suit, waking early with what turned out to be a completely unjustified case of jitters. The exercise went off as smoothly as possible and three agencies that had never worked together meshed as a team. It was like watching them fall in love before our eyes. As soon as the customs officers identified the drug-laden suitcases at the airport, they notified their police and treasury counterparts, who began tailing the suspects. Those units, radioing ahead for assistance, succeeded in tracking the smugglers to their hotel. There, a task force from the three agencies was waiting to make an arrest.

On the flight home, we ticked off the few things that could have been better: a point on identifying smugglers, a point on making sure all the agencies involved used portable radios tuned to the same frequency. We would have plenty of opportunity to work out any kinks. When we sat down in Washington a few days later we found requests from a dozen countries for our class.

The State Department, reviewing the Rome case, agreed it was a success and promised to continue to fund us. The BNDD's fledgling program was off and running. Medwid and I sat down to plan a grueling schedule of almost twenty overseas courses for the next year, and two of the extended domestic schools. Our bosses negotiated a State Department budget of about $1 million for our effort. In the years ahead the program would grow to have a staff of fifty and a multimillion-dollar budget. In six years of constant traveling we visited seventy countries, many of them twice or three times. Medwid, his Blue Boxes and I at times would travel from Seoul, South Korea, to Belgrade, Yugoslavia, to Buenos Aires, Brazil without ever touching ground in the United States.

But from the start we paid a price for the State Department's involvement. The Secretary of State's Coordinator for International Narcotics Matters almost daily used his budgetary clout in an attempt to influence who was picked to attend our courses in Washington and which countries made it onto our packed itinerary.

"We're funding you, we have the right to say who goes," Sheldon Vance told me at one acrimonious bargaining session in 1974.

Often Vance, his predecessor and their deputies succeeded.

In late 1972, as the United States negotiated to pull Egypt into our orbit and strengthen our influence in the volatile Mideast, we were ordered to Cairo. Anwar Sadat's country played no role in the trafficking of drugs to the United States and Egypt's drug problem was largely confined to the widespread domestic use of hashish. But Sadat, and the intelligence he could provide, were important to the United States.

Squandering resources to bolster political policy in the Mideast continued throughout the early 1970s. On another trip we found ourselves entertaining Jordan's King Hussein and his brother Prince Hassan as the United States inched toward another attempt to resolve the Arab-Israeli conflict. Hassan had toured BNDD headquarters and been allowed to use the pistol range. He was impressed and the State Department promised we would train Jordan's anti-drug forces.

The State Department's influence did not stop at such wasteful, if relatively harmless, meddling.

As early as January 1972, our agents, who had established a bureau in Panama, had identified Lt. Col. Manuel Noriega, the chief of the country's ruthless intelligence forces, as a suspected drug trafficker. In reports to our Washington office, they outlined his suspected involvement in protecting the final leg of one route used to bring heroin from Turkey into the United States. For protecting traffickers from our agents, Noriega received a huge fee, probably in the hundreds of millions of dollars. On top of that, he gave the dealers the entrée they needed to launder their dirty money through his country's banks.

But the State Department told the BNDD in no uncertain terms that Noriega and his boss, Panamanian strongman Omar Torrijos, were too important to be touched. They provided critical intelligence on Soviet influence on Latin American and Caribbean Basin countries. My bosses agreed to cooperate with Noriega and soon I found myself in his office of knotty pine, shaking hands as he thanked me for bringing the training course to Panama.

"I am honored. Panama is honored," he said. "We welcome our role as host to your overseas training school." I struggled not to show my unhappiness at having to spend the next two weeks as his guest.

The agents based in Panama were angry. They felt foolish because their government refused to allow them to arrest Noriega. "But it is war. How can we win it if you won't let us fight it?" they complained at a meeting with our boss, John Ingersoll. "This man is a valuable intelligence asset," they were told. "You can't arrest him." The conference room momentarily lapsed into silence. Out of frustration, someone offhandedly suggested, "Then assassinate him." In this case, that was out of the question. Eventually Noriega assumed the dictatorship and became so valuable an intelligence asset that our support remained solid despite his regime's torture, money laundering and deceit.

My agency reached an accommodation and Noriega began to supply us enough information to make cases against some of the traffickers who passed through Panama. We suspected they were those in competition with the dealers who paid Noriega, but that was of no consequence. Noriega was given the protected status we usually gave other informants—he would not be prosecuted. The only difference between him and these other informants was that we could not extract a promise that his own illegal activities would cease.

Because of their injudicious suggestion that Noriega be assassinated, our agents stationed in Panama were subjected to a BNDD internal affairs investigation. It determined that the suggestion had not been serious, so I got to return twice more to Panama. Noriega liked the course. He also liked playing host to the American agents. At night our rounds included parties, banquets and endless drinks. The consummate host, Noriega also offered women. Thankfully, no reports of an agent accepting ever surfaced.

The bending of policy to accommodate Noriega came back to haunt us, but for the most part, the overseas strategy was a success. Nixon withheld aid from Turkey until it halted opium production, and that, combined with the crackdown on shipping that came in Italy, France and other nations we visited, reduced, for several years, the flow of heroin into the United States.

Aware, as the war there drew to a close, that Southeast Asia was a growing source of heroin to the United States that could replace the Turkish route, we stepped up our anti-drug efforts in Thailand, Vietnam and the Philippines. The cooperation between our agents and Southeast Asian police officials proved excellent.

But in 1972, while the overseas efforts were progressing, the Nixon administration and the anti-drug forces were bracing for very heavy weather at home. The drug agents would survive, although the going was rough.

I got one of my first glimpses of just how difficult it would get for the administration on June 18, 1972. Nixon's counsel, John Dean, and I were about to begin a one-night stop in San Francisco after completing a three-week training course in the Philippines. Dean, who had befriended my wife and me at a Washington cocktail party, joined me during the final week and delivered the graduation lecture.

"I have to check in with the office," Dean said as we sat in the airport lounge. When he came back, his face was ashen.

"You stay on, I've got to get right back," he said. "It looks like a couple of people got caught burglarizing the Democratic campaign headquarters at the Watergate hotel. Now they are trying to pin the job on the administration."

That was how I learned about Watergate. Its significance I honestly wasn't to understand for more than a year. By that time, despite handily winning reelection in 1972, no amount of success against drugs was going to save the Nixon presidency. Meanwhile, I returned to Washington where the BNDD was engaged in its own set of domestic intrigues—many involving the same administration officials as the Watergate conspiracy.

These were under way before I even was picked to head the overseas training efforts. At the time, our administrator, John Ingersoll, was fiercely fighting with the president and his advisers over what appeared to be two minor issues: the development of a new program to involve the BNDD's United States–based agents in street-level arrests; and a squabble with the Customs Service over jurisdiction of cases that began at the border but continued into the United States or required enforcement overseas.

At first glance it might have seemed Ingersoll was fighting too hard to win points that better lent themselves to compromise. But there was more to Ingersoll's battles than was immediately apparent. He was fighting for the autonomy of his agency.

In Myles Ambrose, both the head of Customs and Nixon's top adviser on drug policy, he had a formidable adversary. Ambrose had two goals. He wanted to increase the jurisdiction of his agents beyond their stations at border crossings, and he wanted to implement the plan to use the BNDD, in conjunction with Customs investigators and local cops, to wage a street-level war we thought was better fought by municipal police.

Ambrose had a high stake in the joint street-level task force. In his role as policy adviser he had dreamed it up in response to the president's desire for his agents to fight back on the street. The word in the law enforcement rumor mill was that Nixon got the idea after watching the street-fighting antics of the roguish cop Popeye Doyle in the 1971 Hollywood release *The French Connection*.

Nixon liked the Ambrose task force plan and Ambrose was the person he intended to command it. In their grand view, Ambrose was to become the most powerful voice on drug policy and the person in charge of all domestic anti-drug efforts. The head of BNDD would, in effect, remain a top commander, but his power at home would be restricted by Ambrose's control of the agents. Abroad he would be reigned in both by Ambrose's influence and by the heads of other agencies, including the State Department.

Ingersoll was alone in his fight. The president's other advisers—G. Gordon Liddy, John Ehrlichman and Egil (Bud) Krogh—also wanted BNDD agents back making nickel-and-dime street arrests. They had a set of self-serving reasons that fitted nicely with Ambrose's. They wanted a public relations campaign showing the government was doing something to take back the streets as well as stopping the drug flow from overseas. Ingersoll's arguments that the plan was a poor use of BNDD agents were crushed by this political juggernaut.

Unswayable, Ingersoll continued to refuse. Over his objections, the plan was set in motion and institutionalized as its own Justice Department bureau, the Office of Drug Abuse Law Enforcement. On January 18, 1972, Ambrose resigned as Commissioner of Customs and was named Special Assistant to the President and Assistant Attorney General in Charge of ODALE. One of his first moves was to reassign 500 BNDD agents to ODALE, virtually stripping Ingersoll of domestic agents in the field. Yet, somehow, Ingersoll, struggling for what he saw as our agency's future, found the courage to survive through the tenure of Attorney General John Mitchell. On February 15, Mitchell resigned to head Nixon's reelection campaign. Richard Kleindienst replaced him as head of the Justice Department. Our agents worked on the street arrest task force under the direct supervision of the Justice Department's prosecutors. In a sharp break with past practice, the lawyers ran the investigations that they would later take to court.

Kleindienst kept Ingersoll on as head of the weakened BNDD but began immediately to groom his successor, John R. Bartels, Jr., the son of a New York federal judge, a confidant of Ambrose's and one of his two deputies at ODALE. Meanwhile, Nixon set in motion a plan to resolve the border squabbles by merging the 1,200 BNDD agents with the 500 investigators of the Customs Service who worked on drug cases and the entire ODALE unit, creating in effect the legislation for the current mechanism of fighting drugs with one agency. Ambrose appeared a very big winner. By virtue of his position as head of ODALE and Special Assistant to Nixon, and his management of BNDD and Customs through hand-picked successors, he emerged as the de facto drug czar.

But by June, when I returned home from the Philippines, and before the czar could accomplish very much, a leak to Washington columnist Jack Anderson and subsequent reports in the national news threatened to depose him. The accounts alleged no wrongdoing by Ambrose but linked him to a wealthy rancher and Republican party supporter embroiled in an illegal gun-smuggling case along the Texas border. The negative publicity ended Ambrose's effectiveness. He was allowed to stay in government, but was stripped of his power. Later, he resigned.

ODALE continued as a Justice Department task force, but now under the supervision of Kleindienst and Bartels. Meanwhile, the merger designed to settle the border clashes between Customs and BNDD was completed in April 1973 when Nixon signed Executive Order 10257, reorganizing all anti-drug efforts under one agency. News of the reorganization was lost as the Watergate investigation deepened and on April 30, H. R. Haldeman, John D. Ehrlichman, John Dean and Richard Kleindienst resigned. But it took effect on July 1, and when it did the Drug Enforcement Administration was born. On June 30, Ingersoll, the first and only administrator of the BNDD, resigned. The new agency, with John Bartels as its first administrator, was heralded in press releases that promised success against traffickers now that all enforcement was under one roof, that of the BNDD's direct descendant, the DEA. Ingersoll, who had lost every battle, resigned knowing that in the long run he had won the war—narcotics agents, not Customs agents, FBI agents, politicians or prosecutors, would be in charge of the government's war on drugs.

But the ink on the press releases was not dry before the first full-scale congressional inquiry into the DEA had begun.

With Ambrose out of the picture, the former Customs agents felt they had been reassigned to the DEA against their will. Despite Bartels's efforts to appease them by replacing several former BNDD bureau chiefs and field office supervisors with agents fresh from Customs, they began a vicious rearguard action, leaking to Congress and the media allegations of DEA excesses overseas that included illegal kidnappings of drug suspects and gunfights with suspects in violation of our own rules.

Two congressional investigators were assigned to look into these abuses by the infant agency—one that was asking for an increased budget to add 300 more agents and had close links to members of Nixon's reelection campaign and his top aides.

Soon the scope of their inquiry would grow as other disaffected agents added allegations of corruption, personnel mismanagement, poor budget practices, questionable undercover tactics and abuse of the 1970 "no-knock" law, a piece of Nixon law-and-order legislation that allowed us to kick in doors without announcing the raid.

At the start, these detractors got plenty of help in smearing the DEA as a result of a botched case that took place just as the legislation forming the agency was being drawn up.

One April morning in 1973, a team of BNDD agents working in an ODALE task force had kicked in without warning the doors to six homes in and around the quiet suburb of Collinsville, Illinois. Within days, reports were surfacing that the agents had roughed up the occupants, torn up their furniture and detained some for as long as seventy-seven hours without charging them.

I returned home from a trip to read these charges in gripping accounts by a very unsympathetic press that had dubbed the botched case "The Collinsville Incident."

The raids had been staged as part of a coordinated search in a seven-month national cocaine investigation. Somehow, in a way that was never satisfactorily explained, agents had raided the wrong addresses. None of the families were involved in the sale of cocaine or narcotics. Nor had the searches of their suburban homes turned up drugs or evidence of wrongdoing. They simply were innocent. Several of the families pressed criminal charges and eleven agents were indicted on charges of conspiring to violate their constitutional rights. Agents across the nation were sweating with fear as the trial date approached.

The trial took place in March 1974 in Alton, Illinois, in an atmosphere hostile to the narcotics agents. During the trial an Internal Revenue agent present at some of the raids testified that several BNDD agents drank beer and shot at imaginary snakes during the break-ins. The press reveled in our "Nazi stormtrooper mentality" and "Gestapo tactics." Ultimately the agents were acquitted of wrongdoing—no evidence was found that they had done anything other than make an honest mistake. Cleared of roughing up the occupants, tearing up their furniture and a litany of other allegations, the agents sued for libel. They won based on the fact that they had done none of the things alleged.

But by the summer of 1974 the one-year-old DEA had taken the heat for too long, the admittedly ill-conceived raids just one more serious blot on the agency's already tarnished image.

Each time I returned to my Washington office I heard a new howl from one of the factions and the loudest were about Bartels. He had, by all accounts, run amok, appointing cronies to key positions, using friendship to decide promotions, and generally bending the agency rules and tarnishing its image. It was difficult, with Bartels at the helm, to counter the charges against us by asserting that for the most part we were a disciplined force.

One telling instance of Bartels's mismanagement was appointing Vincent Promuto, a former professional football star, to be the $29,000-a-year public affairs director despite allegations that linked him to organized crime. Promuto allegedly maintained ties to gamblers and underworld hangers-on that he had formed during his days with the Washington Redskins. Promuto was a wonderful guy, and the allegations, including that he interfered in a local police investigation of gambling at a sports bar where he hung out, never amounted to much.

But they were well known in the world of law enforcement. In August 1974, they were brought to Bartels's attention, but his top deputies felt he did nothing to clear them up. If anything, Bartels seemed to actively stand in the way of a thorough internal investigation of Promuto. The allegations about Promuto and Bartels were leaked to the press and added to the pattern of abuses that congressional investigators were uncovering.

By January 1975, the Senate's permanent Subcommittee on Investigations, chaired by Washington Democrat Henry (Scoop) Jackson and co-chaired by Illinois Republican Charles Percy, had begun executive sessions on abuses by the DEA.

The subcommittee started by looking at Bartels's hiring of Promuto. With Percy on the subcommittee, we knew it was only a matter of time before the bungled raid in his home state was also raised as a serious issue. An agency that could be so mistaken surely ought to be disbanded, we felt certain Percy would say.

As the subcommittee sessions began, a second congressional inquiry by the Senate Select Committee on Intelligence was also proposed. This probe would question the DEA's links to the CIA in three areas: why a cadre of former CIA agents was employed as investigators in our internal affairs office; why Nixon began a project that allowed the CIA to fund some drug operations overseas, creating drug agents who did double duty as spies; and why assassination equipment was reviewed for possible purchase by one DEA agent who had been a CIA spy involved in an early Vietnam intrigue and a recent Watergate operation.

In any era, the first two items would have raised questions, but the DEA might have been able to answer them without further tarnishing. In the conspiracy-marred mid-1970s, we were at a loss when they were tied to the third item: the disclosure that the acting director of DEA special operations had reviewed assassination equipment for domestic use. This earned the DEA the dubious distinction of being the first federal agency caught even considering such unconstitutional armament. The list was chock-full of secret agent, super-sleuth items including exploding telephones and booby-trapped rifles. The director who reviewed it was Lt. Col. Lucien Conein. Conein had been the Chief of Station for the the CIA in Vietnam in 1963 when the assassination of President Ngo Dinh Diem and the overthrow of his regime paved the way for our deepened involvement. Conein's name had come up in Watergate committee testimony when it was disclosed that one burglar, E. Howard Hunt, had met with him at a time when Hunt was gathering information to prepare bogus cables implicating President Kennedy in the assassination. Years later, Conein would say that he had in fact passed on the message from President Kennedy to the friendly opposition that if Diem was assassinated the United States would not interfere.

In 1975, his actions while at the CIA, his activities for the DEA and his links to Hunt were quickly painted in the most sinister light and leaked to the press.

Beneath the bold headlines, "U.S. Aide Was Briefed on Assassination Equipment" and "High-Level Backing Cited in C.I.A. Drug-Unit Spying," it was easy to miss, amid the wealth of detail about Conein, that the weapons had never been purchased and the overseas component of the BNDD funded by the CIA under orders from Nixon had been shut down in 1973.

It was also easy to miss the point that the majority of the former CIA officers on the staff had been hired under Ingersoll to help our internal anti-corruption efforts. Ingersoll felt they made good moles since they had no long-term ties to other narcotics agents, many of whom had spent more than a decade working with each other. The detractors, quoted anonymously, were allowed to paint these moles as fabricating charges of misconduct against their co-workers and ruining the careers of those agents.

It all became fodder for the congressional inquiries, which would laboriously consider each activity before concluding which was justified and which was not. For the moment, those panels were in the evidence-gathering stages of their investigations. My own few months at the CIA before joining the DEA did not come in for any scrutiny. Fortunately. Because we didn't need any more headaches.

All of us knew that, scrutinized in an unsympathetic climate, our track record would look terrible: the New York office, wracked by corruption in the late 1960s; the Boston office scoured clean after a similar investigation in the early 1970s; Bartels's abuses; kicking in the wrong doors in 1973—maybe the DEA should be disbanded. The inquiries had all the earmarks of a replay of the Knapp Commission, which just a couple of years earlier had ferreted out corruption and forced the disbanding of the New York City Police narcotics unit.

Soon after Nixon resigned on August 9, 1974, Gerald Ford tried to undo some of the damage by disbanding the tainted ODALE operation. In April 1975, another damage control move was made. Promuto, by now the subject of several unflattering press accounts, was transferred out of Washington and given a low-profile position in the New York office. "I did nothing wrong," he said in an interview after his transfer. But he stayed in the minor post until he resigned from the DEA. On May 30, Bartels resigned and was replaced by an interim administrator, Henry S. Dogin, a former assistant district attorney in Manhattan.

By now the public mainly thought of DEA agents as cowboys, rogues and dirty scoundrels—worse, if possible, than the dope traffickers we were supposed to be hunting. Senate investigators were digging back as far as the mid-1960s in their effort to document a pattern of recklessness, lawlessness and corruption by federal narcotics agents.

Senator Jackson, rather than comment on the forced resignation of Bartels or the appointment of Dogin, used the opportunity to herald his subcommittee's upcoming public hearings.

"The issue of the effectiveness and operations of the Drug Enforcement Administration remains crucial," he said in a statement. "We expect these in-depth hearings to examine, for the first time, the total Federal narcotics law enforcement effort and result in constructive recommendations to assist the Federal Government in combating what knowledgeable sources see as an upcoming narcotics epidemic."

The hearings began on June 9, 1975. In his opening statement, Jackson made very clear that the very future of the DEA could hang in the balance.

"I see a threat of a lack of professionalism running through this operation. We are not prejudging it. The testimony will come out, and it will speak for itself."

It did, filling five volumes with 1,435 pages of criticism, commentary, observation and charts about every facet of the DEA's operation and the operations of its predecessors. The hearings did not end until August 26 of the following year, 1976. And as they stretched on, the investigators kept digging.

With the hearings lumbering into their sixth month, in December 1975, President Ford announced that he had found his candidate for a permanent DEA Administrator. Dogin, the interim administrator, had held the reins for seven months while this search took place. Peter Bensinger, heir to the Brunswick billiard table fortune, Yale-educated, a liberal Republican, had accepted Ford's nomination. In February 1976, he was confirmed as administrator of the embattled agency.

Bensinger knew he had inherited a mess, and at his first staff meeting, held the day he was appointed, he told us he intended to clear it up and pave the way for the agency to heal its wounds and continue its global mission.

"I'm not bringing any outsider in with me," he told a dozen senior agents at the meeting. "We are in this together. Our only goal is to keep this agency alive." It was reassuring news.

I had been in Washington for another of my battles with the State Department, which wanted total control of the domestic training program. It intended to change the selection process so that instead of high-level police officials from countries where drug trafficking was significant, the program would serve police officials from any country where the department wanted influence even if they were unimportant to our overseas drug strategy. I was still fending off the diplomats a couple of days after Bensinger's first staff meeting, when I gave a commencement speech to our training school's graduates.

Bensinger, as the head of the agency, was present. Afterward he called me to his office. He said he had reviewed the program and found it was running well enough that it could continue without me. My skills as a speaker would be better used in Washington. He explained that he wanted me to persuade Congress that we could carry out our anti-drug mission. I was to portray a positive image of the DEA and try to alter the apparently inevitable outcome of the congressional inquiry—our disbanding.

"Because, Bob, if we don't change the public and congressional perception of us, then anything else on our agenda doesn't matter, because we won't be here next year." I saw his point. Overseas training wasn't going to do much good if the agency was destroyed. I became the first agent put in charge of congressional affairs. Medwid was asked to continue the overseas course without me until a new supervising team could be picked. He did, but he was tired of the job and asked to go back into the field as soon as he could. A few months later, he returned to the field as a supervisor in our Bangkok, Thailand, office.

Bensinger, meanwhile, gave me a mandate to open our doors and our files to Congress, invite the various lawmakers to briefings, and promise his presence at the briefings and on any overseas fact-finding trips they might need to take. It was a bold maneuver, and at the pace at which the hearings were proceeding it had come not a moment too soon. It looked like the committee's findings would be ready just before the up-coming presidential election.

No sooner did we set to work than the final pieces of bad news developed. First, Senator Mike Mansfield of Montana succeeded in attaching an amendment to the Foreign Assistance Act forbidding the DEA to be at the scene of overseas arrests. Designed to combat the alleged overseas abuses, the law badly crimped our agents' ability to work with their foreign counterparts. Worse, it sent the message that DEA agents were not trusted by their own country. In the United States, publicity surrounding the legislation only darkened the shadow of mistrust in which we were portrayed.

Next, the Senate investigations into the stream of allegations of overseas kidnappings disclosed that the BNDD and DEA did in fact forcibly remove suspected drug traffickers from their home countries for trial in the United States. A rift soon developed in the Justice Department between those who sided with the use of the tactic and those who found it questionable.

The tactic was a simple one: Upon identifying a major trafficker and developing a case against him that stretched from overseas into the United States, our agents and embassy officials would convince a foreign government to hand over the dealer. As soon as they did, the trafficker, his own nation's constitutional guarantees and extradition proceedings brushed aside, was shipped to the United States for prosecution.

In June 1976, *Newsweek*'s Washington bureau reported that about 150 drug traffickers had been shipped against their will to the United States. The report by correspondent Anthony

Marro detailed the furious internal Justice Department debate over whether the procedure was legal. It also reported the outrage of defense attorneys. Finally, it captured in great detail the snatching by Chilean police that has become known as "The Wrong Choy Case."

Chino Choy, a tailor by trade who was illegally living in Chile, was minding his own business when police invaded his village and asked, "Are you Choy?"

He answered yes.

In the custody of police, Choy left his village for the less comfortable climes of the West Street federal jail in Manhattan. Chino Choy had nothing to do with the drug trade. He merely shared a very common name with a drug trafficker. The name had been enough for the Chilean police. And it turned out after three months in jail to be enough for the arraignment judge.

"Are you Choy?" the judge asked.

"Yes," he again answered and was whisked back to prison to await trial. The news magazine and a series of newspaper articles brought Choy's plight to light. The government tried to get him out of jail and return him quietly to Chile, but that created more problems since Choy had been in Chile illegally. While it took less than a week to get him out of that country, it took almost a year of fighting red tape to free him from jail.

Although the tactic, "involuntary expulsion," was later upheld in court, the debate surrounding it did not make our first entreaties to Congress easy. The questions the tactic raised about the DEA's potential for even greater abuse of our powers turned the first meetings, intended as get-to-know-you sessions, testy.

But by the time the Choy abduction and the internal Justice Department debate reached the news media, Bensinger and I had found in Representatives Charles Rangel, Ben Gilman and Lester Wolff three legislators willing to give us a fair hearing. With Wolff as the chairman, and Rangel and Gilman as members, the House Narcotics Committee had begun to listen to the DEA side of the story.

We explained the frustrations of narcotics cases, the need for special powers overseas and the risks that agents took. We put the CIA rumors to rest. We admitted our mistakes and showed the minority of corrupt agents and occasional cases of mistaken identity against a tapestry of successes, including the drug enforcement training we gave municipal police, the overseas schools and the impact we had limiting heroin production.

Then we took the three on a twenty-one-day fact-finding trip to Western Europe, the Mideast, Turkey and Pakistan. We showed them the heroin routes, the fields of poppies and the efforts of our agents. We instructed the agents to meet with the congressmen independently and to answer every question.

By June, we had made similar trips with other key members of Congress and began to notify the senators and congressman each time we were ready to complete a case in their district. If they wanted to, they could be part of the announcement of the success against the drug traffickers back home.

With this exhausting campaign Bensinger and I managed to extinguish some of the congressional hatred before the final sessions were held. On August 23, 1976, Bensinger addressed the subcommittee at the opening of those sessions.

"I think the Drug Enforcement Administration, more than anything else, needs stability," he began. "DEA has come through a number of traumatic experiences. Some are related to management and management changes. Others are related to congressional hearings such as this. DEA, in my opinion, was placed in the position of having to meet unrealistic expectations. That, I think, was a principal problem.... One of the other problems, one that has not been focused on specifically but one that is important, has been, I think, the historical role DEA has played in terms of its relationship with other federal and state law enforcement agencies. I do not think it assumed the decisive leadership role which was delegated to it.... But now DEA for the first time is."

Bensinger, his statement completed, proceeded to undergo a thorough grilling from Senator Sam Nunn, who by now was presiding over the hearings. His answers were thorough and honest, but he carefully put each of the agency's faults in a context and demonstrated everything, from increased internal security to increased hiring of minorities, that the DEA had done to redress them.

The subcommittee hearings ended three days later with the recommendation to the White House that the DEA be preserved.

Instead of disbanding us, the subcommittee suggested restrictions in line with the Mansfield Amendment that curbed our involvement overseas. In most instances, agents would be limited to gathering intelligence. It also suggested revised hiring practices and a greater compliance both with the mission and image of a United States governmental agency.

We had survived, and under Bensinger we began our transition to a new era. We were 2,100 agents strong—all our budget requests had been granted despite the battering we had taken.

No sooner had we begun to dig out from under the rubble of our mistakes than Jimmy Carter was elected and the DEA entered a four-year spell of benign neglect by an administration indifferent at best to the issue of drug abuse. Our only allies would be the ones we had made in Congress. Fortunately, they would prove formidable. The day after Carter was elected, Bensinger, Rangel, Gilman, Wolff and I left for Latin America. As the plane took off, Bensinger told the congressmen, "Well, guys, this may be the last time I see you." The three assured him that they would do the best they could to make sure that did not happen. These three influential Democrats pushed Carter to reappoint Bensinger.

We would get no other help from this administration though. As positions in the DEA became vacant, we were not allowed to fill them. By the end of the Carter years, our forces would be down to 1,700 agents. The Nixon foreign policy of curbing opium production was dropped. Soon, unhindered by our severely restricted agents, a new flood of heroin came across the border from Mexico.

For the first two years of the Carter administration I worked with Congress, taking its members to our field offices and overseas bureaus to make the case for aggressive drug enforcement. It seemed I spent most of my time on planes, hauling legislators to the sites of drug production: Hong Kong, Thailand, Burma, India. In reshaping our image and arguing for stiff enforcement, it did not hurt one bit that the locations were often exotic. While it would be nice to say that all the legislators were as genuinely concerned as Rangel, Gilman and Wolff, for some the overseas trips were merely another junket.

Chief among these were Representatives Billy Lee Evans and John Jenrette. These two men and their wives were my charges on one trip to Thailand. The idea was to show how we needed a coherent policy that did not reward with foreign assistance a military that spent most of its time escorting drug caravans out of the mountains of the Golden Triangle—Burma, Laos and Thailand. We felt that policy, plus the allies we had made of individual, honest Thai police officers, would go a long way toward stopping another influx of heroin.

Any serious purpose was completely lost as soon as the two lawmakers' expensive shoes touched the ground.

"Tell our wives you're takin' us on one of those missions tomorrow so we can get rid of them by tellin' 'em it's too dangerous. Then we'll go see some of them prostitutes," one of them said. Fine, I agreed, figuring I'd take them to play golf and get drunk and they would forget about the prostitutes, still one of Thailand's most available entertainments.

But golf, in this case, was a walk in the country spoiled by more than the game. As the two lawmakers reached the ninth hole, I watched as the caddies, young Thai women, knelt and performed oral sex on the men, who then zipped up their flies and teed off.

"Boy oh boy," one of them said, when I felt it was appropriate to catch up, "no wonder these Asians love golf."

As I said, for the DEA it was worth it. But I never said it was pretty. We did not succeed in pressuring the Thais into increased cooperation until the administration of Ronald Reagan.

Looking back, I am on the whole proud of the gritty job I did because it gave the agency in which I believed a chance to come of age. Congress had every right to mistrust us. The drug agencies had for years been so secretive and adamant about not providing information that the lawmakers had been allocating funds for drug enforcement on the basis of crude guesswork. For drug enforcement to truly mature, it had to be able to endure greater scrutiny. My job was to provide access, but not for free. For each piece of information, I sought in exchange a measure of good will and clout on Capitol Hill.

Along the way, I made friends. One was Rangel. The black legislator from Harlem had an advantage over his more bigoted colleagues in understanding the drug issue: He didn't have to wait for it to leave the ghetto to see its vicious effects. Whatever cures or Band-Aid solutions we proposed, Rangel wanted to make sure they were as effective for the underclass and for the struggling black working class as they were for middle America.

It was Rangel's guidance that helped me to see how most legislators merely wanted to push the drug problem back into the ghetto. This was a big help in shaping a DEA policy that sought to avoid that trap. The result was that by 1979, I, along with the DEA, had matured enough to see that drugs were a public health menace, not just one to be solved by more jails.

Bensinger and I began to push for the greater involvement of other government agencies, fully aware that when drug enforcement became a part of an overall public health policy, the bulk of the anti-drug money would go to social service agencies. It is a method of combating drug abuse that I continue to firmly believe is the only one that will yield a lasting result, although as yet I am not convinced of the virtue of trying decriminalization or legalization, which might logi- cally seem to follow. I'm not sure that social programs alone will be effective in the long run. And I, for one, still think it's worth a shot at keeping drugs from becoming even more accepted in the fabric of life in our country. To that end, I favor a mix of effective law enforcement, prevention, public education and widely available treatment. By early 1979 I felt it was time to try my hand at implementing these ideas. The best place to test them was back in the field.

Portrait of a Narc: Special Agent Everett Hatcher as he posed for his final official Drug Enforcement Administration photograph. *(Courtesy, DEA)*

Dressed to Kill: Costabile "Gus" Farace, moments after his second marriage. His tuxedo-bound muscles are still hard from prison weightlifting and a steroid-enhanced diet. *(Courtesy, DEA)*

Crime Scene: Shortly after Special Agent
Hatcher was killed by Farace on Tuesday
night, February 28, 1989, *New York
Newsday* photographer Ken Sawchuck arrived
and made this haunting image.
(Copyright © 1989, Ken Sawchuck/
New York Newsday)

The Agent's Widow: Mary Jane Hatcher and her sons, Zackery and Joshua, standing by her husband's gravesite at the conclusion of the burial services. *(Copyright © 1989, Jon Naso/New York Newsday)*

The Early Years:
Special Agent Bob
Stutman (*center*) and
his raid team
following a shootout
in Washington, D.C.
No one was injured.
(The authors' files)

The Creds: The badge and
credentials Robert Stutman
was awarded by the Justice
Department.
(The authors' files)

Bad Move: Elvis Presley
pictured in a set of similar
BNDD credentials that
President Richard Nixon
cheapened when he awarded
them to the drug-plagued
singer. *(The authors' files)*

Friend or Foe? Suspected as a drug dealer and money launderer throughout his more than two decades of cooperation with the DEA and CIA, Manuel Noriega was finally brought into custody. Photo was taken in the cargo bay of the plane that brought Noriega to Florida. *(Courtesy, DEA)*

DEA SENSITIVE

NOFORN

HQS ATTN: PS; DO

HQS PLS PASS TO AMEMBASSY BOGOTA

POST FOR DEA

SUBJECT: GONZALO RODRIGUEZ–GACHA

RODRIGUEZ–GACHA HAS ALREADY SENT "HIT TEAMS" TO NEW YORK FOR THE PURPOSE OF ASSASSINATING THE HEAD OF THE NEW YORK DEA OFFICE, THE UNDERCOVER AGENTS INVOLVED IN RECENT SEIZURES OF COCAINE IN NEW YORK, AND THE GOVERNOR OF NEW YORK. THESE "HIT TEAMS" ARE COMPOSED OF YOUNG PEOPLE TRAVELLING AS STUDENTS. SOME WILL ENTER THE U.S. AT NEW YORK CITY, OTHERS WILL ENTER U.S. ALONG U.S.–MEXICO BORDER. THE MURDERS ARE TO BE CONDUCTED IN SUCH A WAY THAT THE CALI CARTEL WILL BE BLAMED.

Death Threats: This reproduction of a teletype is formal notice of an impending assassination attempt on Stutman by the drug gangsters. *(Jim Keleher/Sloan-Millman, based on material in the authors' files)*

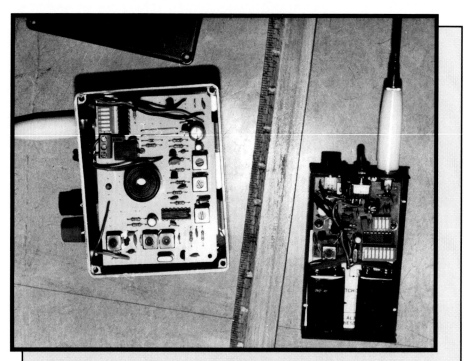

Detonators: After the threat issued by Gonzalo Rodriguez Gacha, the now-imprisoned head of the violent Medellín cartel, these detonators—modified garage door openers—were seized in New York. *(Courtesy, DEA)*

The detonators, a fleet of rental cars, maps and information concerning the execution of the threat were seized from four men who have since been deported. The bombings, as noted in the teletype, were to be blamed on the rival Cali, Colombia, drug cartel. *(Courtesy, DEA)*

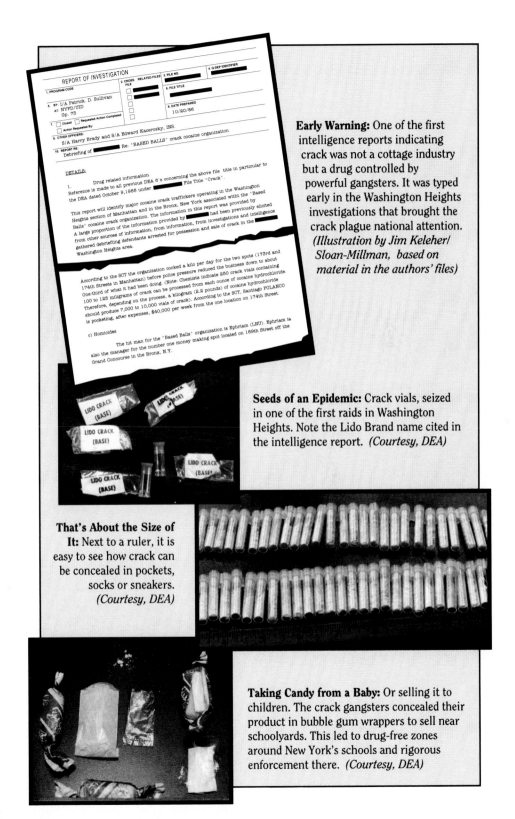

Early Warning: One of the first intelligence reports indicating crack was not a cottage industry but a drug controlled by powerful gangsters. It was typed early in the Washington Heights investigations that brought the crack plague national attention. *(Illustration by Jim Keleher/ Sloan-Millman, based on material in the authors' files)*

REPORT OF INVESTIGATION

BY: I/A Patrick. D. Sullivan
AT: NYPD/UID
Gp. 73

DATE PREPARED
10/20/86

OTHER OFFICERS: S/A Harry Brady and S/A Edward Kacerosky, INS.

REPORT RE: Debriefing of ███ Re: "BASED BALLS" crack cocaine organization

DETAILS:

1. Drug related information
Reference is made to all previous DEA 6's concerning the above file title in particular to the DEA dated October 9,1986 under ███ File Title "Crack".

This report will identify major cocaine crack traffickers operating in the Washington Heights section of Manhattan and in the Bronx, New York. The information in this report was provided by the "Based Balls" cocaine crack organization. The information provided by ███ had been previously elicited A large proportion of the information provided by ███ had been previously elicited from other sources of information, from information, from investigations and intelligence gathered debriefing defendants arrested for possession and sale of crack in the ███ Washington Heights area.

According to the SCT the organization cooked a kilo per day for the two spots (173rd and 174th Streets in Manhattan) before police pressure reduced the business down to about One-third of what it had been doing. (Note: Chemists indicate 250 crack vials containing 100 to 125 milligrams of crack can be processed from each ounce of cocaine hydrochloride. Therefore, depending on the process, a kilogram (2.2 pounds) of cocaine hydrochloride should produce 7,000 to 10,000 vials of crack). According to the SCT, Santiago POLANCO is pocketing, after expenses, $40,000 per week from the one location on 174th Street.

c) Homicides

The hit man for the "Based Balls" organization is Ephriam (LNU). Ephriam la also the manager for the number one money making spot located on 169th Street off the Grand Concourse in the Bronx, N.Y.

Seeds of an Epidemic: Crack vials, seized in one of the first raids in Washington Heights. Note the Lido Brand name cited in the intelligence report. *(Courtesy, DEA)*

LIDO CRACK (BASE)

That's About the Size of It: Next to a ruler, it is easy to see how crack can be concealed in pockets, socks or sneakers. *(Courtesy, DEA)*

Taking Candy from a Baby: Or selling it to children. The crack gangsters concealed their product in bubble gum wrappers to sell near schoolyards. This led to drug-free zones around New York's schools and rigorous enforcement there. *(Courtesy, DEA)*

The Littlest Victims: On Hart Island, New York, inmates unload a ferry full of coffins holding the bodies of infant victims of the twin epidemics of crack addiction and AIDS. The infants will be buried in Potter's Field.
(Copyright © 1988, Alan Raia/New York Newsday)

Living Large: Twenty-year-old George Rivera, known on the street as Boy George, is dressed to party in this photograph taken the night of his Christmas Eve cruise. The cruise around Manhattan was a treat for key members of his heroin ring. *(Source: NYPD detectives)*

Gather Round the Boss: Boy George's cronies, decked out for the cruise with gold belt buckles, gold watches and bracelets, gold-trimmed sunglasses and cellular telephones. *(Source: NYPD detectives)*

A.C.E. PRODUCTIONS

_____ ACM _____ ACM _____ TIME 6:30 PM - 11:00 PM

P.O. #:_____ CLIENT CONTACT: _____

NO. SHOWED _123_ TOTAL BAR SALES: $ _____ 1ST DECK:$ _____

2ND DECK: $ _____ 3RD DECK: $ _____ NAME:_____

CAPTAIN_____ CHEF: _____

NUMBER OF BOOKS SOLD: _____   WEATHER: cold/ rain/ fog

CHECKS DOWN: _____   CHECKS IN: _____

DID CHEF VISIT TABLES?   YES   NO

RE: CRUISE (GENERAL), GUEST COMMENTS (SPECIFIC):

Guests began arriving in stretch limos as early as 6:30PM.
When they were told they couldn't board until 6:30, they got
back in their limos and went for an hour ride. We started
boatriding about 6:15 — those guests who stood on the pier
were anxious to get on... No one smiled. No one spoke to one
another. Those that arrived together stayed together
in their cluster... and stared across the room at one
another.

———— At 10:00 pm we left dock for a 2 hour cruise
that was quite memorable. Needless to say, this
was a tough cruise — Oh yes, before he left, the D.J.
said, "I think these were crack dealers."

Ship's Log: This record of the cruise speaks for itself. Boy George's idea of a good time was seen for what it was—a nightmare—by the crew member who kept the log. _(Reproduction by Jim Keleher/Sloan-Millman; source: NYPD detectives)_

Spoils of War: Sgt. Billy Cook points to $15,000 worth of stereo amplifying equipment in the trunk of Boy George's Porsche. The Porsche was seized in the final raids on George's heroin ring. Close inspection revealed other modifications including hidden compartments for guns or heroin and devices to spew tacks or oil in front of pursuers. *(By Phillip W. Schoultz, Jr.)*

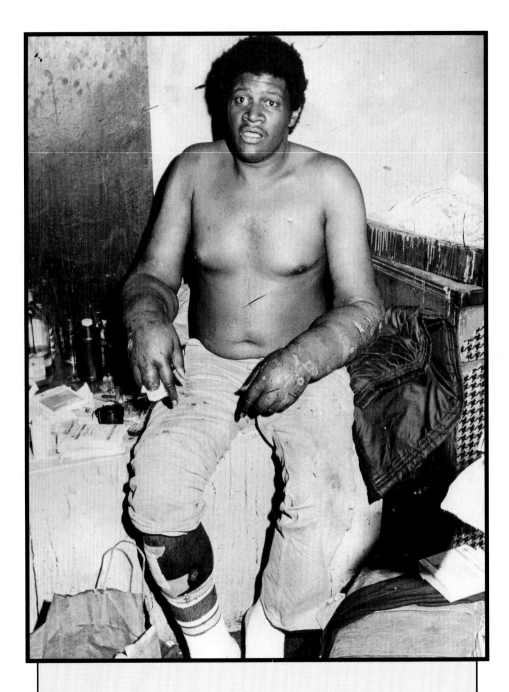

Portrait of a Heroin Addict: This photograph, of an addict nicknamed "Gloves," serves to remind New York State Police Senior Investigator Robert Donovan of the reason he combats heroin dealers. The original hangs in Donovan's office. *(Courtesy, Robert Donovan)*

The Cocaine Connection: Moments before it was raided, this photograph was taken of an upstate New York farmhouse. Inside the farmhouse, ring members extracted cocaine base from chunks of charcoal, purified it, dried it, pressed it, cooled it, and bagged the finished product for shipment across the United States. *(From investigative files)*

Air Cocaine: This map shows its routes. A clever shipment scheme allowed Aart Vanwort's Air Cocaine ring to ship cocaine aboard commercial flights from Brazil to the United States. Dozens of airline workers, all looking for a fast buck, assisted the ring. *(Illustration by Jim Keleher/Sloan-Millman)*

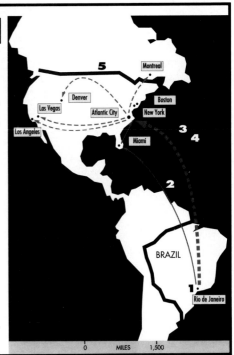

THE DISTRIBUTION NETWORK

How ring distributed up to $1.5 billion in cocaine

1. Cocaine was processed at a laboratory about 80 miles from Rio de Janeiro.

2. Contact brought luggage packed with cocaine to Rio de Janeiro airport, giving luggage tags — but not the luggage — to courier. Luggage would be checked on Pan Am Flight 202, which flew either to Miami and then onto New York, or nonstop to New York.

3. Courier and luggage would arrive at Kennedy Airport. Contact would switch domestic tags with the international tags on the luggage to bypass customs inspections.

4. Contacts would take luggage to a nearby hotel to repack cocaine into smaller quantities in other luggage.

5. Contacts would take repacked luggage to Kennedy for shipment to Denver, Boston, Los Angeles, Montreal, Las Vegas and Atlantic City.

Montreal · Denver · Las Vegas · Atlantic City · Boston · New York · Los Angeles · Miami · BRAZIL · Rio de Janeiro

0   MILES   1,500

An Agent's Guide To Conspiracy

1. The agreement is a violation.

2. To agree there must be two or more competent people.

3. A participant must have knowledge that the success of the conspiracy depends on the actions of others.

4. The participant need not know the number or identity of other co-conspirators—one is enough.

5. In narcotic cases, knowledge that others are involved is inferred.

6. Mere association with conspirators and or knowledge of the conspiracy does not constitute joining.

7. A participant need not join at the start of the conspiracy.

8. If the only other co-conspirator is a government agent there is no conspiracy—exception under many statutes.

9. Acquittal of all but one co-conspirator at a joint trial (absent evidence of the involvement of another) is acquittal of all—rule of consistency.

A Guide to Conspiracy: Above the desks of Special Agent Bill Klein and Port Authority Det. Mike Molina, the men who cracked the Air Cocaine case, hung this simplified set of rules to establishing whether a conspiracy did in fact exist. *(Illustration by Jim Keleher/Sloan-Millman)*

Arrest of a Capo: Drugs from the Air Cocaine and upstate farm case found their way to Wall Street via traditional organized crime, which used low-level hoodlums, including Gus Farace, to sell their drugs. During the final stages of the hunt for Farace, intense pressure was brought to bear on the mob. In this photo, reputed mob capo Gerry Chilli, who had served prison time with Farace, is arrested in his bathrobe. The photo was taken during a raid on Chilli's home. *(From investigative files)*

Gunned Down: Finally the pressure grew too great and the mob had Gus Farace killed. Taken a few moments after the convulsions that marked the ebbing of his life, this photo shows a bearded Farace, flabby and almost unrecognizable as the same man in the wedding portrait. Emergency medicine had proved fruitless and Farace died on the ambulance gurney. *(From the files of government agents)*

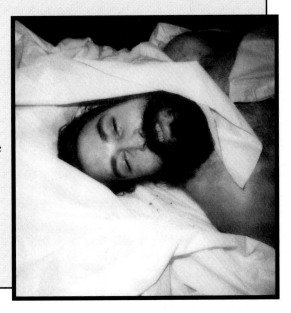

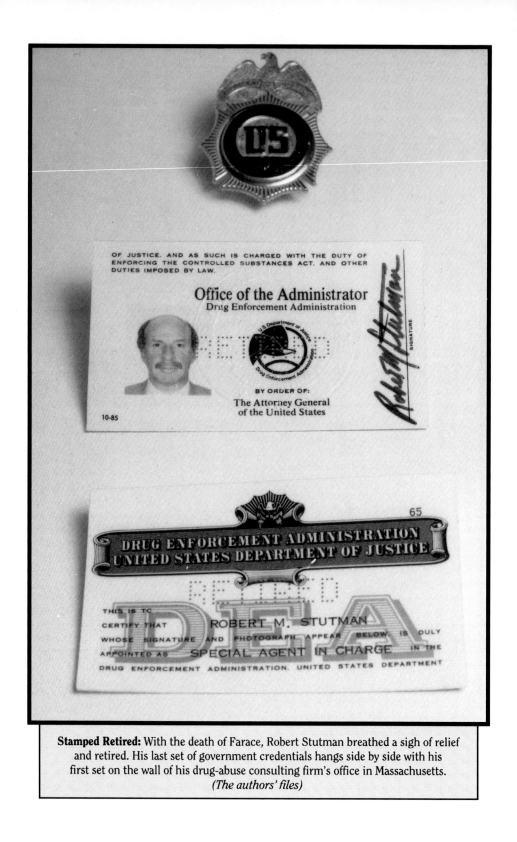

Stamped Retired: With the death of Farace, Robert Stutman breathed a sigh of relief and retired. His last set of government credentials hangs side by side with his first set on the wall of his drug-abuse consulting firm's office in Massachusetts.
(The authors' files)

NINE

A New Agenda:
1979–1985

I'd had enough of Washington. After eight years of grinding out policy—most of them on the road—and after fifteen years as an agent, almost all of them spent making speeches, training other agents and sorting out the political pitfalls that could waylay a federal agency, my own education was complete.

Peter Bensinger and I, toward the close of the Carter administration, felt the DEA had developed a fresh approach to attacking the nation's cyclic epidemics of drug abuse. We envisioned it as a two-pronged war. The DEA would launch a coherent set of domestic and foreign law enforcement initiatives that would put major drug dealers on the defensive. As soon as this attack began, we would use each case our agents made to rouse people to fight against drugs. DEA officials would stand behind the seized drugs and speak out.

"If we want to stop this, we can't rely on cops alone. We need to get the schools, hospitals, city, state and federal governments behind us to figure out why people use drugs, and develop treatment programs that are effectively showing them how to stop," we planned to say.

With this phase under way, the second front could be launched. We would use that public fervor and our allies in

Congress to push the government to expanded research, education and treatment as the primary weapons against the drug scourge. If we succeeded, we thought the proper role of law enforcement would become enforcing the laws governing a much broader public health policy. As things were, punitive law enforcement was the sole policy option.

In a way, I had come full circle from the days under Leroy Morrison when I first realized that arrests alone were a dead end. I would spend most of the final decade of my career pointing that out to the public as I implemented the strategy the DEA had conceived, one that used cases to illustrate the need for a wider anti-drug effort.

I began asking to return to the field in mid-January 1979. By mid-summer, two posts had come open—Bangkok and Boston—and Bensinger felt the timing was right. National attention was beginning to shift back toward actively combating drug abuse and away from the laissez-faire attitude of the Carter administration. Ronald Reagan captured the new mood and said all the right things about forming a national anti-drug policy. There was no way a Reagan administration would be less sympathetic to us than that of Jimmy Carter.

During the Carter years our forces were cut by 400 agents, we were hamstrung overseas by a refusal to back our efforts, and little was done domestically to heed our early warnings of the need for drug treatment or prevention. On top of this, Carter's adviser on drug policy, Dr. Peter Bourne, repeatedly pressured Bensinger to endorse the legalization of marijuana. And the keynote to a Carter fund-raiser was provided by Greg Allman, a heroin addict, and the Allman Brothers Band. To an agent, it seemed the administration encouraged drug abuse. To my mind, no better example of its disregard for our agency can be found than Bensinger's first meeting with President Carter.

Midway through the Carter years, Bensinger was summoned to the White House to meet his president. As they shook hands Carter asked Bensinger what government job he held. "I'm the head of the DEA," Bensinger answered. "What's that?" Carter asked, and moved on to the next guest without waiting for a complete reply. To be fair, Carter's Attorney

General, Griffin Bell, had been even-handed in all of his dealings with the DEA. But the prosecutors in key positions under Bell, including Phil Hyman, the head of the Justice Department's criminal division, while all bright, well-meaning and honest, seemed more concerned for the suspects than for the DEA. Inside the agency we joked that we were now working for the Public Defender's Office.

With the Carter administration out of the way and me commanding an active field office, Bensinger agreed that we would have the perfect test of whether the DEA could expand its impact beyond mere prosecution to the larger social welfare issues.

But Bensinger had a worry. "Bob, I want what is best for you, but I can't afford a screwup right now," he said before getting to the meat of our discussion. My days in the field were long past and few of the agents still there had been on the job back then. The younger agents would view me skeptically— from their point of view I was a desk-bound manager with no accomplishments on the streets where the dangers and the scope of the anti-drug efforts had increased dramatically. The number of heroin addicts, estimated at 242,000 in the late 1960s, had grown by the late 1970s to more than 500,000. The amount of heroin seized had grown from about four tons annually to almost seven as a result of the DEA's efforts.

On top of the doubts the agents would have, Bensinger had his own reasons to worry: The last Washington confidant he had sent into the field turned out to be a royal screwup. Appointed Special Agent in Charge of a small DEA office in Texas, he failed to stand up under fire. When he and a team of agents were involved in a gunfight with drug dealers, his leadership, according to the agents, allegedly consisted of hiding under the government car. Repeated denials did nothing to stop the story and its worrisome message from spreading: This was the kind of man Bensinger had sent; this was the kind of agent that dwelled in the comfortable offices of headquarters. Bensinger could not afford to have another close associate even appear to fail in the field.

His reservations on the table, Bensinger spent a few moments with me kicking around the choices.

While Thailand offered the appeal of the exotic and plenty of good heroin cases, it was too far from the public eye. Boston seemed the better place to begin because of the attention we thought our cases and ideas would get on television and in the newspapers. There was the added appeal of being back in New England, close to my parents and my wife's parents. The office was also badly in need of an overhaul. It would be a challenge to shape it so it could stand up to the public scrutiny we anticipated. The prospect was exciting. So Lee and I put our house in Randallstown up for sale, called our parents with the news and began to shop for a home in the suburbs outside of Boston, settling on one in Sharon. It was close enough to Providence that we could see our families on weekends and help repair some of the damage from my years on the road. Settling in would also spare my kids any dislocation now that they were approaching junior high school. That Lee and the entire family would be in a familiar place that felt secure would ease my mind.

I spent the remaining weeks in Washington familiarizing myself with the problems of the insular New England office. A thirty-five-page, single-spaced report by DEA Chief of Operations David Westrate spelled those out:

A failure to rotate agents out of the office had resulted in a good-old-boy network sprouting up between agents and defense attorneys. The network fostered corruption that senior management had failed to notice. The reason was these top commanders had no direct contact with the agents, only their mid-level supervisors. Westrate's report summarized a housecleaning that had begun at the start of the decade and included a criminal probe completed in 1977 with eight agents prosecuted or fired.

But two years later, the taint of corruption, low morale, and management style of the old leadership—the Special Agent in Charge whom I replaced had run the office since the 1960s—were still evident. Those problems were mine to solve now, as were the newer charges of racism against the largely Irish-American force of agents. They had to be solved before Bensinger and I could begin to take our plans public.

Those thoughts were firmly in mind the first day I walked

toward my new office whistling a favorite Harry Chapin song, "Copper." Just then it was the most fitting expression of all I felt about the way a group of these agents had brought shame on the agency by developing a new version of the old protection racket—taking cash in exchange for leaking information to the targets of investigations.

> *Yeah, I grew up and it came clear to me,*
> *all the smart cops on the make.*
> *You get a silver badge not an old tin star when*
> *you're on the take.*
> *It's pimps and whores*
> *Punk gang wars,*
> *Robberies and homicides.*
> *When you walk the beat with the creeps on*
> *the street*
> *Well there ain't no way to hide.*
> *I spent half my life without no wife ridin'*
> *herd on the scum of the earth . . .*
> *And when I send my kid to college someday*
> *he'll have guys like you to thank.*
> *Yeah, ten bucks a week on your grocery store*
> *means you don't have to worry 'bout crime.**

I swung open the door to the John F. Kennedy Federal Building and my whistle stopped. While the housecleaning had swept out the corrupt few, I'd inherited a bunch of federal agents with no morale. There was no way to hold up these agents as role models to the nation.

I descended to the DEA's basement offices. Waiting inside the windowless warren were eighty agents, almost all, unlike most DEA agents in other offices, shrewd enough to have escaped our transfer policy. Instead they served in the city where they were born and raised. I called a supervisory staff meeting and kept my agenda simple.

"I want you all at my house Saturday morning," I told these senior agents, letting them know quickly that I was in charge and I had the power to alter their lives. "When you

---

* © 1979 Chapin Music

come, I want each of you to bring a list of all the extra paperwork, above the minimum required by our manual, that our agents have to perform. Saturday we'll eliminate most of it. Monday you'll tell the agents about it." In my review of the office I had noticed that the agents were required to submit voluminous daily reports accounting for everything from where they parked their cars to how they spent each hour. On top of these, plus the monthly reports required by Washington, the senior agents had piled a required quarterly report. It would be easy to trim the load.

Monday morning, these same supervisors who had never provided leadership would be carrying half of my first message to the agents: If you work with this new guy Stutman, he can make your life easier. The fact that the supervisors had to use their weekend to decide what paperwork to eliminate was the other half of the message: Or he can make your life miserable.

"Now there's one more thing," I said, once the weekend assignment was dished out. "A person I'd like you to meet." An agent named Carlo Boccia walked into the room.

"Meet my second in command. Your new exec," I said with a smile and all the warmth in the world.

Boccia, by contrast, seemed incapable of a smile. A pencil-thin mustache was the only thing that punctuated his handsome, sharp-featured, tight-lipped face. A tall, muscular mountain of a man, Boccia was blessed with a head of thick brown hair which he swept smartly back. He wore immaculate clothes and completed his image of what to Irish eyes must have looked like the height of dago chic with ten trim, manicured fingers that sported a set of very decorative gold rings.

I watched as he ran his eyes across the supervisors' madras jackets, green polyester pants and ruddy faces, and the effect was as if Sylvester Stallone had raked his machine gun across the room. The ruddy faces looked downcast. Boccia was the head of my team to bring them hard into line. After several gun battles, he had earned an agency-wide reputation for ferocity. The respect he'd earned from a hard-bitten group of Newark, New Jersey, cops assigned to his task force had also garnered him a reputation as a tough commander. Boccia, like me, replaced a boss who had been in place since the 1960s.

A few months later, in case anyone had missed the idea that we meant business, I brought in a person who would force them to confront even more.

"This woman," I announced at her introductory meeting, "is a very good friend of mine. Gloria Woods. She's your new training director."

Gloria Woods was very beautiful. And very black. She favored the same pastel greens, pale blues and pinks that these Irish agents enjoyed, only they looked a lot better on her. There were many times when the agents and supervisors could not contain their racism. At first, some threatened to boycott her classes. Others, when they thought she was out of earshot, referred to her as "that nigger bitch."

But Gloria Woods, while she fretted over the racial hostility in private, was tough enough to win their respect. With her help, Boccia and I would complete our shakeup. I also had other, personal reasons for picking Woods as my training director. I trusted her and delighted each time I listened to the story of her climb from the housing projects of West Dallas, Texas, to the rank of supervisor in the DEA.

It was not for nothing that her friends had nicknamed her Story Book.

At a very young age, Woods told everyone who would listen, and told them often, that she would somehow graduate from college, get married to the right kind of man, would buy a house after being married exactly two years, and after having lived there for one year, she would have her baby.

They all thought it was a fantasy, and the nickname reflected that. It didn't reflect her ambition. Through hard work at school and good grades on her civil service exams, she made it reality. She even had her baby on time. In a way, it *was* a storybook, an adolescent dream come true, but those same friends who scoffed, helped provide Gloria with its ending.

From the day she began her first job as a Dallas cop, until the day her achievements helped win her a place at the DEA, Gloria Woods successfully arrested almost every member of her high school graduating class she ran into. That included her best friend. It also included locking up the girl who narrowly beat her out in the vote to win the class title "Most Likely to Succeed."

Each time she told the story Woods allowed herself a thin smile at that one. And, she pointed out, despite her hard work, her marriage continued to thrive. Whenever possible, she cooked for her husband—an old-fashioned guy—his breakfast and dinner. "The things you do at the beginning, when you fall in love, you should always continue," she explained. That, not the meals, was the secret to her success at home and at the DEA.

I had picked Boccia and Woods because they represented everything many within this insular group feared—the outside world—and everything they needed to confront, accept and work with to be successful DEA agents. We needed to work in the black ghettos, in the Italian neighborhoods, among the Colombians, and we had to work there with understanding and compassion, not hatred. So first we had to integrate ourselves. Boston, in the federal government as well as within all the local police agencies, was far behind the times.

It would take two years to complete the overhaul of the Boston office. But to give proper credit, the agents themselves, once shown what they could do, began performing like the professionals they had become, consistently making cases against high-level drug pushers.

With my management team in place, the process of reestablishing our authority in the field and developing new targets for the agents to investigate began almost immediately. I decided to complete the demonstration that our new management was tough but firmly behind our agents by going into the field on a few cases.

One of the first was against a mid-level cocaine dealer who was set up to deliver drugs to an undercover agent in the parking lot behind the Howard Johnson's just outside the College of Holy Cross campus in Worcester, Massachusetts.

"He'll be a pussycat," the agent, Pat Meade, told me. It turned out she was wrong. As the suspect got into his Ford Bronco after purchasing the drugs, two of our cars—mine and Meade's—boxed him in. Then we got out, guns ready. His brake lights went on. We heard the engine roar as he gave the truck more gas. We saw the rear end lift as the brakes struggled to hold it in place. I shouted, "Look out, he's gonna fucking kill us!" Meade and I were already backing up as he rammed through our cars at full force.

Meade was hit and sent flying as I opened fire, emptying my revolver at his truck. She landed on her back, breaking it. My shots damaged only the sheet metal and it took carloads of agents and troopers to run him off the road a few miles away. It would take Meade fourteen months to recover and return to work.

I knew the case would generate attention, so I called Bensinger right away and told him of Meade's injuries and my own actions, which, because they were unusual for the head of an office, were sure to be singled out.

"Look at it this way, you didn't hide under a car, so I'm not too worried," Bensinger said.

The case did bring attention. The attention continued as I began to use our cases to illustrate the larger anti-drug effort the DEA wanted. I was hoping for a reaction from local politicians but one of the first reactions I got was from a state prisoner named John O'Masters.

"I saw you on TV, and you were like a rose among thorns," O'Masters said in a telephone call from prison. "Come see me, I can help you. I like the sound of you." I did see him even though he was serving twenty years for walking into a bar, cutting off a dog's head, then cutting off the testicles of a man who failed to pay what he owed.

It turned out while he was in prison O'Masters's son had become an addict. This had turned him against his cronies who sold drugs. If we would free him from prison, O'Masters would deliver them to us. We knew he could. In Massachusetts, the Mafia and the Irish were close allies. Despite his Irish background, the rules had been broken for O'Masters, and he was so connected that he had been made a member of the Italian organized crime groups.

We freed him from prison and began, in 1980, a series of cases that would net us dozens of organized crime figures and lead us to target Frank LePere, one of the top mob drug traffickers in the region. Slowly, over two years, we built the case against LePere. It began by introducing our undercover agent into his trafficking organization, a move that was engineered by O'Masters, on whose word that "this guy is good" the other gangsters relied. But each time we got close to LePere, he slipped away. We began to suspect someone in our office was leaking our plans.

So we installed a wiretap on his telephone. The day we did he made a series of calls and said, "Did you hear about our friends who are starting to deal drugs? I would never do that. I think it's terrible." This, we knew, was a conversation designed to provide ammunition only for his defense attorneys. He clearly knew the wiretap was in place.

Next, we put a video camera atop the telephone pole nearest his house. The following day, the lens was painted over.

Finally, despite these efforts to thwart us, we had enough information by 1982 to prepare an indictment. As we did, LePere vanished and became a fugitive. Two more years passed before a tip came in that he was living under an assumed name on the top of a mountain overlooking Lake George in upstate New York. In the middle of the night Boccia and I assembled a team of agents and boarded a government plane for Lake George. Using the darkness as protection we climbed four miles uphill through the rough countryside to a sprawling villa that LePere had occupied.

When we kicked in the door, he came quietly. It turned out that during his years at Lake George, LePere had posed as a respectable member of the community, going so far as to sponsor Little League teams. Facing a long stretch behind bars, LePere, in exchange for a reduction of his sentence, agreed to tell us who tipped him to our investigation: "The guy who heads your prosecutors."

David Twomey, the chief federal prosecutor on the case, was the person who had destroyed the case his own lawyers were preparing to try. He had done it in exchange for large sums of cash. Twomey was convicted of obstruction of justice.

Through the four years this case took, my agents made

dozens of other successful cases. Each time I pleaded for greater education and anti-drug treatment.

By 1983 my public appearances had grown to well beyond what I had ever done before. School groups, community groups, editorial board luncheons, television panels, charities, local police groups, after-dinner speeches at charitable functions; I did them all. A similar pace during my overseas years led my agent buddies to jokingly call me "Senator Bob," but in Boston, people seriously speculated that I had political ambitions. I did, but not for myself. I had no interest in running for office. I was using the same methods as a candidate to politicize the drug issue. The moment that led to an overhaul of the state's entire approach to drug abuse presented itself quietly one spring day in 1983 when I walked down the halls of Brookline High.

Brookline was in one of Boston's many wealthy suburbs that are so close to the center of the city that Governor Michael Dukakis took a streetcar ride three stops from his home near the school to his office downtown in less than half an hour. But even in that prosperous suburban environment, drug use was on the upswing. Inside the school's halls instead of the evocative odors of chalk, disinfectant, moldy lunch and drying milk that is the memory of school everywhere, I smelled marijuana. In my walks on the school's campus during a two-day lecture question-and-answer session with students and teachers, I spotted dozens of burned marijuana cigarette butts on the lawns. Then, during one of my talks, I met a young girl I call Stacey, although that is not her real name.

Stacey had stayed on after one of my morning sessions to ask some questions. She was precocious, her questions were very intelligent and from the moment I laid eyes on her it was apparent that Stacey was whacked out of her tree at one o'clock in the afternoon. I stared at this child in Sassoon denim jeans, Frye leather boots and a cotton Calvin Klein top, the pride of any family. I saw ten years down the road a life lost.

I asked her, "Stacey, why are you doing drugs?"

"Mr. Stutman, because nobody has ever told me why not to," was her reply. She had started using drugs, amphetamines, at age twelve. At fourteen, she had just received her first education against drugs. Until then, all her information had come from her friends and it was all pro-drug.

I left Brookline bewildered. How, I wondered, could a child from an intact family, living in a wealthy suburb and attending an excellent public school, never receive any warning or advice about drugs? It turned out she had been swallowing several diet pills a day.

Upon reflection, I realized that I had found the example that I needed. Only education could help curb drug abuse, and if we did not put it in place other children like Stacey would fall by the wayside. I decided I would use the case study of Stacey in my presentations.

About a week later I attended my monthly law enforcement breakfast, one hosted by a Boston priest whom I only remember as Father Quinn. The way he organized the breakfast reminded me of the orderly, scholarly priests who had taught and disciplined me and my largely Irish-American classmates at Providence College.

I told the story of Stacey at the breakfast.

Charlie Barry, the state public safety director and a father of seven, listened. Afterward, he pulled me aside. "What you said surprised the hell out of me," Barry said. "I've put all these kids into school and I should know what the heck is going on in some of the schools around the area."

"Well, Charlie, most parents think that way, but the fact is, do you really believe the kids will tell their parents the truth? Look at the national polls on the subject—most kids, something like 80 percent, say there is widespread use of drugs in their schools, yet most parents, something more than 60 percent, say that they believe there is *no* problem with drugs in the schools their children attend. Someone is lying to someone. From my own observations I see that it is not just the high schools—drugs are moving into the grammar schools as well."

We parted after breakfast. I went to my office, he to his, each of us still thinking of Stacey and the schools.

The next morning, first thing, my office telephone rang and it was Charlie Barry.

"Bob, I went home last night and I thought long and hard

about what you said: grammar school kids; that means you're talking about kids only twelve years of age. Start hooking these kids at that age, there's no hope for them by the time they reach nineteen or twenty. Come over if you don't mind, I'd like to talk about it some more and figure out what to do."

Governor Dukakis and his wife, Kitty, had attended Brookline. Now both their daughters went there, Barry told me at the beginning of the meeting. After that he asked me to explain the DEA's ideas for combating drugs. I laid out the plan developed under Bensinger for treatment, prevention and education. Then I added that kindergarten was not too soon to start drug education. My ideas seemed to allay any suspicions that Barry, a rail-thin Yankee, might have of a conservative Republican agent prowling the halls of a Democratic stronghold. He agreed that if handled the right way, the program could be an excellent agenda for change, but if handled the wrong way it could create an alarm that drugs were flourishing under Dukakis and turn into political dynamite. As always, Barry was polite, charming and to the point. He ended the meeting by saying, "Okay. Fine. I want to whip you over to see the governor and you'll see him today."

Dukakis greeted me in shirtsleeves. A rooster of a man, in person he exhibited all the fine qualities of a rational manager that somehow became transformed into a stiff, ill-at-ease style whenever he stepped in front of a television camera.

"You've got a problem, Governor," I began. My style is as hot as his is cool, and I can't imagine what he thought as I stood in front of his desk wagging my finger in his face as I spoke.

"I'm talking to you not just as the regional director of DEA but I'm talking to you as a parent in the town of Sharon, who's got kids in the schools." He listened stoically to this fast talk by a federal agent, inserting his comments only after I completed the story of Stacey and Brookline High.

"Hey, maybe there's something out there we can do, maybe we can really get young people involved," Dukakis said. But first, he suggested, the state needed to do its own survey. Dukakis was not the kind of man to take a stranger—possibly an alarmist—at his word, but, it would turn out, he was the kind of man to act forcefully when the facts were in.

We parted company and I kept my peace until the survey results came back. The report showed that the drug problem was worse than even I had thought, and worse in the affluent neighborhoods than in the inner city. Everywhere in Massachusetts drug and alcohol abuse by the state's youth was well above the national average—more than 60 percent of the students, in virtually all but the lowest grades, had tried illegal drugs. Dukakis called a meeting and said, "Okay folks, let's go." Massachusetts was declaring war on drug abuse.

Once Dukakis saw how widespread the problem was, he moved quickly to lay the groundwork for what became the Governor's Alliance Against Drugs. It was, when completed, the finest program of its kind in the nation. Later, it became the model for the DEA's own school substance abuse program, which was developed toward the end of my stay in Boston.

In presidential histories, Michael Dukakis might be marked down as a loser, but in the war on drugs and alcohol, his personal contribution was heroic. He began fighting alcohol right after his inauguration as governor in 1983, founding Students Against Drunk Driving chapters at a number of schools and personally leading a tough crusade against drunks on the roads. A few months later, he was set to personally lead the war against drugs.

While in many other policy areas he and George Bush had much in common, had the vanquished become the victor, the solution posed to one of our nation's most pressing problems would have been very different.

"You've got to take the lead if you're in charge," Dukakis told me. "You've got to do this. It can't be delegated. Young families want help. They don't want a big spending program, they don't want a lot of bureaucracy."

The premise of the Alliance was simple: The governor would lead the crusade, developing an anti-drug message and delivering it in a speaking schedule almost as exhausting as my own. Meanwhile, as Dukakis spearheaded the program with public appearances, his staff plunged in to solve the difficulties of designing a curriculum for the schools and an agenda to force the criminal justice and education bureaucracies to work together. This research and development was methodical, grueling and painstaking.

When it was completed, the plan was brought to the state's educators and criminal justice establishment. By then, the meaning of the Governor's Alliance had become clear: An effort by everyone in the state was needed to stop substance abuse. The people of Massachusetts took the program to heart but fierce battles erupted behind the scenes as entrenched bureaucracies tried to fend off change. Dukakis waded into the fight to back his staff with the full weight of the governor's office. He threatened to withhold funds from powerful prosecutors and judges to show that he was serious about hacking through the undergrowth of these formidable interests to get what he wanted. He took an equally strong stand when the same battles were fought over schools. He personally lobbied school district superintendents who refused to believe they had a problem—despite the survey results. At the beginning, just eighteen of the state's 337 school districts were willing to admit they might have a problem.

By the time the Alliance was fully under way more than 95 percent of the school districts implemented kindergarten through twelfth-grade drug education. Peer counseling, a great antidote to the sometimes dangerous peer pressure, was in place in many schools. Expulsion was ordered for students who repeatedly violated the anti-drug rules at all the schools, a harsh measure, but one I favor for the message it delivers. In a very real sense, the threat of expulsion serves as the law enforcement function in these schools, policing the edges of a well-conceived drug policy. Juvenile drug offenders caught by police were sent before judges who knew their funding depended on the quality, not just the quantity of their sentence, so community service, counseling and mandatory attendance at treatment centers or self-help groups became the rule, not the exception. All of these measures, to one degree or another, had been carefully thought out during the early planning sessions.

During this time dozens of meetings between Dukakis staff and the DEA were held. Dukakis wanted the federal agency to play an active role in shaping the policy. I attended most of those meetings and every management meeting Dukakis was to hold on drugs for the next two years. I helped set the goal of drug education in 100 percent of the state's schools and grades by 1992, helped develop the guidelines for the relationship between law enforcement and education, helped write the new school anti-drug policy. This close relationship went a long way toward making federal and state efforts a coherent whole. Once done, we took a back seat on the education and prevention fronts and watched Dukakis's program fly. That mission to suppress demand was the perfect companion to our drive against drug suppliers. Reducing demand and supply at the same time was our goal. Each time I spoke at one of our press briefings, I was able to offer concrete proof to support my talk on prevention, treatment and the role of law enforcement. I pointed out that Massachusetts's educational effort was the only one of its kind in the country. That message was picked up by the national media. Dozens of congressmen, senators and governors descended on the state to take a look and to steal some of the ideas.

Unfortunately, the next few years would show, few had the willingness to lead that Dukakis had shown. The result was evident when I left Boston in the fall of 1985 and went to New York. There, despite a number of fine local efforts, statewide leadership by Dukakis's political ally, Governor Mario Cuomo, was not nearly as strong as it could have been. Where Dukakis had succeeded in heading off a problem before it truly blossomed, New York would fail. Which was one reason why later in 1986, crack was $5 or $10 a vial in New York and $35 a vial in Massachusetts—there was no market, hence the drug was scarce and expensive. The drug use that surveys indicated was reaching epidemic proportions in New York, Washington, D.C., and Philadelphia was on the decline in Massachusetts. It would continue to decline five years after I had left the state.

At home, meanwhile, I and the governor had substance abuse problems to which we had been blind. His, unfortunately, exploded in a full-blown crisis for his wife, Kitty. Mine, luckily, was nipped in the bud.

I had given one of the innumerable speeches to school

groups that marked the Alliance years when, as I made my way to the back of the room, in a school in my own suburb of Sharon, a woman stopped me: "How can you stand there and give these speeches when I know that your son Brian has smoked pot with my son?"

I was devastated. My own son smoking pot? Despite everything I had ever uttered about parents and drugs? I didn't want to believe it. I said something I barely recall, probably that I would question him and bring it to an end if it were true. Then I drove home frustrated, angry and wondering how I would handle this situation that was thrust on me.

I thought I could put aside my anger and talk to Brian as calmly as I had talked to others his age—he was in eighth grade at the time. I was wrong. As soon as I saw him I confronted him in a roar: "Brian! How could you? Marijuana smoking is everything I am against. Damn it, I'm your father," I recall shouting. He had hurt me.

He sheepishly confessed, but I had to throw in one more fatherly remark, "It's okay if you tried it, but if you ever do it again I'll kill you."

He stood there cowering, and said: "I said I'm sorry."

I finally realized I had better ease up. "It's okay. I am the head of the drug enforcement agents in this state. You can't expect that if you try drugs I won't find out. I'm just upset."

My method of talking to Brian is not the method I recommend, and in retrospect I'm amazed that it didn't misfire. But I was fortunate. Brian and I have spoken about the use of drugs many times since, and he has never, he assured me, felt the desire to try them again.

The point was that, like all parents, I led a busy life and, in my case, I had even missed the trailing off of Brian's grades and the other obvious signs that he might have been having social problems or looking for adult attention. I had forgotten, until the incident surfaced, how much time I had spent apart from my son during his early years. Fortunately, the experience was an isolated one. I chose not to make it public then for the same reason that I chose not to use Stacey's real name: There was no reason to cause either of them unnecessary pain. The insights I gained from each encounter were enough to lend greater depth to my speeches and to convince me that, to be fully effective, kids had to address the problem not only with adults, whom they mistrust, but with each other.

In the end, my talks and the work of Michael Dukakis and his staff were enough to create what was truly a miracle in Massachusetts, a state where drug use significantly declined while in many other states the epidemic was growing.

But there was more to the price my family would pay for the high profile I had maintained. Death threats poured in and I realized something remarkably easy to overlook. Drug dealers are an integral part of the global village and they watch television too. All the reports on glowing successes of the Governor's Alliance and of the piles of cocaine my agents had seized were beamed straight to the living rooms of Cali and Medellín, Colombia, where they were viewed by the billionaires of the Colombian cocaine cartels. At a meeting of the drug lords in Peru attended by one of our informants the order was issued, "Get Stutman." The informant couldn't say whether they meant to kill me or kidnap me. He said it not because of the DEA's seizures, but because of my constant appearances on the news.

If our intelligence analysts had not rated the threat as serious, it would have been an entirely comic report from a country so savaged that when comedy is sighted, it is to be savored. But I had a wife and family to protect. Before I could take the action I knew was necessary to further hurt the barons' wounded pride, I had to gather my family to safety. It was too risky not to. I called Lee and told her that there were agents coming to the house, not to worry and that I would be home later. Of course, being agents, they came with big guns since this was rated a big threat. Lee worried anyway as they put down their shotguns in the hall, drew the curtains and sat at the kitchen table to wait with their revolvers.

"How long?" she asked.

"Until it's over, Mrs. Stutman," one of the young men said. "At least a couple of weeks."

"I can't believe this is happening," she said, looking at how agents had grown taller and broader in the shoulders since my day. She took out a pencil and paper. "Will you be staying for dinner?"

Gloria Woods, an expert with a handgun, put aside her training responsibilities for the duration of the emergency and became Lee's personal bodyguard. I took comfort in knowing she now shopped for groceries with my wife. Once, while wheeling her young daughter atop her shopping cart, Gloria came face to face with a man she had put in jail. He glowered. She reached into her purse as she passed between the paper towels and the Pampers and said, "I'll blow your ass away right here in this aisle." He filled both hands with canned goods. She took her place in the checkout line unhindered.

Once Lee was safe, I called Brian at the convenience store where he worked. "Go home. Something came up at work. I'll explain it to you when I get there." There was no need to cause alarm and interrupt the browsing customers with an agent's arrival. Then I sent an agent to Kim's friend Jessica's house where my daughter could always be found. She also went home. But she was unhappy. If it was a serious threat, how come we didn't hear about it? We hear about everything, the young women explained to the agent.

Now I could act. I announced the threat on television. What words I used were not important—the message I stressed was that we took the threat seriously, so seriously I would walk with bodyguards to each television studio and newspaper office that wished to see me. I think I visited every one in the region, many twice, and took to announcing even the smallest case.

"This is another small dent in the drug barons' profits," I would say, knowing that the barons would hear my words that night.

My agents also had their lives upset by the threat. The Boss's Threat, as they called it, required many weekends of work and many nights accompanying me on speaking engagements. They began to make office jokes: "What would happen if the drug lords carried it out?" one agent would ask. "Maybe the next guy would go back to a policy of silently carrying out arrests and work would go back to being from Monday to Friday," another would answer. They decided to put the issue to a vote. "Terminate or Kidnap? How would you get rid of Stutman?" they asked each other in an announcement posted on the bulletin board. They used "terminate" because that is the official word for an assassination. They left lots of room at the bottom for votes and comments.

The vote was fifty-three to terminate, twenty-seven to kidnap. Kidnapping, the experienced agents knew, meant long hours of stakeout duty. Better, they thought, to get the whole thing over with quickly. After all, federal agents do not get paid hourly overtime.

Despite their laughter at the vote, the agents kept their guard up until the threat receded a few months later. By then, New York had beckoned. This time the DEA wanted me in the top job, Special Agent in Charge. New York is the largest field division in the agency. It has more supervisors than Boston has agents. Altogether more than eighty supervisors and more than 400 field agents and city police officers work there. It was also a disaster. The office was completely out of touch with the drug crime and drug-related violence that was corroding the city. It had the lowest number of seizures per agent of any field office, the fewest arrests, poor coordination between its various groups and task forces and weak relationships with local police and prosecutors.

When the call from Washington came, I knew I had to go. It came on Independence Day, 1985. The administrator's office reached me as I stood behind a barbecue spit at my sister Gene's house in Rhode Island. After years of perfecting it, my own version of Mumbo sauce is a spicy, sticky mix that makes me a hero around the house. Each bit of chicken brings back fond memories of my first days in Washington, when after arresting the heroin dealer at the takeout chicken store I learned that good cases alone don't make for good press. The public needs time to get ready. The time was right for New York, Lee agreed between bites. With Kim and Brian almost grown she had no reservations about moving.

"I guess we should call Medwid," I said. She just smiled. My partner, now married, and a supervisor in the New Jersey office of the DEA, suggested northern New Jersey would be the best place to live.

"It's where a lot of the agents live, Bob. You can't get anything for your money in New York." Medwid has always been very value conscious. Once, on one of our trips from Washington to Korea, he saw a half-price sale on Prestone antifreeze. For the next 12,000 miles we carried three gallons of it beside our seats. "You'll never get it on sale in Washington this close to winter," he explained.

Who could argue? "If it's all right with you, partner, I'll take the house and the job," I said. "Sure," said Medwid, "I kind of miss you." I listened to his advice and within a couple of months we found a house that we liked in Wayne, about two miles down the road from his.

Once my replacement was selected, I announced the move to the newspapers and television stations, whose crime reporters took it hard. I had been in Boston almost six years and the reporters and I had developed a comfortable rhythm that, where possible, allowed everyone enough time to have lunch between innings of the ongoing crisis. Reporters delivered fond obituaries to a talkative and controversial federal agent— their favorite kind aside from an exposed scoundrel. The *Patriot Ledger* published an editorial praising me for raising the level of awareness about drug abuse. The mayor, the FBI and the police all presented me with public service awards and Lee and I began to pack. At the beginning of September we moved our household to New Jersey, and I began to immerse myself in the problems of New York.

But Boston was not quite finished with me yet. For almost a decade, I had worn a hairpiece. New York was no place for that, I decided. The ridicule would be more than I could bear. I had seen the TV images of troubled Queens politicians with polyester hair looking foolish as they tried to keep their rugs smooth and give alibis at the same time. I had seen pictures of federal prosecutor Rudolph Giuliani standing with his hand on his head in a breeze trying to answer questions. None of that for me. I would not be handcuffed by a coverup. I had also seen pictures of Mayor Ed Koch, the Mr. Natural of politics, who was free to use both hands while he talked. I opted to go bald and save myself a lot of headaches. I began, first at home, prowling around with my polished head and monk's fringe of red, hoping to ease into the world of New York unnoticed.

An overweight Boston writer, whom I'll call Fat Lady, singled me out for a comic column and spoiled my plans. Her piece was accompanied by pictures that showed me in all my different hairpieces and how I looked now that I had gone natural. Stutman's cover blown, was the tone of what she wrote. Compared with what I would face in the rough and tumble of New York, it was a goodbye kiss.

TEN

The Explosion:
1985

John Maltz walked softly into my office with the tiny, blue-capped vial lost in the caverns of his broad right hand. He extended the hand across my desk and opened it palm up to reveal his treasure while saying in a droopy baritone, "Bob, this is some new shit we seized up in Harlem." A watery sadness clouded his eyes. Then he unceremoniously dropped the vial onto my green desk blotter, stepped back and swiped at his long unkempt mustaches with the back of the same hand.

It was October 26, 1985, and I had been in New York barely a month. I stared down at the vial in wonder.

"I don't know too much about it, but you oughta see how they're using it on the street," Maltz said. From his appearance you would have thought the vial was an offering from the proprietor of a psychedelic poster store. It was as if through some time warp Maltz had survived the 1960s untouched except by the weight of memory. A tangle of gray hair, thin at the top, fell to his shoulders. His voice held a gentle confidence. He was the supervisor in charge of all our joint operations with state and city police. He saw the results of all the street-level cases the New York office of the DEA developed.

I picked up the tiny glass vial and stared at the slender shavings inside—curled whitish flakes, resembling scrapings of soap or peelings of paint.

"It's crack, Bob. We've been seeing it for a few months. I think you ought to get to know about it. On the West Coast they've seen it for a while. It hasn't gone anywhere. But here the cops say we're going to see more and more of it."

In that vial, I realized I was seeing the seeds of a fresh drug epidemic. The rest of Maltz's report confirmed my worst fears. Maltz drew a picture of hallways littered with these vials, of an entire cottage industry that had grown up unnoticed in the kitchens of squalid apartments throughout the city. Crack, potent and cheap by the dose, was already filling the lungs of the city's inner-city youth. Nothing more than prepackaged, smokable cocaine, it would prove nothing less than a nightmare in the months and years ahead. The epidemic had already begun.

"Thanks, John. I'd better find out some more. Let's get the chemist up here."

Paula Higgins, a DEA chemist, stayed for two hours, educating us on the chemical properties of crack. By cooking cocaine hydrochloride with baking soda or ammonia, she explained, dealers returned the cocaine to its potent, smokable freebase form. While cocaine hydrochloride—powdered cocaine—can usually only be snorted, and must slowly work its way through the mucous membranes before dripping into the bloodstream, the freebase, heated and smoked, would be delivered directly to the capillary-rich lining of the lungs. The high was intense and instantaneous. Because the drug was absorbed so fast, the crash into depression was as deep and almost as fast.

"So basically," I recapped, "it hits the brain faster. Whacks them up higher. Then crashes them through the floor."

"That's right," she said. "And of course, at five bucks a vial, it appears cheap." But for the dealer, crack was a gold mine. An ounce of pure cocaine, purchased for about $1,200, treated with adulterants to double its weight, then cooked for a few minutes, became 600 to 1,000 $5 vials of crack—a hefty profit per ounce. The users, eager to prevent the harsh crash that came when a dose wore off, quickly learned the strategy of buying a half dozen or more vials at a time. This rapid learning curve, like that of monkeys rewarded with food when they push the right button, guaranteed that addiction would be swift. It also guaranteed the dealers would be doing a huge volume of business.

I dialed Dr. Arnold Washton. I had met the treatment expert at a Boston conference. Now I wondered what Washton was finding in his three private drug treatment centers in New Jersey, Westchester County and Manhattan.

It turned out Washton was then preparing the first report to the medical world on the properties of crack.

"I'm starting to see it clinically," Washton said. "I've had two or three teenagers come to me, brought in by their parents. They all basically had the same story. They told me they had experimented with marijuana but that now they were smoking cocaine. I asked how they made it, you know, did they use ether? Ammonia? To change the cocaine hydrochloride into something smokable. They each said, 'What are you talking about? I don't make anything. I buy it and smoke it. I'm smoking crack.' All three of these kids are from wealthy Westchester families."

"Thanks, Arnold," I said. It was clear that crack had already struck the suburbs as well as the inner city.

The emergence of crack completed an unholy trinity that would occupy my case agents for the next four years. Heroin and cocaine seemed here to stay. Now crack had arrived.

I knew from the moment Washton finished speaking that I would have to act fast to attack the monumental problems of New York. There would be no luxury of a two-year period to get the office into shape. Since October 1, the day I had officially arrived in New York, I had sensed that the job ahead was large. When I stepped off the elevator and into the DEA offices at 555 West 57th Street—nineteen floors above a Ford dealership—the words "Christ Is Coming" greeted me. They were scrawled in thick blue ink across a *Boston Herald* article that agents had posted on the office bulletin board.

Headlined "Assertive Bob Stutman," the article portrayed me as "a man who easily blended the roles of administrator and street agent," a man who fostered "unprecedented" coop-

eration among New England's hodgepodge of law enforcement agencies, a man who single-handedly stepped up the
war on drugs and a man who pioneered drug education
among children in the state. It recounted an incident where I
had drawn my gun on a drug dealer I'd confronted in a bar,
slapped a whiskey from his hand and snapped the cuffs on his
wrists. What a man, I thought. Could I do that? I certainly
would find out in New York.

Then I smiled at the cynical caption the agent's hand had
added. New York's were the toughest agents in the world, and
the smartest. Their humor had survived years of administrative neglect. As I saw for the first time the evidence of it, I
knew this was a powerhouse office waiting to be led. I was
grateful New York was the largest office of the DEA's nineteen
field divisions, yet it ranked nineteenth in terms of the number of arrests per agent. I believed now that the reason lay
with the special agents put in charge. The nearly 500 agents
and cops assigned there had been poorly led for years. As a
triple-threat drug crisis threatened to envelop the region, the
office had stood on the sidelines.

This in a city where my favorite tabloid, the *New York Post*,
shouted "GIVE US BACK OUR CITY" on page one, and
most New Yorkers did not need to look at the inside story to
know it said, "from drugs."

This in the city where the heroin trail ended. The street
corners had more addicts than anywhere else in America. For
the first time in decades, those addicts could again be seen
nodding in public, sleeping off the effects of increasingly
potent doses. This meant so many big shipments were arriving
unhindered that the dealers could afford to give the addicts
stronger drugs without cutting into profits. When shipments
are stopped, the addict's $10 package contains only 1 percent
heroin and 99 percent adulterants. With heroin pouring in,
the $10 dose was 40 percent narcotic.

This in a city where cocaine use was widespread. The
drug was sold openly in every borough. In Bronx bodegas,
where fava beans have a twelve-cent-per-can profit margin,
drugs with a profit of $10 on a $40 packet took over the
shelves. In Brooklyn social clubs, where horse betting was

mourned as too closely monitored to be routinely fixed, the designer sweatsuit gang began filling their pockets with ounces. Outside the corruption-scarred Queens courthouse, lawyers rubbed their noses instead of their hands. On the campus of rural Staten Island's college, drug purchasers caused traffic jams at the gates. In fashionable Manhattan offices, night spots and workplaces, including the Stock Exchange on Wall Street, the art of politely wiping a runny nose became a necessary social grace. Of America's estimated five million cocaine users, two million were in New York, wearing out their shoes by running up and down in double time until they collapsed.

This in a city where the illegal drug market was so notorious that a clique of Pakistani immigrants had taken to buying pharmacies, then heavily stocking them with drugs purchased at auction from other defunct pharmacies. Since there were only the barest of records on those inventories, this allowed the clique to illegally dispense prescription drugs, selling barrels of Valium, Librium, codeine tablets and Percodan pills to anyone with cash—no prescription necessary. But don't bother trying to buy shampoo, or tissues, or contraceptives, since they were never available because there was not enough profit. It was a city where the average drug user began experimenting as early as twelve, where much crime was attributed to the need for drug money and others to drug-induced psychosis. This was a city where the police felt besieged.

The city cops, absent our assistance or expertise, responded in the best way they knew how: with assault waves dubbed "Operation Pressure Point." The first attack used helicopters, personnel carriers and hundreds of cops to claim a beachhead on the streets of one lower Manhattan slum, the Lower East Side. From January 1984 to August 1985 the daily attacks resulted in 14,285 drug dealers and users arrested. During that eighteen months the police succeeded in reclaiming the ravaged neighborhood. But the rest of the city remained in the grip of fear. While the police presence led to a 37 percent decline in the number of burglaries, a 47 percent decline in robberies and a 60 percent decline in murders on the Lower

East Side of Manhattan, that simply meant that the dealers and users had already moved and set up shop in other less-protected neighborhoods, notably Williamsburg, Brooklyn, which was directly across the East River. There, a quick trip away by bridge, they began the killing and stealing all over again. The price of stopping them was too high. There was no way the police, stretched to the limit and breaking the city's overtime budget, could guard each corner day and night and work their way up to the drug wholesalers. They could not even begin to shut these operations down, nor was there any way to keep up the pressure. The police force is not designed to be an army of occupation; the courts and jails are not able to hold large portions of the population. With crack use on the rise, it seemed obvious that the grip of fear would only grow tighter, perhaps tight enough to squeeze the life out of the nation's largest city. Meanwhile, on the Lower East Side, a new problem demonstrated there are no easy answers to drug abuse. In the now very safe neighborhood, long-time residents were being threatened with eviction by landlords eager to claim the higher rents their apartments could command. While the police had made the neighborhood safe for $1,000-a-month tenants, the ones who had paid $150 were threatened with homelessness. Gentrification, which began before Pressure Point, now blossomed.

I knew how I wanted to respond to New York's drug abuse problem. The methods I had honed in Massachusetts, used here, could bring the national attention the problem deserved. The DEA's new administrator, Jack Lawn, agreed that it was the place to fully implement the ideas that Bensinger and I, seemingly an eon ago, had first hatched—education, prevention, treatment as well as law enforcement were needed to combat drugs. New York was the perfect platform from which to launch a campaign for a coherent national drug abuse policy. With Lawn's blessing, I set to work the moment I got off the elevator to revamp the office, revitalize it and get a grip on both the city's problems and the attitudes of its key law enforcement executives, treatment experts and educators.

The DEA in New York was a big office to command. To simplify this, the 300 agents and 200 city and state police officers were divided into a command structure of ten divisions. Each division roughly contained five groups of ten agents and a supervisor. The five supervisors reported to the division chief. The ten chiefs reported to me through my three Associate Special Agents in charge. One of these associates handled all administrative matters—payroll, informant fees and the like—and another, John Maltz, all joint task force operations with city and state police. The third was my chief of all federal operations from this regional office—in effect the second in command.

I began my overhaul with a shakeup of our intelligence division, the nerve center of a field division. New York's, over the past decade, had been turned into a dumping ground for the borderline incompetent, terminally drunk and incorrigibly lazy. These agents sapped morale from the competent agents remaining in the unit, and drastically reduced its efficiency. The office had not a clue as to who was buying or selling drugs or even at what price in the nation's largest drug market. For example, the office was unaware of what, if any, inroads the Medellín Cartel had made into the New York cocaine market. Nor could it identify the top Asian heroin distributors. Yet drugs arrived in New York from everywhere but especially from Hong Kong, Thailand, Colombia, Peru, Mexico, Turkey and Afghanistan. It arrived by boat, plane, truck, car, train. The drugs came stashed inside of purses, shoe heels, anuses and vaginas, suitcases, statues, furniture. People swam the merchandise ashore, airlifted it in and simply drove it to warehouses, apartments and nightclubs. Couriers, anonymous ciphers from every race and nation on the globe, carried the drugs into town undetected.

Next came the revamping of our technical section. Designed to provide surveillance equipment for our agents, it left them ill-equipped to even properly keep track of the traffickers who had lived in town for decades. The agents assigned there had little, if any, training as technicians and they had not taken inventory of our equipment for three years. It turned out, when we did check, that there was not enough wiretap equipment, or equipment to record the numbers of incoming or outgoing calls from a suspect phone. As a result, agents had stopped requesting the equipment and these valuable practices had fallen into disuse.

Then came a shakeup of our priorities. Just one team of ten agents had concentrated on developing cocaine cases, leaving the lieutenants of the Colombian cocaine barons, the most notorious of all dealers, free to come and go almost at their pleasure. This had gone on for almost ten years—since the day the Senate subcommittee recommended that while DEA not be disbanded, it focus on heroin, not the recreational drug cocaine. The cartels had used the time well. A combination of investments in local businesses, the ability to offer lucrative jobs and a code of silence enforced through murder and kidnapping—all the tools perfected by the Italian Mafia—had won them a more solid lock on the Queens region that is their East Coast headquarters than the Democratic party, which also has a stronghold there. The code of silence and our lack of aggressive enforcement ensured that fewer members of their solid organization were in jail than those heavily investigated politicians.

Then came a review of the kind of cases we were making. While the majority of the agents ostensibly were working on heroin cases, the old Turkish connection had been battered since 1972, and no one had penetrated its replacement, the up-and-coming Chinese heroin networks. After thirteen years of prosecution, the majority of the established Italian Mafia and American La Cosa Nostra heroin bosses were behind bars or out of business. Ethnic Chinese heroin traffickers had quietly moved in to fill that gap and by now had almost exclusive control over the local Southeast Asian heroin market. While the Italians, who sold Southwest Asian heroin (from Turkey and the surrounding region), had once controlled more than 90 percent of the New York market, we would soon learn that at least 40 percent of the market was now controlled by the Asians, whose heroin came from the Golden Triangle region of Southeast Asia. Yet our so-called Chinese expert spoke no dialect of Chinese and we had almost no Asian undercover agents.

Finally I had to make all the factions of the office into a whole. In a smooth-running DEA office, with good informants, a good lab and a good use of our overseas bureaus, it is possible to track a drug shipment from the moment negotiations for its purchase begin, across an ocean, to the United States distributor, right down to the dealer on the street. In New York, the agents assigned to the regional office, which was supposed to make importation-level cases, did not even speak with the agents and police officers assigned to Maltz's local task force. As a result, the two teams could not effectively track shipments or make cases against an entire network from wholesaler to retailer. When the task force made a case, the distributors would stay free to await the next shipment. When the regional office made a case, any drugs that slipped through could be sold with relative impunity, since the task force did not know to look out for an increase in the availability of a particular substance. Neither group, of course, bothered to work closely with intelligence, which, if it had an ongoing relationship with the two enforcement units, should have been able to evaluate the quality of each piece of information and help develop high-impact cases by sifting through it all.

A week after I set foot in New York, the beginnings of this structural reorganization were under way—the three associates and ten division chiefs had received their orders. Now it was time to bring all the divisions and their internal factions together as a single group and let the agents know that I would hold them responsible for making cases that would stand up as a cornerstone for an office that I envisioned at the center of national attention.

I ordered an all-hands meeting. "This has been the worst office in the country," I told the assembled cops, agents and support staff. "You haven't made enough arrests, you haven't seized enough of the property of the dealers you do arrest, you haven't paid attention to the needs of the region. You don't even know how bad the drug abuse problem is in New York. Soon we are going to be the best office in the country. You will see a real change. You will be a part of it."

Then I introduced my new number two man, Kevin Gallagher, who would be the associate in charge of federal operations. The exact opposite of Carlo Boccia, Gallagher came in smiling. I would be the tough guy in New York. Gallagher was known as the best case agent in the DEA. He'd earned this through his ability to conceptualize at the start of a case the methods it would require, all the possible investigative tangents it might take—overseas and in the United States— and the desired result. He would show these guys how to make long-term cases and make those cases stick. I freely admit that my strength is in demand reduction, education and developing the right environment in which law enforcement can work. I would never, after almost an entire career spent as a senior manager, pretend to have the wisdom of a detective that a great case agent must have.

"There will be no questions," I said in closing. "We'll have plenty of time for that. Thank you very much."

On the way out of the room, I had to wake my aide, Dick Driewitz, from his chair in the corner. Driewitz was a loyal, bright agent who knew the system in New York inside and out. A trombone player in a jazz band, on Mondays he played long nights with Woody Allen at Manhattan's Michael's Pub. The result was his only fault: He sometimes made up for the lack of sleep during the day. Once he had fallen asleep behind the wheel of his car on the way to work. To unsnarl traffic, someone had to bang on his car window. But Driewitz planned to retire in six months to a year, so I picked him for his institutional knowledge. If I hadn't figured things out in New York within six months, I'd be packing to leave too and not worrying about his replacement.

The next day I began reorganizing the case load. I assigned three groups of agents from the regional office to work on cocaine cases, assigning a Hispanic agent to take charge of each. Until then, these agents who understood the language and culture of the cocaine barons had been wasting their expertise working on heroin cases. Now they could shift their energies to understanding what was going on in the Colombian cocaine cartels' branch offices in Queens. It would turn out to be a good deal more productive than attempting to have them infiltrate Asian-run heroin rings. For that, a different group would be used. Within the task force I shifted 25 percent of the agents from heroin to cocaine.

The moves met with resistance. "This is bullshit," shouted one supervisor. "Cocaine is not as big a problem as heroin. Besides, it's kiddie dope. You'll see, cocaine arrests are so easy to make that soon nobody will bother making the heroin cases." I didn't see, but I understood the prejudice. It was the same one that at the end of the 1960s kept us chasing marijuana cases even as heroin use soared—the comfort of the familiar.

The New York office was so heroin-oriented that it was dubbed "The Bureau of Heroin" within the DEA. Despite this emphasis, there was more heroin then ever on the streets of New York and the DEA was doing little to combat its traffickers. One result was that nearly half the nation's estimated 558,000 heroin addicts—250,000—were believed to be in New York. Yet when I asked one supervisor how many heroin arrests he made and how many cocaine arrests he made, his only answer was "I don't know." That launched me.

"Then how do you really know what the scope of the problem is?" I began. "Those 500,000 heroin addicts we've been saying there are in America—we don't even know if that number is real. Everyone in law enforcement has been using those same goddamned numbers since we developed the statistical model so that Nixon could declare war. We arrived at it the same way they count fish in a pond. By pulling out fish from a small area and multiplying the catch by the approximate size of the pond. Well, nobody arrests heroin addicts anymore. So we don't even know where the edge of the pond is."

I got the whole idea out in fewer seconds than it took to switch channels on a television set. There was no attention span in America too small to hear an entire idea delivered this way. The agents noticed and began to call me rubber mouth.

In the months ahead, the agents would hear me give hundreds of presentations to the media as I attempted to call attention to the drug scourge. Still fresh from the success of Massachusetts, I set out to prove that it could be replicated nationally. With my office on the road to running smoothly, I wasted no time in pointing out its new accomplishments against the drug traffickers and using those cases to illustrate the full scope of the drug abuse problem. For the agents, this was a radical change.

Bruce Jensen, my predecessor, had kept the profile of a mole. A wonderful person who walked around with a coffee cup, he did not belong in New York. Despite the agency's problems it did make heroin cases regularly, but Jensen never called attention to the DEA successes.

As a result, in a city with four major daily newspapers, he had been mentioned perhaps a dozen times in four years. There were funerals that received better coverage than the DEA. The agents nicknamed him "Hands" Jensen. When there was a press conference, the DEA did not get credit. Instead, all you saw on TV were Jensen's hands as he passed the seized drugs to the U.S. Attorney or police official who took credit for the case. This kind of behavior had helped destroy morale. It took no time at all for one of the agents to point out that they had gone from living with Hands to living with the Mouth.

But before I could launch a full-blown media campaign, the agents needed to see that the Mouth could do more than roar. In the first week of November, three weeks after the all-hands meeting and a few days after Maltz walked into my office holding the vial of crack, I completed the shift in priorities at a week-long retreat in the Catskill Mountains.

When we returned, in the second week of November, I was ready to go out on the streets with my agents. I had never lost sight of what I learned under Bensinger—they needed to at least see me on the street before they could develop any trust in me.

While no longer a case agent by any means, and far from qualified to directly supervise a case, I thought street work was still fun as well as good management. I could see firsthand the conditions they worked under, feel and smell the streets of New York during a chase. I wouldn't do it every day, but I would do enough of it that some of the agents were bound to discover that I wasn't such a bad guy. Others, of course, would suspect that I was trying to spot flaws and "do them" on the street. To do someone, in cop talk, can only mean to do them harm, since no untried boss could be counted on to do the right thing.

The first case was a small one by New York standards. A group of Puerto Ricans had turned a set of bodegas and tenements into fronts for the selling of cocaine to the Bronx. It was a low-level ring with only the slenderest of connections to the drug wholesalers. But to crack it involved simultaneous raids on twenty-two doors, behind which these small-time dealers cut, packaged and sold their cocaine. It pleased me that it was a cocaine case because I felt the DEA was finally correctly positioned to use our muscle against this newer threat as we had against heroin.

I squished into a car with an agent named Fred Sandler, a former pro football player, who fit his large frame behind the wheel and said, "You got nothing to worry about, I'll take care of you, boss."

I admit I was nervous. Twenty-two warrants, I was thinking. In my whole career I hadn't served twenty-two simultaneous warrants needed to knock down twenty-two doors.

"Who's got the warrants, you or one of the other supervisors?" I asked.

"Warrants? Don't worry, boss, in New York you don't need warrants in advance, you can just phone the request in to a prosecutor when you start banging the doors. Keeps things simple," he explained. "There's too many cases going on simultaneously to figure out what warrants you'll need in advance."

I almost collapsed. That was my true welcome to New York. In Boston if we didn't show up with warrants already signed, a judge would lock up the agents and set the suspects free. In New York, the agents and prosecutors worked very closely, so that at the last possible minute—once the agents were certain what warrants they needed—the prosecutors could have them filled out, signed by a judge and raced back to the scene of the raids.

We pulled up on 161st Street in the South Bronx. It was late at night, and Yankee Stadium cast a deeper shadow over the surrounding squat buildings. The raid signal was given and the ram teams began crashing the doors.

Some tried to flee the rushing agents and Sandler spotted one driving down the street. We chased the swerving car and as we pulled in front and cut it off Sandler slammed the brakes and I leaped out, gun drawn, and ran at the suspect, who had climbed from his car and started to run. "Freeze, or I'll kill you," I shouted. Nothing much had changed since my first raid. Then I looked at the suspect. He towered over me. I looked for Fred. He was still in the car.

That son of a bitch Sandler must hate me, was my thought. He's set me up to get killed. Not even a boss on the street is immune from the suspicion that someone is out to do him. But within seconds of my paranoid thought, Sandler was free of the car and behind the suspect with gun at his head and handcuffs at his wrists. Sandler's door had been stuck shut and he had to struggle across the seat to get out the passenger side. I brought home the lesson I needed from the streets. I had begun to feel them from my agents' perspective. I tried never to forget that as I waited for them to return from their raids.

Satisfied that my office was in shape, as the end of November approached I made the rounds of the criminal justice establishment. I went hat in hand, seeking to buy a little time and win a little good will.

The task was done against the steady background noise of Mayor Koch screaming for action. These were the Reagan years and if the president of the United States had declared war on drugs, where was the money, the mayor said to anyone and everyone. "Whadda ya think, we grow opium in Central Park? We don't grow opium in Central Park, it's a federal problem." Since I was the head of the federal drug agents in the region, it would not be long before he was screaming at me. I knew that as I made the rounds.

So as I did, I reflected on what Koch was saying. Although people were still cheering him—the quintessential New Yorker, he was cocky, arrogant, funny and aggressive—it just happens that on this issue he was wrong. While he was busy blaming other people there was much more that he could do, beyond exhausting the resources of the police department. He had educated few children against drugs. He had offered few abusers or addicts the treatment needed to turn them back into human beings. "No money. Not our job," the mayor regularly said. Instead, he drained the city to pay the cops, courts, jails and hospitals necessary to preserve the ugly status quo.

Three years after I took over the New York office, he would still be screaming. By then, I had outlined clearly to reporters attached to most of the nation's news organizations exactly what kind of public health solutions could work. Those solutions were quickly promised by both contenders for the presidency. I had met with virtually every official in the city, presented my plan to every educator, and discovered that in New York no one outside of the police was willing to do anything. Ed Koch, through it all, never called. As a federal agent, it was not my position to call on him to help—it was, after all, his city. Yet, he was a mayor too proud to call a cop, until his desperate and unsuccessful bid for reelection. Then, as Everett Hatcher lay unburied, he called from a car to mix his condolences with a job offer in one breath. He wanted a city drug czar. With Everett Hatcher beneath my feet I would finally fit his needs. I declined.

My first stop in November was the office of an old friend—Special Narcotics Prosecutor Sterling Johnson, Jr. He held the purse strings for state narcotics buy money, which I would need to bankroll cases. His office also had state court jurisdiction in all five counties of the city, so many of my task force's cases would be prosecuted by Johnson.

"Hey ya!" He said it in a rogue's baritone as I strode into his warren of offices. He was standing at the tobacco-colored door to the entire paper-littered mess, swinging a nightstick from its leather thong and then tucking it under the right armpit of his pinstriped suit as he finished greeting me. "Good to see you again, Bob. Come on in to my office and we can talk.

"So, what is it you know, Bob? And what is it I can tell you?" he asked once we were comfortable. I laid out my plans and my promises of DEA investigations that were targeted at the city's problems. "I need some time, Sterling." It was easy to ask him for it. We had known each other since 1971, when he worked a few doors down from me at the BNDD's offices in Washington. We had shared plenty of dinners and plenty of thoughts on how the nation's drug abuse ought to be curbed.

"You open your checkbook for my undercovers. I'll bring my best cases to you when they don't have to go federal. I know you always prosecute hard." I promised the prosecutor the one thing he wanted. Good cases. Then I waited to see if the horse trade was acceptable.

"Your guys stop acting like we're second-class citizens and Sterling will treat you right," said another voice. It was Bob Silbering, Johnson's chief assistant, who had slipped in and sat quietly off to the side. I nodded. Sterling rose. Business was over. The message that I would work with the local law enforcement agencies would quickly be passed to the other officials in the city. Johnson would see to that.

I kept my pace quick and took my lumps in stride. I visited the Police Commissioner, key judges, the district attorneys and the U.S. Attorneys for the two federal districts covering the downstate region. From the federal prosecutors what I wanted was an agreement that the DEA would announce its own cases, not watch them be announced at the courthouse. The judges, whom I met at an early December party in the basement of St. Andrew's Church, a little house of worship sandwiched in between the federal court, the federal prison and police headquarters, told me what they wanted. "When are you going to make cases worthy of this court?" was how one judge put it. I promised it would be very soon.

My final important stop on this jaunt was the Eastern District courthouse in Brooklyn. The Eastern District, often overshadowed by Rudolph Giuliani's Southern District courthouse in Manhattan for Wall Street and organized crime cases, was a mecca for narcotics prosecutions. I waited until bantamweight former West Point boxer Andrew Maloney took over from the outgoing U.S. Attorney, Raymond Dearie, and then I visited. His Chief of Narcotics, Charles Rose, was present.

Over lunch I explained the DEA's new mission in New York—an attack on crack, on Asian heroin rings and on the Colombian cartels—then listened to Maloney ignore the agenda.

"I don't give a shit about cocaine," Maloney said. "All I'm interested in is guinea heroin cases on Pleasant Avenue."

Charles Rose shook his head back and forth throughout the meeting but said nothing in front of his boss.

"Can you believe that shit? Guinea heroin cases on Pleasant Avenue. He thinks he's still in 1972," I afterward told my aide, Bob Strang, who would replace the retiring Driewitz. The Italian-American heroin dealers of Manhattan's Pleasant Avenue had not been major traffickers in over a decade. But I had chosen not to argue with Maloney; he was, after all, the U.S. Attorney. Despite his initial archaic view of the drug-trafficking situation, his office would later prove to be very helpful.

The round of initial meetings was a success. The later meeting with Maloney was also fruitful. They bought me the months I needed to start making cases and getting the cases into the press.

Already, my agents had begun identifying the current crop of heroin and cocaine dealers. I returned from my tour to a harvest of reports that outlined a glum picture. To defeat a ban on the export of refining chemicals to Colombia, coke dealers had begun installing highly explosive refining labs all across the state. These labs used hundreds of gallons of ether—easily available in the United States—to turn gummy cocaine base into the snortable white powder, cocaine hydrochloride. The old-line La Cosa Nostra had established a strong connection to the Chinese and was acting as a middleman to heroin distribution groups to which the Chinese still did not have a direct tie. Some city police were involved in a Staten Island drug ring. Colombian cartels were behind an increasingly high number of murders in Queens.

The crack plague, meanwhile, began to make its way onto the front pages. "A New, Purified Form of Cocaine Causes Alarm as Abuse Increases," read the headline of a front-page *New York Times* account published on November 29, 1985. The report, by Jane Gross, summed up the problem insightfully:

"Previously, free-basers had to reduce cocaine powder themselves to its unadulterated form by combining it with baking soda or ether and evaporating the resulting paste over a flame.

"Since crack appeared on the streets of the Bronx last year, spreading throughout the city and its suburbs, new cocaine users have graduated more quickly from inhaling to free-basing, the most addictive form of cocaine abuse.

"In addition, dealers in crack have found a ready market in people reluctant to intensify their intake by intravenous injection...because of fear of AIDS."

The article went on to identify the kitchen factories where crack was created, the crack houses where it was smoked and the slogans like "Crack It Up" that street corner hawkers used to market their wares. It summed up much of the problem that would occupy large amounts of the DEA's energy for years to come.

Soon after crack began to dominate the news, the results of reshuffling our case priorities began to filter in to an intelligence division now equipped to understand them. Even though crack loomed large, the first hard information on the severity of the Chinese heroin problem was sifted. Heroin too would be a growing problem.

The quarterly intelligence report for December summarized that while the traditional organized crime figures, the Italians, still distributed plenty of heroin, the traffic in New York was dominated by the Chinese. Untouched by law enforcement, the report noted, the Asian traffickers had begun using violent Chinese youth gangs to distribute their wares and carry out their murder contracts. It also showed that the Chinese traffickers had branched out from Manhattan's Chinatown, extending their reach across New York harbor to what then Manhattan Chief of Detectives Aaron Rosenthal called "the new territories of Queens." There they blended into a growing community of honest Asian-Americans on whom they would prey just as the Mafia had preyed on New York's Italians.

With a refocused plan of attack on the heroin problem, a freshly shaped assault on cocaine and the identification of the coming crack epidemic, I felt that my initial agenda was complete. The DEA in December 1985 was ready to battle drugs in New York. With an epidemic brewing on three fronts—heroin, crack and cocaine—we were ready not a moment too soon. The inside story of that battle is the agents' story. It is one best told in their voices, the voices of their informants and the voices of the suspects.

THREE

Inside Stories

ELEVEN

An Informant's Tale

In my first days in New York I heard that Richard LaMagna, an agent assigned to the Paris bureau, was up for a transfer. I called headquarters and learned he was the renowned linguist who spoke two Chinese dialects and several other languages. I asked for his promotion to supervisor. "I need him to run a heroin group in New York concentrating on the Chinese," I explained. LaMagna would be the force behind our crackdown on the Asian-run heroin rings.

He arrived with a firsthand knowledge few could match: He was running a high-level informant within the Chinese drug-importing hierarchy. The informant was known as Ah Fat. LaMagna, through his deep interest in China, and genuine concern for Ah Fat, had over the years earned the informant's confidence. With diligence, he used it to extract from Ah Fat a saga that dated back to the years preceding the formation of the People's Republic of China, information needed to crack the highest levels of the Asian networks. Coupled with cases made by our local task force this would complete an attack on both ends of the new heroin pipeline.

Ah Fat's life was the story of modern Asian heroin smuggling. It is presented as he told it. At times, the narrative, reconstructed from seven days of conversations in various Hong Kong hideaways, has been condensed. Comments have been inserted as needed.

I was born in 1930. My father, Yao Chung, was a general in charge of army transportation. When I reached between six and seven the Japanese took over the major part of China, so we had to run away to Chungking, the wartime capital. But even with the war we were living quite well; our family still had two cars. From a very young age, I start to meet a lot of high-ranking people. All of these people wanted deals, business with the military, so they have to come to pay the bribe money to my father. And they came to pay by the suitcase. That maybe made me get used to dealers.

Still, the first few years of war were really bad because the Japanese bombs keep coming, bombing all the time until the U.S. Air Force comes to China and drives them from the sky.

My father was a Buddhist and he had seven wives. My mother he cherished; she was the first wife in the family, so she was supposed to be respected. But the last wife, Yu Ming Shu, was an opera performer in Chungking. She was young. My father loved her very much, so she thought she was supposed to be the biggest wife in the family. One day, my mother, Chang Hang Ling, was playing mah-jongg for four hours and her feet got swollen and she needed hot water to make her feet more comfortable. But at that time we don't have any, so she asks the young mother to boil it. She does. But then she got into a quarrel with my mother and poured the water out on my mother. I was so mad—I was only fifteen, but already I played with guns—I just ran back and shoot her in the shoulder. This made my father angry. He doesn't want to send me to the police, so he decided to send me away to England as a navy officer cadet.

I left with a group of 216. Together, we fly out from Chungking to Calcutta, India. Boy, that flying was rough—it was my first time on a plane, and such small plane.

We reach Calcutta at night. The next day we tour the city and see an old lady with what must have been one hundred bananas. In Chungking bananas are so expensive that for almost a dollar U.S. all you get is one piece. We tell the lady—we all spoke a little bit of English already—we wanted to buy $5 U.S. of the bananas. That old lady just took the $5 and ran, saying all the bananas were ours. Welcome to Calcutta.

We stay for five days, then travel to the British Victoria Barracks in Bombay. There the military supply officer in our traveling group was my mother's brother. My father arranged to put him in this job to let him make some extra money. We got pretty good living money but the supply officers paid us only 60 percent and kept the rest for themselves.

So I go to see my uncle, the fourth brother of my mother; his name is Chung Gee Ching. I told him, "I know exactly what is happening. Unless you give me some special deal, I'm going to have to write a letter to the top minister and give him the whole story. I have two good friends, you're going to supply us with food in a Chinese restaurant each night. And I'm not going to pay anything; you're going to pay all the bills." My uncle had no choice: "Okay, you guys go to eat every day and I pay the bills." I know now this event with my uncle was where I learned to have the courage to be a drug dealer. We stayed happy in Bombay for three months, and then we traveled to Liverpool, England.

This is 1945. When we reach Liverpool I realize I never had such cold weather in my life. We stay in England two years until finally our training is over. Then we picked up eight torpedo boats from the British and put them aboard a ship called the *Empress of Australia* to travel to Shanghai, our naval base. It took thirty-seven days. I was a second lieutenant, in charge of the Number Three boat. At that time I was only seventeen and the war between the Chinese Communists and Nationalists was getting really hot.

My father by now is getting worried and starts taking whatever he has and putting it all in cash. After a year, I left the navy and started going to Shanghai as a playboy, fooling around with all these big gangsters. I got to be very close friends with To Yua Sun, one of the biggest gangsters in China. The Shanghai gangsters didn't like using force; they went into business, making loans, running gambling games, owning nightclubs. Because my father is so powerful, he is important to them, so they accept me. I enjoy fooling around in their nightclubs, buying and selling gold in the black market, then spending the profits playing cards. This is when I started to be a big gambler.

By 1949 the Red Chinese had come very close, so our family decides to run away. To Yua Sun chartered a 29,000-ton ship sailing from Shanghai on May 4, 1949. Since he knew my father very well he said we could go with him. We hurried to leave but with only seven days before we're ready to go, my father had to leave a lot of gold. He asks my older brother to drive to Nanking to pick up the rest of the gold, but when my brother tries to return, the Red Chinese had already crossed the Yangtze River and they arrested him and held him for two years. Then they asked him, "Do you feel sorry about your life?" My brother replied that the East tiger eats people; the West tiger also eats people. So they killed him. My father should not have sent him back, because he had more than enough money already. Why send your son back?

We traveled with To Yua Sun's family to Hong Kong in July 1949. From there we went into Taiwan where the national government had moved. At that time Taiwan was nothing, it was a peanuts place. It was dirty. When it rained, it got muddy and when dry, it got dusty. I hated the place.

I say goodbye to my family and I go back to Hong Kong with $1,000 U.S. in my pocket. I began selling imitation jewelry from a tiny shop, the Hankow Company on Hankow Road, an area with lots of nice shops. One day a big shot walked into the store. I saw how he is dressed and I told my partner, "This guy must be very rich." Then he started talking and said he was from the Rockefeller family. So I raise my price one hundred percent. When I started telling him the price, my partner kicked me on the bottom. "What the hell," I said, "this guy, if you sell cheap, he don't want to buy." He picked up $3,000 in jewelry—imitation jewelry. You know how much capital I started with to make that $3,000? I think less than $200. I know how to make money.

The way I made it began to change because of a meeting with Captain Grant, an American pilot from Korean National

Airways. One day he walks into my store, buys some jewelry and starts talking. I offered him a beer and we sat down.

"You know," I said, "I think I got a good personality, people like me."

"Yes, you do," he answered. "You're a young kid, you have spunk, speak English well." I was twenty-three.

The next Tuesday morning he comes back and tells me about the profit that could be made on English woolen goods bought in Hong Kong and sold in Korea.

"The price here is approximately $6.75—that's what the Indian people sell to me for," he said. "I don't know how much they make. You think you can sell to me at the same price? I'll order from you; I don't like them. I also buy cheap watches. I buy maybe 4,000, 5,000 each time. Since you're a businessman I don't think you'll have much of a problem with this. You should make a very nice profit. But you need to do one thing: All businesses need an export license."

At that time, Hong Kong is a thoroughly corrupt city. Not like now, Hong Kong is very clean. So I got to one of the British inspectors in charge of the customs people at the airport and we make arrangements. For $1,500 Hong Kong every week, I will not need an export license. Then I checked the price of materials. I found out that the profit—if I sold at the price the Indians sold at—would be about 20 percent since I wouldn't have to pay export taxes. That's a hell of a good profit when the total business is about $80,000 a week. That means you can make $16,000, and after you pay all the bribes and workers you make $10,000 U.S. a week.

I called Grant: "I tell you frankly, I don't want to sell to you at that price."

"You can't do it?"

"No, I'm going to reduce the markup to 10 percent," I said. "I'll make $5,000 a week; I feel that is plenty." He had given me a good opportunity. I knew if I was not greedy he would send more business my way. I thought, this way my business will last a long time. Somebody else can't come and take it because who can make a better price than me?

I flew to Korea with Captain Grant and I started meeting all these U.S. Air Force pilots. In the future I would use them to ship my drugs, but now I use them to smuggle watches and cloth and avoid export taxes on woolen goods and import taxes on the watches. Through pilots Grant introduced me to, my smuggling grew to $15,000 U.S. profit a week. I figured that one of every two people who bought a scarf, fabric or a suit in Korea bought one shipped by me. I'm not kidding.

But in China, in that type of business, your good life can not last forever. So now it's 1957 and the pilots tell me there are two planes coming to Japan to be repaired. When completed, they will stop in Hong Kong and then go on to Korea. I could have whole empty planes. I could make a big shipment. I decided that would be my last shipment. You remember that. In any kind of a smuggling business or dope business, don't ever make a wish that a job is your last. Once you make that promise to yourself, you always get caught. Later, when I got caught with the heroin, I had also said the same thing: "This is my last job."

I put 160,000 watches and I don't know how many yards of material on these two airplanes. But the airmen are U.S. Air Force intelligence. They warned the Korean embassy. When these planes arrived in Seoul, the intelligence people, the customs people, the U.S. embassy people, they all were waiting. I was arrested and I lost everything I had. One of the biggest shipments I ever made in my life, and I lost it all. The only good thing was that I had Hong Kong identity papers. If I was Korean, I would have been put in jail for at least ten years. Instead they just shipped me back to Hong Kong.

But I was feeling so bad at that time that I stayed home about six months, and did not even do any work. Then I began to try to go back to making my own living. At that time, there was a gold-smuggling boom, from Hong Kong to India. And I thought, Here I can find a way of making big money. And that is the beginning of how I tricked the gold smugglers.

I did not intend to do any gold business, I was just trying to cheat the smugglers. Just listen to the story—you'll think I'm a genius. It was 1964 or 1965. I met a girl called Elsie; she was a middleman, looking for a way to ship gold from Hong Kong to India. So I told her, "I have a special connection. The U.S. embassy flight. It's 100 percent safe." She said her boss wouldn't take my word, I had to show him something. I had nothing to show. But the next day I walk into the U.S. embassy and meet a man, I believe his name was Baker, and I start telling a story. Since when I was young I had been making up stories, but I still built a reputation for telling the truth. I said, "I have a big smuggling group. They're smuggling gold from here to India and they're shipping opium and morphine from India to Hong Kong. Is your office interested?"

Even back in 1965, the United States was interested in drug smuggling; not that much, but a little bit. So Mr. Baker told me, "Yes, you do interest me with a case like this."

I told him I need an embassy pilot to go out to have dinner with this smuggler boss so I can start working on this. "Okay," this Baker said.

"Just have him carry a U.S. passport showing that this job is that of a U.S. embassy pilot. And have him wear a full U.S. Air Force lieutenant colonel's uniform," I said. I also warned him not to talk about the drugs because they were very cautious about the drugs. I tell him, talk only about the gold. (Actually, if he talked about drugs they would've gotten up and left, since they had no drugs.)

So the lieutenant colonel, who uses the name Meese—I'm not even sure he's a real pilot—myself, this Elsie and the smuggling boss, Mr. Andrew Hsu, we go to a restaurant and we start talking. At the end Andrew Hsu says, "This is a good opportunity." He agreed we'd do 300 ounces every trip; the pilot would get forty-five ounces and I would get forty-five ounces also. That's a lot of profit. Everyone was happy. Later I told Baker, "I need a few weeks to confirm before I can contact you again." I never even tried to contact him.

I got a piece of letterhead paper from the embassy, and I wrote a letter: "I am a friend of Lt. Col. Meese. Unfortunately he cannot make the next flight. I will be the pilot. He told me all the details, and I think I want to make money also. But under one condition, I want to meet you alone." I had the letter say what time this new colonel was arriving. I had it taken to Japan and mailed back to myself. When it arrives I bring it to Hsu and tell him, "Look, this is the letter. You want to do it? I don't want to do it, it's up to you." So he reads the letter and says, "Yeah we'll do it. But I have to see the pilot. You meet the pilot, talk to him in the lobby. I'll watch and see if the man is good or bad."

That night, Hsu drove a car and I sat in the back with the case of gold. It was so heavy, I could see there was more than 300 ounces in it. I told him so.

"You've got good judgment," he said. "Actually it's 350 ounces. You don't have to tell the pilot."

We stop the car. I walk into the lobby of the International Hotel, pick out the best-looking guy, tall, age around forty-five, dressed well, and say, "Did I see you someplace in Japan?"

He looked me up and down and said, "Are you sure?"

"Yeah, Japan," I said. "I'm in the air force, I'm a doctor there."

"Oh, you are? Are you staying here?"

Before we went to the hotel, I had already gotten a room there under the name of Colonel Anderson. I paid in advance and had the key in my pocket, a very important detail.

"I'm staying upstairs," I said. "Why don't we go up to the room and have a drink. I have a bottle of good French cognac." I had already prepared everything. Before we went up, I excused myself for a minute and asked Hsu, "Do you like that guy?"

"I like him okay," he said. "Okay, you carry in the gold." Hsu didn't know I had my own room. And this guy I'm going up with doesn't know what I'm doing either; he just goes with me, thinking I was carrying a heavy suitcase. I put the gold on my bed, opened the bottle, had a drink with him.

As soon as he left I opened the suitcase. I saw there were ten-ounce pieces, thirty-five of them. So I put five in my pocket and I close the case. I went downstairs, gave the five pieces to Hsu and told him, "Look, I told the colonel the truth because I don't want to cheat. The colonel said the agreement is for 300 ounces; he'll do 300 ounces only." I did this because if Hsu saw I was willing to cheat the colonel he would ask himself, Why wouldn't he cheat me also? I was preparing for the future. Hsu was very happy and drove away. I went back up to my room; there was my 300 ounces of gold sitting on the bed.

The next day I sold that gold to the bank. On the third day after I sold the gold a girl standing in the lobby of a nightclub said, "You're still coming here? Some people want to shoot you. Mr. Hsu already told me that he's going to get some people to shoot you, going to shoot you on the street."

I lay low and don't go out for four or five days. Then I walk into Hsu's office and say, "Look, I was traveling on business outside Hong Kong and was about to come back here to collect my payment but I heard you want to shoot me. What for? Did I do anything wrong?"

"The gold never reached India," he says.

"How the hell would I know?" I say. Then I pretended to get angry and reminded him that doing business with this pilot was his idea. "First, I asked you to meet the first pilot. Second, I gave you the letter. Third, you met the second guy in the hotel. You said you could do it, so I followed your instruction. What's wrong with that? Before I came in here I wrote a letter very clearly explaining what happened and put it in my lawyer's office. If you shoot me, you won't be able to stay in Hong Kong."

"I'm not running this alone," he says. "It's a big smuggling group. So you need to sign an IOU for what you owe me on 300 ounces of gold. Then no one has to shoot you."

"I'll sign an IOU, but on the IOU I'll clearly write that I'm not going to pay it back until I get enough money. I don't know when I'm going to have 300 ounces of gold."

"I don't care," he says. "I know I can never get my gold back but I need the piece of paper so everyone knows it's lost." So I just signed my name. I didn't know when I was going to have 300 ounces of gold, because I didn't know when I would do that trick again. But I did know I had the money I got for the gold in the bank. It's too bad I have such a criminal record, I always say that, otherwise I'm the best instructor. I really can teach these young kids how to be good DEA agents.

At that time the gambling habit was still hurting me. That's how I passed another few years in Hong Kong: gambling, fooling around with my life, doing nothing. By 1967, I again lost almost every penny I had. It was a very depressing time in my life. But from the outside, I still looked like a millionaire. I still dressed well. I still wore my Rolex.

One day I was talking to one of the guys and I tell him, "I feel so bad, I don't have any money to move around with anymore."

The guy, his name is Mr. Paul Sun, he says, "You know you're one of the most clever people I've ever met in my life. Why don't you go to Vietnam? With the war, you could make a lot of money. Why don't you take a chance, see what happens?"

I borrowed $2,500 Hong Kong from him, and I paid extra money under the table to get a Vietnamese visa. By the time I was through, I think I had only $25 U.S. left in my pocket. Empty-handed, I go into Saigon. I head straight for the hotel where all the Chinese business people, gangsters, all the Singaporeans, Thai people, Hong Kong people, everyone who made money from the United States, they all stayed. I sign my name, get a room. I was still a big name so some people recognize me when I come in. A guy called King, a tailor on the U.S. Air Force base in Saigon, comes up and says, "Welcome to Saigon, Ah Fat, we figured you would've been here a long time already." Then he told me, "Come up to the eighth floor, we're playing big games."

I did and the dealer told me, "Sit down, get some chips, and start to play."

"I should go down to my room and get money," I said.

"Oh, your credit is good, you can just pick up the chips, start playing," the guy said. So I played poker and I won $8,000 U.S. and there were a half million American troops in Saigon waiting for me to make money from. I started with no money. That is called luck.

I could start fooling around in Saigon; I could go meet people. Now we're coming to the drugs. At the air force club I meet some old air force people from Korea. One guy I met, Finler, used to be a second lieutenant or some such; now he was a major. (Later he's the guy who goes to jail for sixteen years.) "Now that you've come to Saigon, we can go back into business again," he says. "There's a lot of business we can do flying between Hong Kong and Saigon. We can make a lot of money."

A retired Vietnamese general named Roung was watching us. Since he retired he'd been fooling around with all these Chinese businessmen. He came over and told me, "All of them say they have U.S. people, but they never have big people, they always have just a couple of sergeants. I see your major: We can do business. I have a lot of stuff in Hong Kong. If you have a flight to bring everything back, we'll split the profit."

At first, we did the same thing as in Korea—material, French shirts, the white-and-black pants the women wear, pajamas, cigarette lighters. All for the Saigon black market.

Every day I prepared the cargo, went to Hong Kong, and came back the next day. On one trip, I went to see Paul Sun. He had given me $2,500 Hong Kong; I repaid him $10,000 Hong Kong. I said, "This extra $7,500 is a small gift." In my life if anyone does me a favor, when I can afford it I always return it. I don't want to owe people favors.

Again I had money and was back gambling, fooling around, spending.

Whatever I made, I spent and gambled so I needed more. I knew a lot of people in the drug business in Saigon, so I went to see them. One of these guys, Chen Man Tung, a very old Chinese man from Thailand who'd been in the drug business for a long time, told me, "You have such good connections. Why don't you start doing some business in shipping black-and-white? The opium can go from Bangkok to Saigon and the heroin can go from here to Hong Kong. You could make a fortune. If you're interested, I can intro-duce you to some really big guys in the business. Not the youngsters."

Through a middleman he arranged for me to meet Ah Sue, the biggest guy, big as the king. His full name is Chow Pe Sue, only everybody called him Ah Sue, the Ah being a term of respect, like Mister. Chen Man Tung, Ah Sue and I had dinner at a restaurant under the Bangkok Hotel. Chow Pe Sue said, "I have a lot of people tell me they have a good transportation route to making big money, but most of them just have boats. It's not easy to get good airplane transportation. Also, most of the people are just talking nonsense—they don't have enough money. So if you want to do black—you must do a test trip—I can give you as much as you want if you've got the money." He told me I needed $50,000 U.S. in cash. "If you can do it, you don't have to look for buyers for the opium in Saigon. I'll give you a guy's name; you contact him, say I'm the supplier, and he'll take the black off your hands and pay you the Saigon price. You could make somewhere around 80 to 100 percent profit."

After dinner I go and talk to Finler. "If you want to take a chance, we could make a couple million dollars in one year. From Bangkok to here, it's about $50 profit on each piece, from Bangkok to Hong Kong we'll get $100 to $150 a piece. We start with maybe 500 to 600 pieces. But in the future we'll take a couple thousand pieces."

He estimated he could make $25,000 to $50,000 a trip. He said, "Yeah, we'll do it."

To get the money for the first trip I go see Roung, the retired general. He put up $50,000 and was now a partner. The best thing for him, me and Finler is that Ah Sue told me if the first trip went safely, we'd set up a joint business and I wouldn't need to provide any more capital. The profit would be shared 45 percent for him, 45 percent to me, 5 percent each trip to the introduction person, Little Chu, and 5 percent to Chen Man Tung out of respect for setting up the whole thing. From my share I would pay Finler and Roung. That was the first general agreement.

After the first venture our business grew quickly. Ah Sue was very powerful in the mountains where the opium crop grew—he had deals with all the growers in the Golden Triangle and with the military and police to protect the transportation. Soon we started shipping black opium from Bangkok to Saigon. Then Ah Sue decided we would expand and sell morphine bricks, Triple Nine bricks, to Hong Kong. It had 9-9-9 carved in the top because it was so pure, like the American soap. You needed twenty kilos of black to make two kilos of morphine.

Ah Sue had a big buyer in Hong Kong. But for the first trip I had the pilot just take 10 two-kilo pieces in a small red suitcase, fly out from Bangkok, and meet me in the Empress Hotel in Hong Kong. When the pilot arrived I asked him if he had any problem with the small suitcase. He said, "No, it's very easy. Because I'm a colonel, nobody checked me at the airport."

Ah Sue was so happy he got rid of his other partners to concentrate on our business to Hong Kong. It grew fast. I was making a hell of a lot of money doing a tremendous business between Bangkok and Hong Kong, and also the same thing to Saigon—we're also doing the black to Saigon all the time. That was 1969 and 1970. We also did a route from Manila in the Philippines where they made our stuff into heroin and later shipped it to the United States. I made a lot of money. I bet $100,000 Hong Kong on one horse race at Happy Valley. I lose sometimes. Win sometimes. I wore a gold and diamond Rolex.

In 1971 we had a very big shipment out from Bangkok, 968 pounds. This is the shipment I wished was my last. It was 220 kilos of black and 220 kilos of morphine. There were two airplanes: one was flown by Major Finler and the other plane by a Major Charles.

We planned for the planes to take off from Bangkok. I was staying at a hotel there and when the day came I just put all the stuff out in front of the hotel, right outside the hotel doors. The police were walking in front of these boxes of drugs while I was waiting inside for the majors to bring down the U.S. Air Force trucks to pick them up.

We told everyone that the boxes were filled with blouses for the Bangkok officers' club. Then we took everything by truck to put on the planes. One plane was flying that same day, Major Finler's flight. Charles would be flying the next morning. The pilot and co-pilot were all in the group and were making money, but there was a PFC in the back of the plane who wasn't in on it. He opened a box and saw all these things stamped "9-9-9." He didn't say a word—a good thing for him or they would have thrown him out at 20,000 feet. When the plane reached the U.S. Seventh Air Force head-quarters—at Saigon airport—the PFC reported to the air base commander that the plane was filled with drugs. The base commander told him to just keep quiet because if the first plane from Bangkok was filled with the stuff, the second one must be also. The next day, they arrested them all.

I was in Hong Kong, waiting for the shipments, at the Palace Hotel. They didn't come—one day, two days, three days. About five days later, they still had not come. I knew there was something wrong. Then the funny part comes. The government made Finler send me a letter, saying he got in trouble but only lost his flight's stuff. The other 484 pounds of stuff was safe. The DEA people had told Finler if he didn't get me back to Saigon, and also get Ah Sue, he would go to jail for thirty years. If he got us back he would save half his sentence.

I have to go back. If I lost that shipment, I'd be broke again. I flew into Saigon where I meet the guy who actually told Finler what to write in his letter, Fred Dix, the supervisor of DEA office in Saigon. Using another name, Fred Dix pretended he was an engineer working on the air base, that he was a good friend of Finler's, so he could help me get the stuff out while Finler was in trouble. On first impression I knew he was not an engineer; he was one of those DEA agents. I told myself, Ah Fat, you're craps. Saigon airport is restricted. You're going to die in Saigon, you have no way out. If I ran, I might have had a chance, but the chance was very slim—I know if I run I will get shot in the street in Saigon.

You know, actually I'm very smart. If not, I would not still be alive. So I told Dix right away, "I have another shipment in Bangkok. If you are working along with someone in the air force, can you make arrangements to ship the other 968 pounds out from Bangkok? I can get Ah Sue and ship the stuff right away."

"Can I meet Ah Sue? Together we'll talk business," he asked.

I was almost laughing. "Are you stupid?" I said. "You're talking like you are one of the agents, you want to get both of us. Yeah, you get me to Bangkok and you can meet Ah Sue and we can talk. And we can ship another 968 pounds." In the morning he calls me and tells me to arrange tickets. We flew out by Air France at 5 P.M. As soon as the plane took off, I said to myself, "Ah Fat, you get your life back."

In Bangkok, we are much more powerful.

By the time I reached my hotel in Bangkok I already knew I was being followed by the DEA people. The guy following me, I found out later, was Paul Brown, who became one of my good friends. In the room I called Ah Sue and told him I was followed and I thought the man who wanted to deal was a DEA agent. He said, "Okay, meet him for lunch and we'll make an arrangement with Colonel Prumon to check, because he knows everybody, he's the head of the Anti-Narcotics Bureau. After lunch, I went back to my hotel and Colonel Prumon called. "Ah Fat, run as fast as you can. The guy who had lunch with you is the supervisor of DEA in Saigon."

I called Ah Sue, and he said, "Leave your suitcase, just carry your passport in your pocket. Go downstairs. Walk into the restaurant. The people who are following you, they will not go into the restaurant right away; they will stay outside maybe a couple minutes before they go in to see which table you're sitting at. So just walk in, and go through the kitchen; there's a back door. I'll have a car waiting." I stayed in the room one hour, then walk through the restaurant without even stopping, all the way through the kitchen, out, and there's a car waiting for me. I jump in and am on the run.

I went to the mountains, all the way to the Golden Triangle, stayed there five months in a large house all the way past Chang Mei. In this growing region there was nothing to do except play mah-jongg with the other drug dealers every day or have fun with the girls they supply, young Vietnamese or Thai girls, or go a half mile up from the house to visit the laboratory for making the raw material into heroin.

Sometimes Ah Sue came up to the mountains to talk to me, but I was fed up because all my money's gone. Ah Sue also lost a lot of money on that job, but he was not such a gambler. He still had some money, he had a big house and he owned a lot of land upcountry in Thailand. One day he said, "Maybe everything is cooled down by now, maybe you should return to Hong Kong, see what you can do." Because I had a phony Singapore passport I decide to take a chance.

It is almost the end of 1971. The hideout is in Thailand, but just inside the border. All you had to do was walk a few steps, cross a small bridge, and you are in Burma. For $5 U.S. you got a passport. Without that money, it didn't matter what kind of passport you had.

I returned to Hong Kong by the beginning of 1972. Most people didn't know exactly what I was doing, but they knew I was broke. I met a very old Chinese man, Woo Shu Choung. His nephew, Charcoal Woo, used to be a famous informant for the DEA until he was killed in New York in 1980 or 1981 in his apartment in Chinatown. They killed him because he was involved in a big case helping to arrest people from Hong Kong and Bangkok. Even though he was doing a case, he was careless. He fooled around with the girls he didn't know in Chinatown, and they used one of them to kill him.

Charcoal Woo's uncle put me in his apartment in a dingy part of Hong Kong and I stay there while I try to figure out how to make some money. Like when I tricked the gold smugglers, this time I try to trick the Rolex watch company. I read in the paper that the Rolex watch company was trying to get information on who was making fake Rolexes in Hong Kong; they were willing to spend money to find that person. I figured maybe this is the way I can get some money. I will pretend to show them the factory, but first I tell them they must buy watches to convince the people who make the fakes that we're doing business. So I bought two fake Rolexes and walked to the Rolex office. I met the general manager and managing director, Swiss people. We sat, we talked. And when they saw the fake Rolexes, they asked, "Can you get the place, the factory?"

I told them first we had to buy enough to lead us to the factory. It would cost them a lot of money. What I was planning to do was buy fake Rolexes from Singapore, smuggle them in, and make a profit in Hong Kong dollars and disappear. With the money from the watches and some other help I should get close enough to $30,000 Hong Kong profit and be able to go back to Bangkok. I set up the transaction very nicely. But the guys I hired screwed something up, so there I was on the run again. I head for the airport, but a cop there knows me, he said, "Ah Fat, run, police are already here waiting for you."

I spent the night in Woo's apartment house watching my picture on TV. Then with Woo's arrangements I went to a tiny little room near the waterfront. I waited three days, then a small boat picked me up and took me to a cargo ship. But the men on the ship recognized me from my picture in the newspapers. When we docked in Bangkok, they call Hong Kong and sell me out. The Hong Kong police knew I was at the Bangkok Royal Hotel and sent a detective sergeant and superintendent to Bangkok. That night when I returned to the hotel there were about twenty police cars waiting for me. They told me they were going to take me to court the following morning and then they would take me back to Hong Kong for trial. Ah Sue knew what happened right away, since he had good influence with the police. He got some people to pass a message to me, saying, "It's very unfortunate, according to what I heard. For the case in Hong Kong, you'll be going to jail for ten years. Right now I can't make arrangements fast enough. But I will try to make an arrangement with the judge. You're going to be put in jail for three months for illegal entry so you have to stay here. Three months is much better than ten years."

The next morning we go to court, and when the authorities asked for me to go back to Hong Kong for trial, the judge just said, "No. Three months in jail, this is Thai law." You could see the surprise on the superintendent's and chief of detectives' faces. Ah Sue had passed the word to some big guy inside jail, so as soon as I walked into the place they put me in the foreign building, it's more comfortable. The warden told me, "Look, I know you know Ah Sue so you'll live well."

Anyway, now the DEA tries me. I was still on the run so they decided they could make me work for them. The first person to contact me in jail is Paul Brown. That was the first time I'd talked to him in person. He came and said, "Our office really doesn't care about what you did before, because we're interested in getting you back to work. We think you are very capable. You speak English well, so we don't need an interpreter, and you know a lot of people in Bangkok."

"I can't talk to you," I told Brown, "because if I talk I'll get shot even inside this jail. My partner is too powerful."

The next day, the guy from Washington came with Paul Brown.

"Ah Fat, we want you to work," he told me. "I'll be flying

to Hong Kong to meet the governor to try to get the charges dropped. If I do that, you can start working with us right away." But they came with the Thai police general, General Tren Pung. He was sitting right across the table from me and was saying, "You have to tell the truth." And I was really laughing. "If I told the truth," I said, "you're the guy going to jail first." This is the guy who did all the storage for us when I started coming to Bangkok. As soon as the stuff came in from the northern part of Thailand we all put it in his house. When you came to get the twenty kilos out, then you paid twenty kilos' rent. That's very high rent.

When I got out I still had Hong Kong charge to face, so I knew I was still on the run. Ah Sue called to arrange to help me get away. He said, "You'll go out tonight around eight or nine. As soon as you walk out, a car will pick you up." But at that time I had a suspicion that Ah Sue was worried I had talked with the DEA people. I figured he might just pick me up in the car and send me some crazy place and kill and bury me.

I decide not to go with him; I want to run by myself. At eight when a police officer asked me to go downstairs to take a shower, which is how Ah Sue arranged for the escape, I walked downstairs, passed the shower room. On one side of the shower there was an iron door, locked twenty-four hours. This time, the door was open. I just walked out. But I didn't go to any car across the street—instead I jumped in a taxicab without even a penny in my pocket. The only thing I carried was a DuPont cigarette lighter. Since I needed some cash for taxi money I stopped at a restaurant where I knew the boss lady. I told her, "Look, we're old friends, I need some cash but this is the only thing I have, my cigarette lighter. You can pay whatever you want." The lighter was worth about $5,000, but she gave me $1,000, that's what she had.

I took the taxi to a very small room. I knew I was safe that night. The police wouldn't say anything, and the authorities at the jail would keep quiet until the next morning, then say I disappeared.

From that room I called a missionary, Mah Ting, I forget his last name. He was always preaching, asking people to listen to him and to be a good man. You know what I mean. I had his home telephone number because he was my middleman with the DEA. "I ran away," I said. "Now I really need to get something before I can really run."

"I can't do anything right now," he said. "I'll try to contact the DEA. See me early tomorrow."

I arranged for him to come at 10 A.M. I was waiting at the corner of the street, in front of a telephone place.

"Ah Fat, I give you two pieces of news," he said. "One. Bad news is the DEA can not use you right now, you're too hot. It would kill the relationship between the United States and Bangkok. But the second news I bring you is money. This is from the DEA. You run, and if your luck runs out, contact any office of the DEA, then they'll see what they can do." They gave me $10,000 U.S.

It took me almost twenty-four hours before I reached the southern part of Thailand. But even there the first thing I saw was my picture on all the newspapers. I am still on the run. I contacted the owner of a massage parlor, and he made arrangements to send me to the Malaysia border where his brother ran a whorehouse. He told me, "Don't worry, we'll get you out to Malaysia; it should be no problem at all."

I stayed one night with his brother. The next morning we went to the wire fence across the border. He cut the wire, making a door, then said, "Okay, across the other side is Malaysia. Walk a little bit and you'll find a church. In front of the church, there's a guy waiting, his name is Chang, just let him direct you the rest of the way."

I walked until I met Chang. "When you get on the boat," he said, "it'll take you no time to reach Singapore. But after you jump off the boat, you are on your own." It was a small boat and very fast. I got off the boat and ran, I walked up from the shore. It was all farmers, chickens, pigs. I didn't know the place, but I knew Singapore well, so I kept walking till I saw a bus station and got a bus all the way to the main part of the city.

I have old friends in Singapore. I started doing the electronic smuggling business—TV sets, tape recorders, video-tapes to Indonesia. I already forget about the DEA. I made about $1 million Singapore dollars in about seven months. I was back to my old life again. I got a new Rolex, new suits, I was coming back. So I start fooling around with the higher business people.

I met the owner of a big nightclub, a retired policeman who was also very powerful at the racetrack where he was a big horse owner. We went out, had dinner and went to his nightclub almost every night. There were a lot of Taiwanese singers, pretty girls. Since he owned a lot of horses, he also asked me to go to the races wherever he went, in Kuala Lumpur and also to the Singapore track. His racing tips were tremendous. Almost every time he told me to bet heavily the horse won. You may not believe me, but I won $2 million Singapore, which is $700,000 U.S. in two to three months' time. By now it was almost 1976. I just kept going with him, racing and gambling.

One day he asks me do him a favor. A very pretty singer from Taiwan was going to be singing in his nightclub. He asks me to pick her up at the airport and make arrangements for her to stay in a hotel. Her name was Lee May Kwon; her nickname was the Queen of the Beautiful Legs. She was tall, very pretty and a good singer. When I picked her up at the airport, I did not know that the nightclub owner, Mr. Quing, wanted this girl for his own. So I took the girl to the hotel, and we go out to have something to eat, and she likes me very much. So then we went dancing. Three days later when Mr. Quing returned from Pinang and saw the way she was leaning on my shoulder he didn't say anything but he actually inside gets mad. Starting from then, my luck went lousy. All the tips were losers. And I wasn't only losing a little bit. Because I didn't quit, I kept losing every race. I lost almost all the money I made.

In this trouble, I figured maybe this was the time to think about the DEA again. In August 1977 I called the Singapore office. You know who answers the phone? Paul Brown. He recognized my voice.

"You bastard, where have you been for the last five or six years?" he said.

"I was in Singapore."

"What a life," he said, "I've been stationed here for four years and Singapore is so small—how come I never met you on the street?"

Then I told him I was broke and said, "Maybe I should go back to work, do you still think the DEA wants me?"

"Yeah, we still want you," he said. "Right now the Singapore office is pretty small but you can start and see what we can do. In the meantime I'll give you $1,000 U.S. for expense money."

When I signed for the money that was my first signature to receive money from the DEA. Paul Brown gave me a serial number, SF001, the number I've been using right up to now. That number has been signed to receive money from the DEA for more than 500 pieces of information.

From the beginning of his career as registered informant SF001 Ah Fat worked with agents Paul Brown, Bruce Stubbs, Steve Shea and Richard LaMagna. The cases they developed beginning in 1977 and the heroin networks they identified stretched across a decade. Ah Fat gave the agents entrée to the secretive world of opium growers, crop brokers, corrupt officials, morphine and heroin chemists, fishing fleet owners, greedy pilots and major drug exporters that stretched from Thailand, Burma and Laos through Saigon and Hong Kong to the United States and Europe. The same networks, routes and dealers were still in many cases active when LaMagna came to New York in 1986. By reintroducing Ah Fat into that web, the DEA was able to discover that the networks were supplying a growing volume of increasingly pure heroin. Kevin Gallagher, who supervised these agents and their cases at or nearer their inception, also supervised the cases that were developed by LaMagna in New York.

The first case is going to be one that will make you laugh. There was a guy called Ah Seng. He was selling heroin to the commercial airline pilots, which they took to Australia, Amsterdam and the United States. I didn't know Ah Seng, but I had information from the DEA that he loved to play horses and was the middleman for black-market booking on horses. I contacted him and started betting. Then I took him to a Thai restaurant to eat, started talking Thai with the girls and gave him the impression that I came from Bangkok. With all the names I know in Bangkok, he's no doubt that I'm a drug dealer.

"Do you have the stuff on hand to supply, say, three kilos?" I asked.

"A few kilos, I always can get it," he said.

"In Singapore, a few kilos will get yourself the death penalty; you get death for just fifteen grams," I said.

"It's not that easy to catch me because I never touch the stuff myself," he said. I tell this to Paul Brown and we began the next part of the case. Paul Brown borrowed a uniform from Pan American to show that he was a pilot. Then he made arrangements to meet Ah Seng in the Shangri-La Hotel in Singapore. Everything went very well. Ah Seng was happy to have a Pan American pilot. As lunch ended Brown told him he'd have the flight out tomorrow morning, and he'd be back here after seven days and we would talk again then. Brown later contacted the Singapore Anti-Narcotics Bureau and told them the case was going on. They wanted to put surveillance on the next meeting.

After seven days, I called Ah Seng and told him, "The pilot is arriving, we'll meet in the Holiday Inn." In the lobby, we talked, and he said he brought a pretty big-sized sample, fifteen or twenty grams. In the men's room Ah Seng gave the sample to Paul Brown and gave the price at $40,000 Singapore, which is close to $15,000 U.S., per kilo. Ah Seng agreed to supply four kilos when Brown arrived next time. All went smoothly. As we were ready to leave, Brown whispered, "Everything's fine." But when we walked out of the hotel, there was surveillance outside to take pictures of Ah Seng. They had put the camera inside a big book. As we walked out a flash came out from this guy's book. Ah Seng shouted, "Run," and he takes off. He will never trust me again. The stupid bastard on surveillance ruined everything. Nobody was corrupt, just damned stupid, that's all. Now I could no longer work in Singapore; I was suspected.

Before I left for Bangkok to work for the DEA there, I met a woman called Wong Ping. She used to be one of the most famous dancing girls in Hong Kong. Very pretty. She told me about a big drug dealer named Cheng Ah Kai. It took the DEA a long time but now he's in jail in New York. The deal he did in New York was seventy-eight pounds. But this was the start of the interest in Cheng Ah Kai. Wong Ping told me that she had his telephone number and gave it to me. I told Bruce Stubbs, and he said, "Now we contact Cheng Ah Kai to start business in Bangkok."

So we begin the case, but at the same time, one day I'm supposed to meet Bruce Stubbs at a place called Siam Square, a big shopping area in Bangkok. I got there too early, so after I had lunch, I went into the shops to look at some shirts. At the same time I saw a lady walking with bags of skirts. I didn't pay attention, but when I turned around, I saw it was Suzanne, a girl I used to know ten or fifteen years ago in Taipei. She always liked me; she even kept an old photo she took with me. So she looked over and said, "Gee, it's you. What are you doing in Bangkok?" I told her I was working.

"You know, I've liked you all my life," she says. "Why don't you contact me, give me a call, we'll go out sometime and get to know one another again." So when I got back to meet Bruce Stubbs, I told him about Suzanne and he was surprised.

"You hit the jackpot," Bruce told me. "Do you know who she is? She's Ah Yen's sister. He's one of the biggest targets for the DEA. So how the hell do you know her?"

"I know her for years, and she likes me very much," I said.

"Go ahead, keep this line attached with her and we're really in business," he said.

At around this time, we were having a big dinner, and Cheng Ah Kai brought a couple of his friends. One of the friends was Suzanne's relative and he didn't trust me. He said I was only a guy looking for money.

"I don't believe it," Suzanne told him. "I think you're a guy never use woman for her money. I can tell." When I returned to Bangkok from a trip to Hong Kong with her, all the drug dealers started to see Suzanne was almost like my wife. They had more respect for me. I felt very bad, because I liked her, but I thought if I wanted to get to work for the DEA, I had to do this.

At that time Kevin Gallagher is in charge in Bangkok. One of the guys he really wanted to arrest used the name of Pakyuling; he used foreign couriers, British citizens, Dutch citizens, old men, to ship his stuff out in their golf bags. Pakyuling used to be a big gold smuggler in Hong Kong so I knew him already, but he was very careful. He didn't talk to anybody, only to Cheng Ah Kai. They had deals between Bangkok and Hong Kong. But one day, he comes to play cards at the club, and his wife called and left a message asking him to call back. So he went to make a phone call. I could see the way he dialed. I remembered the number and went to the mens' room to write it down. Then I called Bruce and gave him the number.

A few days later, he told me I got the right number. Now the DEA said to stick with them and get them to put more confidence in me. So I told Cheng Ah Kai I had an American buyer and I want to pick up a kilo of pure Number 4 heroin. I went down, met Cheng Ah Kai, picked up the kilo and brought it back to Bruce Stubbs. He took it to the lab, and they said it was the best they'd ever got—it was up to 97.8 percent pure. Then the next day I went to the club and paid off the money. Somewhere around $10,000 U.S. You could sell this kilo at $200,000 in New York. Things go on like this: meet them, go out and meet more people, get more necessary persons' telephone numbers and most of the drug dealers' names. Still, for a long time we did not do any arrests. In the dealers' eyes, I was starting to become a very big drug dealer, buying a kilo or half kilo as a sample all the time. They didn't have any trouble until three or four months later. Then while we were all playing mah-jongg in the place, suddenly twenty or thirty policemen came, some carrying machine guns, some carrying pistols. Cheng Ah Kai and everybody else was arrested. At the same time another squad of Thai police and the DEA arrested Pakyuling at a pier with three Taiwanese seamen, and thirty-six kilos of brown heroin, not the pure white. I was put in handcuffs and taken with them together to the police station. And Suzanne also had to go down there. Then Gallagher and LaMagna and Bruce all walked in. I was handcuffed to the chair. I sat there and waited. They couldn't just let me go in front of Suzanne. They had to pick out the right people to keep and let all the small guys get out together. They released five or six of us and held five of them and charged them with conspiracy to ship the thirty-six kilos to Hong Kong.

At about two in the morning, Suzanne drives me back. And she is suspicious.

"When the police came in I didn't see any fear or shock on your face. You seemed very calm; you just didn't seem worried. I feel you certainly must have had contact with some people you don't want me to know. And you speak much better English than the average person, which means you should not be in the drug business. Unless you are undercover. Since I decided to marry you, I hope you don't mind telling me. I won't throw you out, but I don't want to be a widow again."

I denied everything. Her family was one of the biggest drug families in Bangkok. If I told the truth I would've gotten myself shot.

When we got home, I called the DEA. They thought I was in trouble, so they suggested I go to Taipei for a vacation. Suzanne went with me for two weeks and she got us a marriage license. So I told her, "You sell me out or not, it's up to you. I'll tell you frankly: I work with the DEA. But I really wasn't involved in any case; I don't know why they're paying all the money to me. You saw on the day of the arrest I was just playing mah-jongg. I really don't know what's going on." Of course she didn't believe what happened, but she was thinking back and she didn't want to be a widow again.

A couple of months later—it's somewhere around the end of 1981—I made a mistake that turned out lucky. I went to help someone with a passport problem at the immigration office. They remembered me there—and they remembered they had a Hong Kong immigration case against me from 1971. I forgot all about it. They sent me to jail for two months. When I got out, I began making cases in Hong Kong again, but soon I had a fight with the DEA supervisor, James Swit. He thought I was still making money in the drug business because I was going to Taiwan a lot with Suzanne and I had connections with the drug business there. Actually it was

Suzanne who had the idea: "Why don't you just make one business trip to Taiwan, do it by yourself, ship a few kilos, and you could make a couple million dollars."

"No, you can't do that," I kept telling her. Meantime, they tapped my phone in Bangkok. They heard our conversations about the drugs so they figured if Suzanne was doing something, it must have been my idea. Bruce Stubbs flew all the way back. He told me that the DEA thought I was back in business for myself. I said, "Bruce, you have to believe me. Suzanne wants to make $1 million U.S., but I really did not do anything." Bruce said he believed me, but he added, "But with the tape, it seems like you're talking about doing some business in Taiwan. Still, you are very lucky you didn't actually do it. If you did, you'd be in jail by now."

So I said, "If your office doesn't trust me anymore I will quit." And I did. I quit the DEA and started a new business, shipping watermelon seeds from Hong Kong to Taiwan. You could make somewhere around $50,000 U.S. for each twenty-foot container if you could smuggle it into Taiwan. I'm starting to do quite well, making a lot of money. The DEA people came to know about it and said they were happy. But one guy, Steven Shea, he gave me his home and office telephone numbers in San Francisco.

"Ah Fat," he said, "I know you too well. Doesn't matter how good you are, one day you'll be losing everything, and as far as I'm concerned, nobody can work like you with the DEA. If you decide to come back, I'll be the first person to welcome you back to the fleet. I know you, you're too brave to do business in a smart way; you put everything in and you may lose everything."

Time goes by until 1986, when I made a wrong move in China. I ordered $1.5 million Hong Kong of watermelon seeds. And the Red Chinese double-crossed me. They shipped me rotten stuff with stones in the bag. Terrible quality, I couldn't ship it into Taiwan. I lost about a million dollars. I was almost broke again.

Then one day I walk into the Hong Kong Telephone Company in Hong Kong side and I see Cheng Ah Kai. They're all out, he told me. They spent a couple million dollars each to prove there wasn't sufficient evidence against them. Even Suzanne's brother, Ah Yen, was out and he was sentenced to life at the first trial. At the second trial it was also a life sentence. Until it went to the Supreme Court which said everything wasn't good enough so he was released. You know why? Their families put some money together—a total of $2.5 million Hong Kong.

So now we met in the telephone company and later we sat down and had a drink. Then he told me he was connected to some big people in Thailand, and they were doing very well. They were using the Thai fishing trawlers to bring back a couple thousand kilos of black, a few hundred kilos of Number 4, pure white heroin. They took opium out from Thailand to sell to the Chinese, and he told me that he had a big supplier. I used this meeting to return to the DEA. I called Steven Shea in San Francisco. "Look, what you said was right, I'm losing all my money and I need money, and I think I'm back to work with the DEA again."

After I talked to him I left for China for a meeting. The DEA put on surveillance and found out the man who was going to meet Cheng Ah Kai was Wichai Chaiwisan. And Wichai Chaiwisan was one of their big targets. Steven told me it turned out the people in Washington, D.C., wanted him to stop working with me because they said my working with Richard LaMagna in New York would be more useful. Then at the same time LaMagna called.

"Old buddy," he said. "We're going to work together again. I've already arranged the money for you and you don't have to worry about what you're doing in Hong Kong right now. You're coming down to New York."

"I don't know anything about New York," I said.

"I've got a hundred percent confidence, I know you can do it," LaMagna says. "We need someone like you to come to Chinatown. There's always someplace to start."

That was the early part of 1987. I had known Rich LaMagna eight, maybe nine years. I never forgot what he always used to say in his cases with Bruce Stubbs. "Whatever piece of information you pick up is always useful for the right person. Unless the agent doesn't pay attention to his work.

Then it is like a piece of trash, slowly going to waste." He always knew how to use what some other agents didn't.

I left Hong Kong on the twenty-second of February, taking United Airlines all the way to New York. LaMagna picked me up at the airport and put me in the Excelsior Hotel, just in front of Central Park, on 81st Street near Amsterdam Ave. "I know you just got here," he says. "Take a rest first, don't rush, look around town, and see what you can do."

So I go to Chinatown, started fooling around with the people, and I met some old guys from Hong Kong. LaMagna had told me that the biggest target was a guy called Sit Tai Hung, in English, Red Dice. He got his name because he was a big gambler. I didn't know how to start, but I knew a guy, Jack Chung in Los Angeles, who used to know me very well. He had made a lot of money as a dope dealer but then he wasn't doing very well. I got his phone number, contacted him, and pretended I had stuff coming to New York, figuring this was a way to approach our target.

When he flew to New York he told me he knew drug dealers, maybe he could make some kind of arrangement to sell the stuff. We try a couple of things. Finally we got a guy named Muk Sat, which means Bedbug. He was crazy, had killed people, was always fighting. But Bedbug was very close to Red Dice.

Starting that day, every meeting for me and Jack Chung we had surveillance; and in addition I was wired all the time. Chung knows nothing. He thought I was a dealer. We met Bedbug and talked about the products and how they were arriving.

Now we had them ready to buy and Richard was very clever. He asked me if by any chance I could go back to Bangkok and get one of the guys there to sell something; then we could arrest the guy in Bangkok and get a case in Bangkok and make arrangements with the Thai police to share the case and use the drugs to sell to Bedbug and Red Dice in New York. It would make a better case. Richard wanted also to come into Hong Kong to make some kind of arrangement to talk business with Cheng Ah Kai and Wichai Chaiwisan. In fact, that was a major reason he went. That way he made two cases.

So we made the arrangements in the spring of 1987. Richard arrived and stayed in the Grand Hotel in Hong Kong. We had two rooms, one for us and the other for the surveillance people from Hong Kong. Richard first met the supplier for Bedbug and Red Dice. Then I met Cheng Ah Kai and told him my buyer had already arrived. Wichai came in from Bangkok and stayed at the Nathan Hotel and we started talking. The surveillance people were following us, taking pictures, and all the talking between me, Cheng Ah Kai and Wichai Chaiwisan was recorded. Still the dealers delayed for two days.

Wichai finally decided Richard could go down to meet them. Richard came in smoking a cigar and with a couple of cigars in his pocket. I introduced him as the Italian gang leader from New York, the big boss. We had a general talk. Wichai Chaiwisan told Richard he had about 100 kilos of stuff in hand and could ship out anytime. He also said he ran a big laboratory in Laos, under the help of the government. For this deal we had to pay a deposit, the U.S. side of the deal, $140,000. They said once they were ready to ship, they would let me know and I would come back here again to make the down payment.

Everything was nice and everybody was happy. LaMagna left for Bangkok and made contact with the other guy in Thailand. As he took delivery of two and a half kilos the police arrested the delivery boy. LaMagna took a half kilo back to the States. I flew back to New York to do the rest of the cases. I told Jack Chung that I had some stuff arriving from Bangkok. At the same time I brought along Tom Ma and introduced him as the guy coming from Hong Kong who worked for me. He was one of the agents in Group 41, the Chinese heroin group. I brought him in to meet Jack Chung because an informant cannot make an arrest. They were going to meet us at the Omni Hotel with the drugs.

That night Bedbug, Jack Chung and one of the other guys, Szeto Kwok-Ching, came together with $75,000 cash. I thought we would just go ahead and deliver the kilo and arrest them. But I was told we still had to wait because the fish was not big enough for a fry. We were waiting for Red Dice to come. So we decided to keep the drugs; they kept the money until morning. They also had a room in the hotel.

During the night, they decided to move their money, since they don't want to keep it in the room. So when they went out, we had to have two cars do the surveillance. We needed to make sure the money was coming from Dice, so we could use the conspiracy law to arrest the whole group. But unfortunately, they found out the car was being followed. Two of them jumped out of the car and went down into the subway, and the car speeded up and disappeared. The agents on the surveillance called me in my room. I called Jack Chung right away and he was afraid. So I kept telling him, "There's nothing wrong with that. Maybe just because it was three in the morning, they were suspected by the local police detective. If it was a DEA tail, they would've arrested all of us by now with the $75,000."

Jack Chung told me he knew the DEA policy, that they didn't take small fish. They were waiting for Red Dice. Jack Chung told me he was going back to L.A. I told Rich LaMagna and he said, "Let him go back to L.A. With all the tape we have, it's good enough to arrest him anytime. Let him go for now. We'll concentrate on the other case we started with Cheng Ah Kai and Wichai Chaiwisan."

I had kept contact with Hong Kong. Around September 1987 I went back there for a down payment meeting, and a few days later Richard comes and Wichai Chaiwisan comes from Thailand. We met again in the Nathan Hotel and we brought $140,000 in cash. We made payments. The day after, Wichai, Cheng Ah Kai, me, we walked to the black-market money transaction center to transfer the money to Wichai's place. We also had surveillance. That was one piece of evidence we needed. We sent the money and Wichai returned to Bangkok. Now we were supposed to get our stuff in one month. But actually it turned out to take seven months. Everybody became worried on this case—$140,000 is a lot of money, even for the DEA. But for this kind of deal, to get Wichai Chaiwisan or Cheng Ah Kai, it's worth the money to do it. Also, Washington wanted to have the case succeed because it involved the Laotian government. The United States wanted to confirm if the Laotian government was really supplying all this dope, as they'd been hearing.

During the case, according to information we got from Wichai Chaiwisan, we learned that the Laotian government was supplying all the raw material to them, without any payment. But after they finished turning opium into product, pure heroin, they paid about $2,500 to Laos on every unit and they had to pay another $500 under the table to the high official and another $200 to the people who were on the factory level, the lower-rank officers. So the actual total they had to pay out was about $3,200 U.S. for just one unit, three units to make a kilo. So the cost was about $7,000 U.S. per kilo. But the selling price in the States was $150,000 to $200,000. So you can see there was a big, big profit.

But while we learned this, we were still waiting for them to notify us when the stuff would be arriving in the States. That would not come until after the end of the year, 1987. I was spending my Christmas in New York; looking at the Christmas tree in front of Rockefeller Center. But I started to get worried before that: I don't want Rich LaMagna getting in trouble because I was the guy doing all the deals. So I kept calling from the States to Hong Kong to check and double-check what was actually happening.

They called me to say the delay was because of heavy rains in Laos, that all the laboratories had been flooded and they had no way to transport anything. So the New York office called the DEA in Bangkok and checked. They said there was no way to transport anything in Laos. So that made us not worry too much.

But now Wichai had gone back to Hong Kong again to talk to Cheng Ah Kai—both were still under surveillance. I called there and shouted at them and they said, "We're not going to cheat you out of your money. With our names, we're worth more than $140,000. It's out of our control because of the flooding. If you don't believe us, you can go down there yourself to take a look. If Richard LaMagna is interested, he can go into Laos to inspect the factory."

Besides the water, we also started getting worried because we had a report from the Bangkok DEA office that Wichai was spending a lot of money and that he was collecting some dope from different friends. So I again called Wichai in Hong Kong. He told me because Laos was very badly flooded maybe the quality was hurt, so he was using his partner in the northern part of Thailand to collect some good stuff from the mountains, which meant the Golden Triangle. That was also confirmed by the DEA people in Bangkok, because they tapped Wichai's phone.

But I was getting very fed up, worrying about this and that. I called Cheng Ah Kai and told him but he said that if Wichai Chaiwisan double-crossed us, personally he would shoot him. He said he didn't believe that Chaiwisan would cheat on him.

Then we got a call saying the two packages were already in the Bangkok airport warehouse, ready to go. Back in the States, we understood that there were two packages marked to send to our undercover company, Dunn and Dunn Corporation in Manhattan.

Finally they called to say the packages were gone from the warehouse, that it must have been on the flight by now. Actually by Christmastime they were talking about the packages going out. On the fifth or sixth of January 1988, the packages finally arrived at Kennedy Airport. There were seventy-eight pounds of pure Number 4 heroin inside.

I contacted people back in Hong Kong, because we wanted to make sure to get Wichai Chaiwisan to come to Hong Kong to collect the money from the other kilos. Otherwise if he stayed in Bangkok, even if we arrested him, there'd be no way to get him extradited back to the States. The Thai police always gave those people some kind of protection. So Wichai arrived in Hong Kong. We got the package in New York and sent it to the lab to check the quality and then to the Independent Commission Against Corruption in Hong Kong, who arrested all of them and charged them with conspiracy to smuggle drugs. My job was finished.

As a result of Ah Fat's cooperation, indictments were filed against Jack Chung, Bedbug and their associates in the Manhattan federal courthouse in July 1987 and in the Brooklyn federal courthouse on January 20, 1988, against Cheng Ah Kai and Wichai Chaiwisan. Convictions were won in these federal cases as well as in several others where the conspiracy indictments were made as a direct result of his case work. As in the past, his information also provided invaluable, corroborating evidence in several other cases. He was, and is, an unusual, if amoral, man. Although he has earned much respect in the DEA, we cannot forget that, as he said, he treated smuggling heroin as if it were no more than an import-export business.

TWELVE

At the End of
the Heroin Trail

Sergeant Billy Cook was standing in the rain again.

For protection he had thrown a blue New York City Police Department windbreaker over his heavy bulletproof vest. That finished obscuring the proud maroon signature of St. Bonaventure University across his white sweatshirt. Across the back of the flapping windbreaker the rain now streaked across bold white letters that spelled out **POLICE**.

Shielded from the elements and stray gunfire, he checked his watch and bided his time until dawn officially broke, although he knew none of the sun's rays would pierce this overcast.

The sergeant replaced the elastic cuff of his windbreaker over the watch face. He would wait; he had not made it to retirement age unscathed by being incautious. Fifteen years as a sergeant, a total of twenty-two years as a cop and the past six spent running this task force for the DEA were ending. This was Billy Cook's last raid.

It came after two years of patient investigation that had led Cook's raiders to the bitter end of the China heroin trail inhabited by a black and Hispanic distribution network controlling fifteen lucrative "spots" in the Bronx. These retail locations each generated $50,000 business a week. The network

behind them also shipped white death as far away from the slums of the Bronx as the upstate city of Rochester, where the deaths of four addicts were blamed on overdoses.

These deaths and this illegal empire were the tragic result of the smuggling machinations of Ah Fat's cronies, who by 1986 controlled a heroin highway that annually delivered thousands of pounds to the United States.

By the morning of this raid in the spring of 1989, those Chinese suppliers were the dominant wholesale source of heroin in New York. They sold the highest-quality drugs at the most competitive price. Their business savvy encouraged a heroin plague that had grown virtually unnoticed by the news media as crack dominated the headlines for more than four years.

The retail network Cook had targeted was the most aggressive group of dope sellers in the Bronx. Its top lieutenants bought pure heroin wholesale from the Chinese, then handed it to $9-an-hour underlings. These doubled its weight by adding quinine and milk sugar, then measured out single-dose quantities of the 50 percent heroin in plastic McDonald's coffee spoons. Spoon by spoon they shoveled the heroin into thousands of glassine bags. The lieutenants then took the heroin back and handed it out in bundles of ten $10 bags to street corner pushers who earned about a dollar-a-bag commission. One $85,000 pound, divided this way, yielded the network a profit of $150,000. The network sold several pounds each week. It was controlled by a murderous and smart dealer so young that his own lieutenants had dubbed him "Boy George."

George Rivera, barely twenty years old when Cook's investigation began, built an organization so lucrative that he registered a fleet of a dozen Mercedeses, BMWs and customized Porsches to one of its corporate shells, the Tuxedo Corporation. He kept loyalty strong in this organization, Cook said with admiration, by distributing cash bonuses, gifts and free vacations—the identical incentives that the head of a legitimate company would lavish on star performers.

But behind the generosity there was a deadly face. At least a dozen homicides, investigators said, could be directly

linked to George's rise to the top. This too built a reputation that encouraged loyalty.

Finally, Boy George had, Cook explained, what is known in the trade as "good product." Early in his murderous rise, one of his employers introduced George to a Chinese wholesaler, one of the dozens whose merchandise came from the organizations Ah Fat penetrated. This introduction was a mistake. George, having made the connection to pure heroin at a good price, abandoned his former employer and soon surpassed him. Boy George's heroin—sold under the brand names Obsession, Delirious, Hammer, Candy Land and Airborne Express—became the only heroin available in vast portions of the Bronx. Savvy management, good product and brute force had won him a virtual monopoly.

But Boy George had also made a mistake. A man close enough to attend weddings with him, devious enough to be awarded the code number "6-6-6" for beeper communications, "cause it's the sign of the devil," George told him, and successful enough to operate as one of George's top lieutenants, was also a government informant. He tipped the cops to the silent menace growing in the Bronx. To protect him, the cops referred to him only as CI One, the first confidential informant in the case.

CI One soon led to three other informants, each yielding a fragment of information on Boy George's network: an address for a heroin-cutting mill, the nicknames of George's most trusted confidants, even the kind of jewelry—a gold ring that spanned three fingers—worn by one of George's most successful dealers.

This went to the surveillance teams and undercover agents. Drugs were bought, observations made that confirmed the informants' information.

In April of 1988, there was enough to seek a court order to set up a monitoring device known as a PEN Register and attach it to a set of telephones believed widely used by members of Boy George's organization. On one of those telephones, 2,884 calls were placed between May 1, 1988, and March 20, 1989, when the monitoring device was removed. Over 40 percent of the calls went to beeper numbers, a large number of those to CI One, who knew that when he saw "6-6-6" on the display screen, he must prepare to work. Other calls went to five public telephones on the streets Boy George's dealers owned.

There was not yet enough evidence to build a box around Boy George. There was enough, however, to go before federal judge Thomas P. Griesa with a ten-page request for a wiretap to be placed on the telephones of Boy George's network. This request, authorized by the Attorney General's office, was approved by Judge Griesa after he read the forty-two-page supporting affidavit by two of Billy Cook's investigators, DEA Special Agent Anthony Farretta and Detective Willie Cebolleros. It summarized the results of the almost eleven-month investigation and spelled out that while there was ample evidence Boy George was running the heroin ring, there was not yet enough to put him behind bars.

On April 4, 1989, the wire intercepts were placed on the network of telephones. A network of agents and Spanish language translators began to listen to the dealers conduct business.

Meanwhile, surveillance of George's mills and distribution points was intensified. Within a month, the investigators realized the wiretaps were being circumvented by the use of beepers, pay telephones and cellular mobile phones. Because everyone occasionally makes a mistake, the taps on the home telephones did yield enough to clarify how the network operated. Since that plus the rich stream of information from surveillance still left them short of an airtight case, Cook's investigators decided to stage their first raid.

It yielded thirteen arrests, seven pounds of heroin, seven guns, $60,000 and a set of thick, gold belt buckles of the kind awarded to heavyweight champions.

"Cheap pieces of shit," Billy Cook told the investigator who handed him the belt buckles, a detective named Jeff Beck. "Gaudy-looking pieces of shit," he reiterated.

Beck took a buckle to an appraiser who told him, "They're worth $8,000 each, give or take a few cents."

"Take it to another appraiser," the unflinching Cook told the persistent Beck.

The second appraiser determined the buckle was gold through and through—$8,000, he told Beck, is the value of the gold. He would not guess what Boy George paid a jeweler to make it.

Cook had been wrong, but he was philosophical. As a sergeant in charge of detectives, he explained, "I am no longer in charge of detecting things. I am now in charge of the supervision of those who detect." That often amounts to ordering a second opinion, or a second search, and sometimes they are unnecessary.

Cook, satisfied no defense attorney would shoot his case down, now embraced the evidence that Boy George was in a position to reward his employees with $8,000 belt buckles. And those buckles became a link in the evidence trail.

A photo album, also seized, showed the heroin gangsters putting the buckles on for the first time when Boy George presented them at a Christmas party held on December 24, 1988. This led Cook's investigators to question their informants, who told them the party was held aboard a yacht that docked in Manhattan. A visit was paid to the yacht charterers but the employees of the Hudson River concern were reluctant to help—they were afraid Boy George's enforcers would sink their boats.

Their records, when subpoenaed, showed they knew just enough about Boy George to have reason to be afraid.

The records indicated that the boat was hired for $60,000, including a disc jockey and dinner for 120 people—Boy George's employees and their guests. Boy George, using the alias John Marciano, had paid in cash. He provided his own entertainment, two well-known rap musicians, including Big Daddy Kane, who was paid $10,000 in small bills to sing two songs. A third singer, who was paid $7,500 for a fifteen-minute performance, stalked off when she discovered she had no private dressing room. "I will not use a common restroom," the singer, Sa-Fire, said, according to seized records.

During the course of the party, a woman was gang-raped, a man stripped on the main deck, beaten and spit on by Boy George for stealing a necklace. A raffle was held with a BMW as grand prize, $20,000 cash as first prize, a Rolex watch as second prize, a week in Hawaii as third prize, a trip to Disney World as fourth prize. Not one of the guests would demean himself by coming forward to claim the paltry $100 consolation prizes—tip money in their world, for some kid to watch your car and make sure nobody scratched it.

As fog drifted across the river and rain lashed the decks, the belt buckles were awarded and coke use became rampant, a dutiful log keeper noted. And as the yacht made for shore at the stroke of midnight, a man attempted to dive off the bow and race the boat on a bet. He was restrained by three off-duty New York City detectives.

The detectives were aboard as part of the yacht charterer's security, and they, Bill Cook pointed out, were most uncooperative. Months later, as the case went to trial, they would remain steadfast in their refusal to testify to what they had witnessed. Cook found that an odd, if not despicable, attitude from a brother cop.

But the ship's log, kept by a crew member, by itself gives a telling account of what Boy George and his tuxedo-clad troops found to be an entertaining enough evening:

Entry One: "Guests began arriving in stretch limos as early as 5:30 P.M.," the log begins. "When told they couldn't board until 6:30 they got back in their limos and went for an hour ride."

"2. We started boarding about 6:15.

"3. No one smiled.

"4. No one spoke to one another..."

Instead, the meticulous recordkeeper noted, they stood in clusters. The men of each cluster wore cummerbunds of the same color—red for one distribution group, purple for another, gold for a third.

Item five indicates that through the night the cliques remained intact, "Those that arrived together stayed together."

"6. ...One of the guests told the D.J. they didn't want any music played until the host showed up. The D.J., being somewhat intimidated by the guest, played nothing....

"8. Mr. John Marciano, who was called George all night by his associates, finally arrived and he was upset that we had security on board but Vinnie Albanese spoke with him and everything was ironed out. John or George assured us there would be no trouble on the boat.

"9. Well, even with the host on board the entertainment hadn't arrived yet. 'Big Daddy' was stuck in traffic. (If you saw his size you'd understand why he has this name.)...It was close to 8:00 and Amor (a group of eight who never did make it and God only knows what they were paid) was never heard from.

"10. Big Daddy finally made it....

"11. Now the host began to pressure me for an extra hour service....It was now 9 P.M. and 11 P.M. still seemed to be a couple of hundred light years away. The guests were getting nervous and that did nothing for me.

"12. At 10 P.M. we left dock for a 2 hour cruise that was quite memorable." It included, he noted, the gang-beating of the necklace thief, dinner, dancing, a raffle and a gang rape and "a nice gratuity for the staff."

The writer closed his log on the seventeenth item:

"Needless to say this was a tough cruise. Oh yes, as he left, the D.J. said, 'I think these were crack dealers.'"

They weren't, but with crack so much on everyone's mind it was easy to understand the mistake. Because from 1986 when that drug first hit, everything else seemed to take a back seat in the public mind. But not to Cook's methodical investigators. They saw heroin as a resurfacing danger, long before middle-class users were again documented snorting it. And they had acted, not certain when they began where the evidence would lead.

With these new fragments, the picture that a jury would need was almost complete: Boy George standing tall at the center of his tuxedo-clad, gun-carrying, heroin-dealing minions.

Another set of raids was made. Boy George and his top lieutenants were dragged in. From their mouths came the first hints that cooperation, not silence, would be the order of the day. From the upper reaches of George's organization would come the final shreds of evidence necessary to complete the box around him. Enough was enough. The extent of the conspiracy was corroborated. Cook sat down to plan his last raids.

These final raids were intended to get every last shred of physical evidence and every possible cooperating witness against Boy George. This was the insurance. By the first days of June 1989, a raid date was set. This morning was the day.

Unfazed by the rain, the sergeant in charge of detectives was wearing a crinkly Catholic schoolboy smirk beneath his brown mustache. He had worn it since 3:30 in the morning when, eyes sparkling and unruly hair still dry, he plugged in the coffee urn, set out the dozen boxes of sugary Dunkin' Donuts and waited for his raiders to assemble in the DEA's seventeenth-floor conference room in Manhattan.

"Okay boys, let's go wreck some zip codes," the ever-smiling sergeant told the seventy raiders at 4:30 A.M. as they squeezed out of the tight lecture chairs packed into the conference room to head for the Bronx buildings whose doors they would crash through. They were still making final entries in their notepads as they stood and Cook admonished them, "Remember! Seize all the paper. Paper, paper, paper! That's what we need to make the case stick."

Cook knew, as younger agents and police officers not fully versed in the nuances of federal law might not, that conspiracy cases are built on little scraps of paper. In a successful conspiracy case it is the paper that ties one person to another without room for a denial. The paper ultimately forms a chain of evidence that ends in conviction, even if no drugs are seized. The exhortation was Cook's guide to conspiracy; succinct and accurate. They could sort out what was unnecessary. The group, an amalgam of federal agents, city detectives and state police investigators, was formally known as the NYPD-DEA Drug Enforcement Task Force. In boat shoes, Reeboks, stonewashed jeans, neatly pressed sweaters or freshly laundered sweatshirts, the raiders looked like a heavily armed group of graduate students—or a bowling team from a very dangerous neighborhood.

The younger ones had strapped ominous seventeen-shot automatics under their arms, hooked a second gun into their belts and in some instances strapped a third around their ankles. A few carried shotguns; a few more submachine guns.

Cook and the other older hands stuck to their small five-

and six-shot Detective Specials. They shoved the snubnosed .38 caliber belly guns where they belonged, neatly to the side of their belt buckles, and were ready for a day's work.

"If there is a clear and present danger, I'll take along a shotgun, but basically, I'm more comfortable with a baseball bat or a nightstick," Billy explained later. His raiding philosophy, he said, was not based on some misplaced pacifism.

"It's a jump ball for me. I've had some scary instances with the shotgun. One of my guys, back when I was in Bronx narcotics, shot a crib. A dog had come out and attacked him. He shot at the dog. It went over the dog and hit the corner of a crib. The baby wasn't in the crib, but it was enough. If the danger is there I'll take a shotgun, I just prefer not to."

As Cook's raiders stood to leave they picked up the last pieces of their assault arsenal: heavy steel battering rams, crowbars and hammers. Then, with the collars of their blue windbreakers that said **POLICE** or **FEDERAL AGENT** across the back pulled up against the expected rain, they headed for the elevators and their parked cars. On the way out, one member from each raiding team filed past a conference table set up by the blackboard next to Cook's podium to pick up a cardboard evidence box, a search warrant and plastic gloves for handling drugs. Seventeen search warrants, seventeen boxes and seventeen battering rams—a set for each door that would come crashing down.

A few minutes later Cook and another investigator climbed in their government sedan for the drive to the Bronx.

When Cook stepped into it, the steady curtain of drizzle that hung from the predawn gray skies of the Bronx did nothing to dampen his enthusiasm. He stood with a knot of supervisors outside the Alexander Avenue police station on the edge of what used to be a teeming shopping district.

At a few minutes before six, Cook again looked at his watch, then broke up the group and climbed back into his car. He tested the police radio before driving to St. Ann's Avenue and the first of two doors that the team he personally led would raid.

"Be safe," a uniformed officer walking out of the station house said quietly. Cook had earlier stopped in at the station house desk and alerted the officers to the raid—a precaution against any of his investigators being mistaken for a criminal and halted or shot by a fellow law officer.

As Cook pulled away, the cop in his raincoat standing in front of the green-shaded torches on the station house seemed to be the last outpost of law in that gutted section of the Bronx.

At 6 A.M. sharp Cook's car and two other carloads of agents had drifted to a halt in front of 474 St. Ann's Avenue. A reputed lieutenant of Boy George's lived there. Cook gave the raid signal: "Notify all units," he said over the radio. "Go. Go! We're going in."

Cook's team, guns and rams in hand, raced to positions at the front door, sides and back of the building. One cop stood across the street to provide covering fire if necessary from a position with a clear view of the roof and of all the front windows of the three-story brick building.

Screams echoed from inside as the ram slammed down the steel-backed door. Spanish was shouted and shouted back by the cops. "Keep your hands up. Police. Nobody move."

Turmoil filled the apartment as closet doors were torn open, beds overturned and any place where a criminal could hide was searched. The frenzy came to an end without incident.

By 6:13 A.M. everyone inside was in custody, seated on couches or chairs in the dimly lit apartment.

They were also in tears. The apartment had contained the grandmother, mother, wife and children of the suspect, Willie Claussen, a reputed Boy George lieutenant.

A litter of half-strung costume jewelry and boxes of beads covered most of the kitchen table. This was important work for the women in lean times. They had kept it up. Now they would need the income again.

A letter from Great Meadows Correctional Facility was mixed in with the beads. Correspondence from one of Willie's friends.

The suspect was not home. He would turn himself in later. But across the longest wall in the living room were shelves that held a shrine to his father. His father, Willie

Claussen, Sr., had been a well-known Golden Gloves boxer. His picture was at the center of a career's worth of trophies.

It ended, Cook told his young investigators, when the father got killed in the ring.

Had he not, said Cook, who knew the city and understood how slender is the thread that can lift an entire family out of its ghettos, Willie Claussen, Jr., might have turned out differently. Instead the son plied a trade that from Southeast Asia to the Southeast Bronx sold certain death, and not in anything so noble as his father's ring.

When the noise calmed down, amid the wreckage of the search, Billy gave out containers of coffee and cocoa to the family and accomplices.

"It never hurts; there could be a payback later for being nice," Cook explained. The minor players very often were freed in exchange for their small bits of cooperation. They were mill workers who cut Boy George's heroin, the baggers who packed it. Their lives had little in common with the lifestyle of a young man who drove a $140,000 customized black Porsche—with a sound system whose preamplifiers took up all the trunk space, gun compartments that slid open to a touch, blinding lights to ward off chasers, and a host of other James Bond goodies, including the ability to drop tacks in the road.

The next raid would make that entirely clear. Cook had saved the raids on the lowest-level workers for last. Paid about $9 an hour to cut George's heroin, or almost three times the wage of a clerk in a fast-food store, Cook knew the workers were viewed as disposable by the dealers. They had no chance of receiving a warning call from a mobile phone carried by a more important suspect who had escaped an earlier raid.

It was a few minutes after 7:30 when the raid took place. This time, the target was a couple. A mill worker and her street pusher husband. They lived in an apartment on the ninth floor of a housing project. Those stationed outside its door endured the all-pervasive smell of urine in the hall. Those outside the building stood in what was now a steady downpour.

This time, Cook knew there was no way out the back and

he expected no resistance, so when the raiding party was in place, he knocked. The suspected mill worker, Desiree, opened the door and let the raiders in. Her children Shakeena and Boo-Boo were at home.

"I'm going to have to take you downtown," Cook told her, still smiling.

"Can I take Boo-Boo to school first, and call my mother to pick him up and watch my daughter?" Desiree asked.

"I'll call your mother," Cook said, by now stripped down to his sweatshirt as the apartment's furniture and drawers were tossed in the hunt for evidence. "What school does he go to?"

"St. Peter and Paul. Please, Mr. Cook, Shakeena is too young to know what's going on," the mother said. Of Boo-Boo, her seven-year-old son, she said nothing. The boy had on a red Braves cap, Nike sneakers and a little black leather jacket. The outfit resembled one his father could be seen wearing in a photograph that lay on the kitchen counter.

"Officer, don't handcuff me," Desiree said to Cook, as the other agents and officers found $3,600 and a pile of food stamps in their search.

The woman and her husband, a slightly higher-level Boy George employee, earned well over a thousand dollars a week in cash, Cook estimated, "But invariably we find food stamps." He said he really didn't want to get philosophical but it was clear these suspects could not be bothered spending money on anything so mundane as groceries. They spent it instead on cars, sound systems, fur-trimmed coats. They lived in a project, but they "lived large" as was said on the street. They wanted nothing more than to wear gold as heavy as that worn by George.

Desiree had seemed resigned and had spoken softly since she opened the door for the police. The screaming began when the grandparents of her children arrived. The grandfather, smelling heavily of liquor at 8:30 A.M., led the charge. Grandmother was also hysterical. "She ain't done nothing. Why you want to arrest her? Who is gonna take care of the kids? Why she have to go downtown for?"

"Okay. You keep screaming and I have to take everybody

downtown. Then where will the kids go? To Social Services," Cook threatened. The city's bureaucracy was more formidable than any set of handcuffs. Once the kids were lost inside, the adults, you could see by their faces, knew they might never see them again.

Still, it took ten minutes of this tough bargaining before the handcuffs were on Desiree's wrists, the children in the grandparents' custody, and the last portion of Billy Cook's last raid was completed. One stretch of the heroin trail was destroyed. Boo-Boo fixed the angle of his Braves cap, adjusted the collar of his black leather coat and walked ahead of his grandparents out the door.

In all more than forty people were arrested in the Boy George case. Almost all waived the right to trial and pleaded guilty to a variety of minor narcotics-peddling charges. Boy George Rivera and several of his top co-conspirators opted to stand trial in Manhattan federal court. In the November 1990 trial they sat at the defense table and listened as another of their crew, Ward Johnson, took the stand, revealed himself as a government witness, and detailed their crimes for the jury. Johnson had availed himself of a shortened prison sentence offered when he agreed to waive trial and cooperate with Cook's raiders. His testimony coupled with the evidence that Cook's team had gathered was enough for the jury. The defendants were found guilty on multiple counts of conspiracy to sell narcotics. On Wednesday, April 23, 1991, George Rivera, now twenty-three, was sentenced to life without parole in federal prison.

THIRTEEN

"When Crack Was King"

Peg Cafolla's clear brown eyes danced across the crowd at the curb, dismissed the figures huddled in a darkened tenement doorway and leapt back to the street. They grew opaque and unreadable as they plucked out the thin young man. Wrapped in an oversized fatigue jacket, his right fist driven in the pocket, the dark-skinned youth leaned into the driver's side window of a red car with New Jersey license plates. He laid claim to the car by resting the tips of the fingers and the heel of his left hand lightly on the roof.

The twenty-six-year-old DEA agent pressed her snub nose closer to her windshield as she sorted out the illicit transaction she knew was behind the half-lit tableau a quarter of a city block away. A smile rippled across Cafolla's face as she watched the dark-skinned youth take his hand from his pocket and extend it into the car. When it came back out, the fist held a small wad of dollars. Her crinkly dark hair and little gold hoop earrings glinted as they caught the glare of a streetlight when she turned and said to her partner, New York Police Sergeant John Jones, "Mar-donne-a. This is us."

The young man in the red car had driven from suburban New Jersey across the nearby George Washington Bridge and into these scarred precincts for but one reason: to buy crack.

The pitted streets of Washington Heights in September 1986 were an open-air drug bazaar.

Jones leaned over and flicked the police radio microphone key to the ON position, linking the two supervisors with the other cars in their raiding party. Cafolla used a high-glossed red fingernail to click a cassette tape into the player set in the government car's dash. Then she spun the volume knob to LOUD.

Cavalry charge. Unheard by the quarry, the throbbing beat of Boz Scaggs's "Lido Shuffle" reverberated through the police radio speakers in all five cars.

> *LIDO, WHOAH OOH Ooh ooooooooooo . . .*
> *Lido be runnin*
> *Havin great big fun*
> *Until he got the note*
> *Sayin toe the line or blow it*
> *And that was all she wrote . . .*
> *LIDO, WHOAH OOH Ooh ooooooooooo . . .* *

When the last notes faded, it was time for the raiders to move. The seller was back at the curb counting what was in his hand. The buyer was driving away.

Headlights flared. One car of agents blocked the top of the one-way street, halting the buyer's car's progress. A second pair of agents left their car at that corner and dog-trotted down the street toward the seller. A third team pulled their car across the bottom end of the block, preventing the buyer from backing out. A fourth stood by them in case the seller tried to run away. The street was now a closed trap.

Cafolla and Jones, waiting in mid-block, got out, locked their doors, drew their guns and ran toward the seller. He was just turning in their direction to escape the two agents running at him from the top of the block. With their left hands, Cafolla and Jones tugged the chains around their neck and pulled their badges from under their shirts. The shields flopped against their shirts as they ran. Ripoff artists were not

---

* © 1976 Boz Scaggs Music/Hudmar Publishing Co., Inc.

unknown on this valuable stretch of the Washington Heights drug bazaar and such an invasion was usually met by gunfire. The badges assured the many heavily armed residents of 175th Street off Audubon Avenue that Cafolla and Jones were not a Bonnie-and-Clyde team. In a rush of seconds the raid was over. The suspected buyer was dragged from his car. The seller was grabbed in a doorway. Then the suspects were thrown by their collars against the nearest brick wall, searched and handcuffed.

The buyer would forfeit his car, the seller his freedom. If they wanted them back, they could try to trade what they knew about the top players in an organization that sold the green-topped vials of Lido brand crack that dominated this stretch of Washington Heights. Those top players, Peg already knew, were four Dominican brothers named Ramos.

The Ramos brothers and their lieutenants had turned cocaine addiction into a thriving million-dollar business headquartered on 175th Street and Audubon Avenue. From basement stashes their brand managers kept busy, night and day, handing twenty-five-vial bundles of crack to their street sellers. Sellers hawked the drug curbside and at the exit ramp to the George Washington Bridge as rapidly as they could remove it from their pockets, hand it into a car, pocket the money and prepare for the next customer. On weekends, each hawker returned to the basement dozens of times in order to have enough drugs to satisfy the unquenchable thirst of these suburban commuters. With a sense of humor, the Ramos brothers named their poison Lido, after a popular Latin American soft drink that also has been known to leave the user thirsting for more.

A city block away from the Ramos stretch of 175th Street, DEA agent Harry Brady was building his case from the bottom up. And he was trying hard not to curse his division chief, who had told him to rummage through all the trash behind the apartment building where the suspects, also Dominicans, lived. Brady was at the beginning of a hunt for evidence against the Ramos brothers' competition, the owners of the Based Balls brand of crack, sold in distinctive red-topped vials. By the narrow beam of his flashlight, he was looking for paper and, so far, all he was finding was plantain peels. The paper, the division chief had said, was the key to linking the suspects to the conspiracy, and the place to start looking for it was in the trash. It was a lesson Brady would find hard to forget.

It had rained the night before, so most of the garbage was wet. But the suspects had just dropped off their trash, and Brady, who had been watching, could be thankful it was still dry: He didn't want the ink to run on any potential record of drug or money transactions.

That was what he sought. But he would be happy with a telephone bill's list of long-distance calls, the name on an electric bill recording unusually high usage (an indicator of the night-and-day microwave usage common in crack cookery), a beeper number, a bank record, a torn stub from a money changer, an ammunition box. Like a sport fisherman hunting striped bass who saves a luckless day with the easy catch of a bottom fish, Brady this day settled for the Gem Star brand single-edged razors and their orange-and-blue wrappers.

With crack they always use the Gem Star blades to whittle it down, he thought. Mockler can show me how to use it as an exhibit in court. Then he put his find in a plastic evidence pouch and flipped off the beam of his flashlight. Brady stretched his legs and his back muscles. He was twenty-six years old and had the tall, fast-moving build of the modern middleweight he was. But all this unfamiliar bending over and digging into trash had made him sore. He got into his Monte Carlo and tried not to kill anyone on the way home. Brady had forgotten his contact lenses again.

The Based Balls crack ring had its origins, Brady knew, back in 1982 when it sold powdered cocaine under the appropriated trademark Coke Is It. But Santiago Luis Polanco-Rodriguez, the gang's leader who went by the street name "Yayo," and his half brother Santiago Antonio Ysrael Polanco-Polanco, or "Chiqui," had early on seen the potential riches of crack dealing. By September 1986, they hardly sold powdered cocaine. Instead, selling crack, Yayo and Chiqui had grown rich. The half brothers had opened two discotheques in their

native Dominican Republic, and their own international money exchange corporation, Sociedad Commercial Financiera Promoción Empresarial, S.A. (FINAPE). FINAPE was suspected of the weekly laundering of hundreds of thousands of dollars from drug profits. After having bought or killed off their other competitors, the Polancos' multimillion-dollar illegal operation and the smaller, but still lucrative, Lido ring coexisted nicely. The Polanco headquarters on 174th near Audubon were but one block away from the Ramos brothers' operation on 175th. Brady wanted to end this happy little nightmare and he had a private grudge that sustained him whenever he felt the task ahead was too difficult.

Brady knew that the job of keeping order among the dozens of hawkers and managers for Yayo and Chiqui fell to a thug named José Roberto Mejía-Muñez, known as Capo to his underlings, who had won the 1981 Golden Gloves title by pounding James (Buddy) McGirt into the canvas. A good boxer at 140 pounds, one who could have made a decent pro, Capo had opted for the indolence of drug money. With its excess he had ballooned to more than 210 pounds.

Brady could not forgive Capo for this affront to boxing. Capo had rubbed the luster off one of boxing's crowns, turning it into a killer's trophy. Brady knew he could beat the guy head to head, but his mission was to beat him with pieces of paper. And the courtroom, for young Harry Brady, was still a foreign arena. He would be back tomorrow to rummage through another load of trash.

The DEA's leading cocaine conspiracy expert, Division Chief Bill Mockler, was the man who had set Peg Cafolla and Harry Brady to work. Mockler could gather the pieces of paper and scraps of buyer-and-seller information and mold them into an iron-clad court case. He looked like a coddled egg as he sat with his soft gray leather shoes on his desk, his swivel chair tilted as far back as it could go, pressing the back of his rough head against the office wall, and his mouth wide open as he screamed again and again into the telephone. From under his blotter he pulled his unfinished charts of

conspiracy. He needed still more pieces. It would take a few more months to find them.

In the meantime, Peg Cafolla, John Jones, Harry Brady and dozens of other street cops and field agents would continue to rummage through trash, kick down doors, photograph, videotape and buy drugs from suspected ring members. They would stop when Mockler had put a name in each box of the Lido and Based Balls organizational charts, drawn solid lines where dotted ones now indicated suspected paths of drugs and money, and put in his files enough evidence to prosecute each member of the conspiracies.

Reassigned to New York from Miami on May 16, 1986, Mockler had spent his first weeks on the streets of Washington Heights sizing up the target. By then the city already had an epidemic on its hands, and the newspapers had picked Washington Heights from among a half-dozen crack-plagued neighborhoods as the flashpoint for outrage: It was the caravan of naive suburbanites arriving in these tough streets that had caught the press's attention. The police were worried too; some doctor's kid was sure to be killed, setting off a furious demand that the police do something they knew was well beyond their grasp. No cop with a gun could stop the craving for crack.

In April, when the precinct's uniformed officers had begun "Operation Clean Heights," they found its major effect was to sweep the buyers only as far as the next precinct. The police brass, in May, had formed a special Anti-Crack Unit and added its roving squad of 101 undercover officers to the neighborhood to attack the sellers.

This team of hardened narcotics cops was successful in collaring low-level and mid-level hawkers and distributors, but with the demand for crack large enough to cause traffic jams, others stepped up to take their places. When a corner became too risky to use because even the cops had found out you could buy drugs there, the dealers just shifted to another spot. It did not take long for frustration to set in among the cops.

But Mockler, working with the unit's commander, Inspector Martin O'Boyle, wanted to do more than just push the entire mess from one city corner to another.

Mockler saw those same young users and low-level hawkers as the beginning of his chain of evidence. He would arrest them and use their information to launch the first systemic attack on crack. He knew his plan jibed nicely with the police's and community's concerns and actions. The kids arrested for buying crack would get relatively light sentences in return for cooperation. To this, the hawkers, hoping for any kind of break on jail time, would add additional information. As the pattern of conspiracy emerged, the millionaire dealers would be driven from the streets.

At the beginning of June 1986, weeks before Cafolla and Brady were set in motion, Mockler stepped into my office at the DEA's Manhattan headquarters to outline his plan.

"I've spoken to Marty O'Boyle, the commander of the Anti-Crack Unit, and I've told him we want to attack these various organizations behind the street sales and he's all for it," Mockler told me. Then the expert puzzle solver laid out what he had discovered—the conspiracies behind the apparently unconnected street corner sales. What had looked like independent street corner pushers were actually the bottom rung of carefully managed organizations. The pushers, and the hawkers who sent business their way, were strictly supervised by managers, who replenished their supply of crack when it ran out and rewarded them with a commission on their sales. The managers controlled enforcers who administered a beating at the slightest hint that a pusher was holding back profits. Above them all were the brand owners, the millionaires who bought cocaine wholesale and turned it into tens of thousands of vials of crack each week. It came as a revelation. Until that day the marketing of crack was thought to be a cottage industry, a low-level blip in the drug trade like the selling of single marijuana cigarettes. Now it was clear that crack was a carefully marketed product designed to lure a vast young set of middle-class and working-class users into cocaine addiction.

By 1986, the drug's glitter had worn off among members of the celebrity set. Sales were down and increased production had left the distributors holding more cocaine than ever. New users were needed to spur flagging sales. It was a case where greed had been the mother of invention. And crack was born diabolically attractive.

At $5 or $10 a vial, it appeared cheap enough. But the user soon discovered a fresh vial was needed minutes after the last in order to maintain the intense high and prevent a crashing depression. Many members of that suburban caravan arriving in Washington Heights were already hooked. The street-level vial trade quickly became a business worth hundreds of millions in profits to the crack kingpins.

In the person of Sergeant George Hanken, a smart cop assigned to the Washington Heights precinct, Mockler explained, he had found a way to speed up the normally tedious pace of laying the groundwork for breaking these conspiracies and arresting the kingpins.

Hanken had been present at the birth of the crack trade and had recorded the growth of the organizations suspected of running it, Mockler explained. But because of a police department policy against making high-level narcotics cases—a policy born of anti-corruption measures installed in the early 1970s when almost every member of the police narcotics unit was found to be corrupt—Hanken could do nothing with his knowledge. Until now.

Mockler asked me to get him assigned to the task force he was building.

"We need him," Mockler said. He explained that the sergeant had determined that there were four major rings dominating the crack trade in Washington Heights, the Conan brand, 007, Lido and Based Balls. Through careful filing and indexing of arrest data, Hanken had compiled what would serve as preliminary organizational charts of each ring. Mockler, with his conspiracy case theory, had just the mechanism for making all this wasted information useful. He would assign a team of agents and cops to each of the rings. Starting with Hanken's information, they would begin gathering evidence necessary to link each vial sold on the street to the hand at the top that profited the most.

I liked the idea immediately and I knew Mockler would deliver. He had been an agent for two decades. He had helped build Miami's major coke cases. He had designed a national cocaine homicide task force that linked agents and detectives from Miami and New York through Washington, a successful project that was killed by internal Justice Department bickering. Mockler still led from the field. After identifying New York's major cocaine traffickers as early as 1978 he had gone door-to-door with homicide detectives to gather the evidence needed to tie the dealers to previously unsolvable murders. He knew the value of good street information. This was behind his insistence on getting Sergeant Hanken. He also knew Hanken's files and the 101 Unit's arrest data would need a context. So he continued to outline what he needed to make his task force effective.

"I need some senior DEA agents to work with these task force modules we are putting together with the police department, people who are in tune with looking for bits of paper, toll call records, and who are used to debriefing informants," Mockler told me. "I'll also want some homicide detectives— since the dealers seem to be racking up a bunch of murders— and a couple of good immigration agents, since a lot of the sellers appear to be illegal aliens."

I said that was all doable. Then Mockler outlined the three phases of his assault. He wanted to begin on the street and work his way up. First he would seize the buyers' cars; this would satisfy the media and the community outcry for action and give the task force leads to the lower-level ring members. Next he would go after these street-level sellers, arrest them and turn some into informants. While both of these campaigns were going on, agents and cops would begin collecting the bills, razor blades, vials and other scraps that would become the paper trail to tie it all together. All of these efforts would be waged so as to appear unconnected. When they were complete, then the third act to Mockler's drama would unfold. The unsuspecting heads of the conspiracies would be arrested in raids on their apartments that would yield the final pieces of evidence—telephone books, bank records, cash, jewelry and weapons—the frame for the already completed puzzle.

I just listened and smiled. I am far from a conspiracy expert. But Mockler laid out the conspiracy and the way he would crack it with the deftness of a morality playwright who introduces good and evil, has the forces clash, but in the midst of chaos leaves his audience sure that good will win out.

Lido and Based Balls, Mockler felt, were the top targets. He would devote most of his resources there. He had already heard of the gold-painted Gull Wing Mercedes cars, mansions in Santo Domingo, discotheques and supermarkets that the Polancos and Ramoses reputedly controlled.

Destroying these ill-gotten empires was the engine driving Mockler. The conspiracy expert could see his way to the top of crack's trail despite a path clouded by money launderers, coded bank records and murky real estate transactions. He saw a big target, and he was, in his own estimate, a big-game hunter. His only fault was that he occasionally displayed a literary vanity. "Certainly there is no hunting like the hunting of man," Mockler was fond of saying. "And those who have hunted armed men long enough and liked it never really care for anything else." To ensure that he was exact in his reference to Hemingway's "A Gulf Stream Letter," he referred to the clipping that he kept, like evidence, in his wallet.

As Mockler outlined the conspiracy, I could feel the power of his concentration. Hundreds of minor defendants, the buyers and interchangeable street sellers, would have to be arrested as he patiently built his case. When it was complete, a more than $40 million a year set of drug rings would be broken and millions more in assets seized.

However, the first objective—seizing the cars—posed a problem.

"Under federal law we have every right to seize them," Mockler said. "But, before I start doing this, where am I going to put them?"

"Well, there's a lot of room on the roof of the DEA garage," I replied.

"If this program goes the way I think it will, within two weeks that roof is going to be full." He laughed.

I smiled. While Mockler had pragmatic reasons for getting rid of the cars, I saw an attractive bonus in this phase of his plan. The publicity surrounding the car seizures would demonstrate that federal and local law enforcement, working together, could have an immediate impact on the increasing problem of middle-class crack use. Users helped create the problem, users should pay the price, I would tell the press.

With each seizure we would identify what kind of people were buying crack and remove once and for all the notion that it was a problem confined to the ghetto.

But before the plan could be put in motion, I would have to go to Washington. Despite the clamoring of local law enforcement for our help, the federal DEA had a traditional resistance toward becoming involved in anything so lowly as street narcotics enforcement. During the first months of Mockler's attack on crack, it would have to publicly appear that street enforcement was all we were doing. I needed to lay out for my bosses in Washington the long-range case that was under way behind the scenes. Even this would not be enough to convince them that my field division needed to do the car seizures. I had to also convince them that crack was more than a low-level blip in the cocaine trade. Otherwise, they would remain unswayed. They would order us back to seeking out distribution-level cocaine cases. We would have to leave attacking the crack epidemic to the NYPD, which, as Mockler and I knew, was ill-equipped to focus on this type of conspiracy.

As a result, while all of New York was engaged in a raging debate over the impact of crack, the extent of the epidemic, the effect on families, children and the city's crime rate, I was engaged in a debate in Washington that would have seemed otherworldly to any hardworking civilian who had to live shoulder-to-shoulder with the crack dealers in Washington Heights.

Is crack a problem that the federal government ought to be involved in? The bureaucrats in the Justice Department kept asking.

Yes, I kept answering.

There was no doubt in my mind that crack was on its way to becoming a national problem. But, to speed up the process of convincing Washington, I needed to make it a national issue and quickly. I began a lobbying effort and I used the media. Reporters were only too willing to cooperate, because as far as the New York media was concerned, crack was the hottest combat-reporting story to come along since the end of the Vietnam War.

Surprisingly, it was only months since John Maltz had walked into my office cupping the tiny vials of poison in his large hands. Between October 26, 1985, when he presented me with the fruits of our first seizure, and the middle of May, when Mockler arrived, the New York field division's intelligence division had compiled every piece of information it could find.

A succinct but thorough bulletin for law enforcement use was prepared. Entitled *Special Report: "CRACK" A New Form of Cocaine Abuse,* the report, issued May 26, brought New York law enforcement officials up to date:

"Presently, 'Crack' is available in all five boroughs of New York City, the Upstate cities, contiguous states and has been prepared in Canada.... The vials are waterproof and may be secreted in body cavities. This is particularly desirable for smuggling the drug into correction facilities.... The purity of the exhibits seized has been between 60 percent and the high 90s.

"In New York City," it continued, "it is estimated that there are over 584 documented 'Crack' locations....A Bahamian publication, *The Lancet,* dated Saturday, March 1, 1986, reports on 'Epidemic Free-Base Cocaine Abuse.'... In summary, the study stated that the cause of the medical epidemic [begun in 1983] seemed to be a switch by pushers from selling cocaine hydrochloride...to almost exclusive selling of cocaine freebase, which has a very high addictive potential and also causes medical and psychological problems."

Not to mention sudden outbursts of random violence.

The report went on to mention just a few of the crimes sprouting up like mushrooms (coincidentally the term the Colombian cocaine dealers use to describe the innocent bystanders they shot): A priest had been murdered by a man who used crack five times a day; three people were wounded in the attempted robbery of a crack manufacturing mill.

It was time to make this information public. Through my spokesman, Bob Strang, I released the contents of the intelligence division report to the newspapers. The reporters dug into the data and found a gold mine of stories in the accounts of the effect of crack on families, the use of crack by teenagers, and the $150 a week the average teenager's crack habit cost. Armed with the report's data they visited crack houses and followed agents on raids to crack mills. The reports they prepared intensified the pressure for federal action that had begun in April with the attention on Washington Heights.

By the first week of June, the national news magazines had put drugs on the cover, with *Newsweek* in an editorial by Richard M. Smith noting, "An epidemic is abroad in America. . . . It is a national scandal."

By the end of August, a bound file of New York metropolitan-area articles begun mid-June and whose sole concern was crack would total 199 pages. All crime in New York except rape was up, and crack was to blame, the *Daily News* reported. The detoxification centers were crowded beyond capacity, *New York Newsday* reported. A surge in cocaine-related deaths was under way, the *Newark Star-Ledger* reported. The murder rate in the Washington Heights neighborhood was up 63 percent, the *News* reported. And all the papers noted that the clergy was fighting the drug wars with street corner rallies.

Mockler's task force, fortunately, would not have to wait for the pressure to build this high. Right after our meeting, DEA Administrator Jack Lawn agreed to come to New York for a presentation on crack. The timing was perfect, although University of Maryland basketball star Len Bias might not have seen it that way. On June 19, the day Lawn arrived, we got the call that Bias had died.

An autopsy indicated that his lungs showed evidence of damage from smoking cocaine. If an athlete in top condition can keel over from a small dose, what effect would it have on the average person? an editorial writer asked. Once again, the coverage of crack took on a new life.

The drug death of a young athlete, with all that signified to an America that worships its sports heroes, had capped the groundwork that had been carefully laid through press accounts and my own public appearances. Crack was a national menace and 1986 was the Year of Crack. From my perspective, Len Bias had not died in vain.

When Lawn arrived, I had Arnold Washton present to outline the medical effects of crack. He had a full-blown presentation with slides and evidence set up. He began by laying out the evidence he had seen in his treatment center:

"I asked these kids where they were getting the crack from and they said they were sneaking out of their bedroom window at night, taking their father's car without permission, running down and buying crack and then missing days of school," Dr. Washton said.

Then I showed Lawn pictures of Washington Heights, the still photographs and videotapes of lines of obviously expensive cars, double-parked, while their young drivers cut deals for vial after vial of crack.

"Crack has put cocaine dealing on the street," Washton explained. "It is a drug that is changing the face of the public image of cocaine. Cocaine dealing was always something that was done between consenting adults in private settings. Until the appearance of crack." While the drug was dealt on the street, Washton quickly moved to dispel the illusion that the drug was limited to the ghetto.

"It is a misconception to think that the majority of people who use crack are black and Hispanic and live in urban ghettos. I will stand by the statement that the overwhelming majority of people who use crack in this country are middle-class employed people, and it includes, of course, all too many high school and college students."

Crack-related violence in the ghetto, I explained, was tied to the economics of poverty. To get the drug, ghetto dwellers had to steal, while middle-class users simply dipped into bankbooks. And to sell the drug, a street dealer had to go to work heavily armed to protect his turf. This always made news, but it misrepresented the nature of the problem. The silent majority of crack users were middle-class and working-class Americans.

The presentation erased any doubts Lawn might have had about my planned anti-crack efforts and he gave them the go-ahead, but asked that I wait on the car-seizure program until he tried some lobbying for resources on Capitol Hill. He wanted the money to put similar task forces at the disposal of any region that needed them.

By the end of July I had his answer.

"Based on what we heard, we were most concerned that crack was a new, more serious problem than just the cocaine problem, which was already serious. We came back to Washington convinced that something had to be done to minimize the spread of crack," he later recalled.

"We put together a request for an enhancement to the [DEA] budget. We requested $10 million, so that we could in a very quick time frame train additional agents and put twenty-four task forces around the country. We sent that [request] to the Department of Justice and it was turned down because the crack problem hadn't reached Washington, D.C."

Lawn was unhappy with the skimping. And in light of then–drug czar Bill Bennett's plans to use DEA agents to police Washington when officials finally awoke to crack in 1989, it was an example of how our national strategists too often do only what is necessary to cover their political asses and not enough to protect the nation. The inaction was a scandal.

But Lawn gave my office the permission to launch the New York seizure program with the full backing of the DEA. He also said he would cobble together a few crack task forces from our existing complement of agents to prepare for an onslaught of the drug across the nation.

On August 4, Police Commissioner Benjamin Ward and the DEA jointly announced the seizure program.

"If you come to New York to buy crack, bring car fare and be prepared to take the bus back," Ward said at a press briefing that announced the seizure of the first forty-three cars in Washington Heights.

The cars included everything from a 1971 Chevy van to a brand-new, two-seat Pontiac Fiero. The buyers ranged in age from sixteen to thirty-nine with the average about twenty-five. In those cars were found the first of the red-topped and green-topped vials that later would be cited as evidence of the Based Balls and Lido conspiracies.

On the street, Mockler's task force of detectives, investigators and agents was busy arresting the most blatant buyers, and dutifully bringing the news to our press officer, who regularly updated the number. Within four weekends, a couple of hundred cars were seized.

Behind the scenes, those same agents and police officers were working around the clock to debrief every suspect to gain the intelligence to move the conspiracy case up from the street.

By the end of October, detailed investigative reports had been filed on Conan, Lido and Based Balls. The 007 brand was an early victim of marketplace dynamics—the sellers of Based Balls had purchased its stretch of a quarter of a block, from fire hydrant to lamppost—for $40,000. Soon Conan would also be absorbed, and become another brand name in the Based Balls conglomerate. While the price might seem cheap for a stretch of street that could generate enough sales to cover twice the purchase price within a week, Based Balls's enforcers made clear it was not really an offer, it was a buyout backed by guns.

Reports indicated that the three brands were doing a booming business at the exit ramps from the George Washington Bridge, on West 174th Street, at boutiques on Audubon Avenue, from telephone booths on Amsterdam Avenue, out of apartments on West 177th Street, on St. Nicholas Avenue, on Wadsworth Avenue, on 173rd Street, across the Harlem River in the Bronx along the Grand Concourse, the borough's main thoroughfare, and along Boston Road, which was one of colonial America's first mail routes.

A quick look at a pin map of the area kept in the police precinct war room showed that on any intersection in Washington Heights, the surrounding precincts and the neighboring Bronx, crack was sold by one of these rings. There were brightly colored red or green pushpins stuck everywhere.

The Conan brand alone pulled in between $70,000 and $140,000 a week, enough so that the street sellers, who were paid $2 a vial, were earning about $1,500 a week. The middle-level managers, who kept about $3 a vial and received a daily stipend of $100 for keeping an eye on things, were netting closer to $2,500. And even after the mill workers and teenaged hawkers—who solicited for the sellers—were paid their cut, the owners came away with a nice minimum profit of $40,000 a week.

Based Balls's owners paid their managers $800 a week plus commission, its street sellers were getting close to $2,000 a week, and again the owners were able to clear a minimum of $40,000 a week. The Lido ring, while less powerful than Based Balls, seemed to be earning a good $20,000-a-week profit.

There was no doubt that Mockler had been right. The crack rings, the evidence showed, were big business.

Phase Two of Mockler's attack was also in motion. While some teams continued to arrest buyers and seize their cars, others were now busy arresting sellers. By the beginning of November, forty-seven sellers and managers from the Conan, Lido and Based Balls brands were in custody. Unlike those arrested in the days before the task force was formed, these defendants faced long stretches of federal prison time that could only be reduced if they cooperated with the immigration agents, DEA agents and police investigators who debriefed them.

Mockler, who also managed all our powdered-cocaine cases, by now had put Group Supervisor Lowrey Leong in charge of the more than full-time job of overseeing the day-to-day investigation.

Leong, aware that the huge piles of evidence and hundreds of statements from defendants were swamping the task force, which spent a great deal of time sorting out what defendant and what evidence belonged to which case, divided the thirteen agents, homicide detectives and investigators in the core conspiracy group into three teams. Peg Cafolla headed the attack on the Conan ring until it was bought up by Based Balls, then she took over the Lido team. Harry Brady was assigned the Based Balls case. This focused approach, Leong hoped, would keep confusion to a minimum.

The reorganization was important because in the long run success would not be measured in the sheer number of arrests. "How many collars do you want tonight?" the agents asked Leong when he arrived at the Three-Four Precinct war room. If he had said fifty, by morning fifty buyers and sellers would be in handcuffs. But now, instead of mass arrests, he told the agents to pick out which cases were important to make—the ones that when added together would prove a conspiracy to a jury.

The teams made progress. Soon they had solid evidence against the owners of the Based Balls brand, the Conan brand and the Lido brand. They knew that at least in the case of Based Balls, all the profits were funneled to Santo Domingo through a street corner money-transfer shop to FINAPE, the finance company the owners had set up in the Dominican Republic. They estimated the ring had already paid for two discotheques, worth at least $2 million each.

They knew something else: the raw power behind the money. They had seen with their own eyes how when Santiago Luis Polanco-Rodriguez, the head of the Based Balls ring, stepped out of his car, for once the traffic came to a halt in Washington Heights. His four bodyguards cleared the streets for the arrival of the muscular drug kingpin and he could stroll, unmolested, through his empire. It was, they now estimated, worth $36 million.

But despite all the evidence already in hand, the conspiracy cases would not be completed until the spring of 1987 for Based Balls and the fall of 1987 for Lido when the final pieces of the puzzle were in place and the raids on the kingpins were ordered.

By then, the car-seizure program had incapacitated its 1,001st vehicle, an ice cream truck that sold crack in front of the local elementary school. By then, many of the major members of the two rings were in custody, awaiting indictment or were fugitives in the Dominican Republic. By then, the police commissioner and I could point to the streets in Washington Heights and say, "While the problem is not gone, we have significantly reduced the drug dealing on the street." Traffic could flow through Washington Heights and a small piece of the city no longer looked like the Marrakech hashish markets.

Peg, despite the grueling case load, retained a gift for looking through the eyes of the buyers and their families to the human tragedy of the epidemic.

"I've become a counselor," she explained to me. "A lot of the kids, they are good kids, they really are, but they made a mistake and I feel bad for them. They come in crying and I tell them, 'It's all right, everything is really going to be okay.' Then that night you take them downtown and you book them.

"A lot of times I call the parents and ask them where did they think their child was going tonight. A lot of times the parents are upset: 'She was supposed to be with her friend, they were going to the movies,' they explain. If they've never been arrested before, we give the car back. But other parents are a sad commentary on where a lot of people in this country are at. They are more upset about their car than they are about the kids. They come down to the Heights and want to give the kid a slap in the head and tell them, 'You're grounded,' and they spend two minutes talking to you about the kid. But when you tell them their car is seized, then they throw a temper tantrum. All of a sudden you've taken something they care about. I just hope their relationship with their children improved after that."

The sad commentary doesn't stop with the parents' misplaced concern for their cars.

It took a continuous prowl through the Heights by Harry Brady, Peg Cafolla and the dozens of other cops and agents to build those cases one arrest at a time. But even the finest effort to call attention to the problem of crack—which I believe the Washington Heights effort was—ultimately fails when it is not attached to mandatory treatment and education.

There is no way for law enforcement to keep up the kind of pressure that we applied to Washington Heights. And that is what increasingly has troubled me about a law enforcement response to what is so clearly a social problem. Months after Peg Cafolla left the DEA—we couldn't arrange a transfer to Atlanta where her husband was put in charge of the Internal Revenue Service enforcement division—all four Ramos brothers pled guilty to charges of cocaine dealing and conspiracy to distribute narcotics. Two other members of the ring fled, and fourteen others pleaded guilty without trial. The case was that strong. But the effect on crack dealing was, in the long run, minimal, because Ramos, General Noriega, the heads of Cali and Medellín cartels in Colombia, are all easily replaceable if America continues to have an insatiable appetite for drugs. No cop with a gun will ever stop the craving, no occupying army can shut off the flow. Four years after the headlines subsided, a drive to Washington Heights told me all I needed to know about crack: "How many?" the kid with his fist driven into his jacket pocket asked.

"How much?"

"Ten dollars a vial," he said.

Police Commissioner Ben Ward's statement from the height of the epidemic, July 1986, still held true:

"The Bolivians are in part correct when they say, 'We grow coffee because Americans drink coffee, we grow coca leaves because Americans use cocaine.'"

FOURTEEN

"The White Line
Down Main Street"

Night-vision goggles dangling from his neck, features darkened by paint and wearing dark clothing to blend with the night, Special Agent Uli Delgado emerged from the upstate New York underbrush. Confident no one was home, he and Special Agent Fred Marano unscrewed the window frame of the expensive Mohawk River Valley farmhouse. A hospital maintenance man from Kew Gardens, Queens, had paid a local real estate agent who asked no questions $310,000 in cash and cashier's checks—a good 25 percent more than the market value and well beyond anything a New York City hospital worker could afford. Soon thereafter, monthly records for the farmhouse showed occasional sharp spikes of electricity use more consistent with cocaine production than the steady drain that was the signature of a working dairy farm. Caravans of cars arrived and left the farm in synch with the rise and fall of usage. Since their discovery of the curious real estate transaction, the agents painstakingly had gathered enough of these additional details to convince a judge in the spring of 1987 that a legal break-in was warranted. Uli and his partner would know for certain if, for the second time in a century, bootleggers had returned to the town of German

Flats. As they lifted the window from its frame, the agents were greeted by the sharp smell of ether.

Special Agent Bill Klein and Port Authority Detective Mike Molina, posing as corrupt customs investigators, lounged on the beach in front of their hotel in Rio de Janeiro. They were waiting for a man whose brother was a Pan Am customer service representative who took early retirement from his $23,000-a-year job at Kennedy Airport. Yet somehow the brother could afford to pay $375,000 in cash for a house in the Netherlands and $37,000 for the BMW he parked out front. Through an informant and an undercover operation at the airport, Klein and Molina had already pieced together the intricate details of a $1.5 billion cocaine-importation scheme that they thought ensured the man's financial independence. Now they needed to link him firmly to that scheme. For that, they had come to this resort capital, the headquarters of the Brazilian Mafiosi who converted the raw Bolivian cocaine base into powder to be smuggled into the United States. The agents had reached the head of the conspiracy, which, as near as they could figure, began in 1980 and by March 1987 involved more than fifty-three airline employees and seventeen gangsters. Most of the airline workers were U.S. citizens, all middle-class or working-class people, who used their jobs to help ship the cocaine aboard Pan Am, Eastern, Varig and Delta airlines to the United States. In return for corrupting the security of the borders they earned about $5,000 a shipment. As the under-covers watched, the Roman Catholic women of Brazil paraded in string bikinis locally known as dental floss. When asked why she didn't just go topless, one explained, "I am religious, that would be a sin." Chris Vanwort, the man the investigators were waiting for, didn't worry about such distinctions. Chris was a party boy, and for twelve days he had kept the two undercovers running day and night from bar to club to dance. Through it all, they asked him dozens and dozens of seemingly innocent questions. "You have a brother? What does he do? What do you do that gives you all this time to party?" the men posing as corrupt customs investigators on vacation asked as they and

Chris drank and danced. Finally, they won his trust. Seeking to impress Klein and Molina with his importance, Chris told them the truth. He explained that he had an important position in a drug-smuggling operation. He proudly pointed out that it was his elder brother Aart who had organized the ring. He grew expansive and said Aart had done it so cleverly that the two of them could live in luxury without any fear of being caught. His brother, Chris bragged, was the link between the sunbaked luxury of the drug lords and the runny noses of users in the United States.

That same spring, Special Agent Terry Van Tassel took her place among the fifty desks in the secretarial pool of the Wall Street brokerage house, flipped her blonde hair out of her face and watched the telephone. She had been hired as an off-the-books broker's assistant after she was told during the job interview, "We don't care what you've done before as long as it wasn't working for the FBI." It wasn't, she replied—truthfully.

"Do you party?" the employer asked as soon as she sat down.

"As a matter of fact, I do," she answered. "And I just ran out of stuff and I have a big party this weekend, do you think you can get me something?"

"No problem."

Terry Van Tassel could not believe her part of the job was going to be this easy.

Informants combined with a couple of years working undercover along the streets of the financial canyons of lower Manhattan had led the DEA to target this firm, Brooks, Weinger, Robbins & Leeds. By the end of her stint at the brokerage house, where cocaine was routinely used to woo clients and to clinch deals, Terry would watch her employers illegally manipulate customers' accounts to the firm's advantage. Business at this 300-broker firm was conducted on a rush of cocaine and with a complete disregard for ethics. In one instance, officials of a company the brokers were about to take public were given cocaine in exchange for $10,000 worth of the newly printed stock. The case against Brooks was called Operation Closing Bell. While the amounts of drugs seized at the firm were small, the abuse of customers' trust was large. And that corruption of trust was somehow worse; undermining a financial institution once called "reputable" by the *Wall Street Journal* was serious. The drug distributors involved in the case were very violent. The violence associated with their network ultimately led to the death of Special Agent Everett Hatcher.

Conducted beneath the leafy swoosh of upstate trees, to the thunder and screech of jets hitting the concrete sprawl of New York airports, in the company of the green glow of financial video display terminals, the cocaine trade had wormed its way into an acceptable part of rural, blue-collar and urban middle-class life.

As former Police Commissioner Ben Ward had pointed out, using cocaine, once the glamorous powder of Hollywood stars, had become as ordinary as a morning cup of coffee. If there had been any reason to doubt that drug money had been as readily accepted, these three cases showed otherwise. In each, the drug trade supercharged an economy and became familiar, like cheating on taxes, so otherwise law-abiding people felt comfortable in turning a blind eye for cash in hand. Cocaine abuse was epidemic, and with a duality of values that was frightening, large numbers of average citizens had become as responsible for making the drug available as the cartel bosses in Colombia.

In a market driven by the mass consumption of crack, an estimated five million people used the drug from inner-city neighborhoods, the suburbs, to the most rural reaches of America.

In New York State, the center of this cocaine marketplace, the demand for cocaine tripled in less than two years, sending the number of abusers rocketing from 182,000 in 1986 to 600,000 by the end of 1988.

To satisfy demand, ambitious cocaine dealers went into overdrive. Their multinational business grew to account for most of the $100 billion that our government estimated was generated by the sale of illegal drugs. Worse, a decade of ill-conceived, politically motivated law enforcement efforts, dating to then–Vice President George Bush's South Florida

Task Force—a costly land-sea-air interdiction failure—had not cut off supply, but merely encouraged suppliers to find new routes and to ship more cocaine to compensate for the occasional seizures. So much cocaine reached the streets that the drug's price in most markets dropped from about $85,000 a kilogram to $18,000. In New York and Miami the drug became so abundant that the cost of getting high had fallen even further. By the vial, a dose of crack and oblivion could be had for $2.

If Sherwood Anderson were writing *Winesburg, Ohio* during this half decade, George Willard, his Everyman on the verge of adulthood, would have looked out the window of the *Winesburg Eagle* and seen a white line of cocaine down Main Street. A line that had distorted values in the town as it would distort his when he followed it as a false path to sophistication.

The plague had been bubbling more than a decade. Back in 1973, I, and most law enforcement officials, were so deeply immersed in a war on heroin that when one federal agent, Pat O'Hanlon of the State Department, raised his hand at a lecture and asked me about the dangers of cocaine, I smugly replied, "Cocaine is not a problem." O'Hanlon has never let me forget it.

Added to our initial blindness to the growing, although still small, audience for cocaine, was the permissive attitude fostered by the Carter administration. Dr. Peter Bourne, prior to becoming Jimmy Carter's adviser on drugs, wrote in his article "The Great Cocaine Myth" that coke was "probably the most benign of illicit drugs." The administration adhered to that line of thought long after law enforcement officials saw the danger signs of addiction.

That attitude only contributed to the growth of cocaine use. By 1977, the number of its largely upper- and middle-class adherents had swelled. There were enough users to fill movie houses across the nation with an audience that knew to laugh at Woody Allen, whose sneeze in *Annie Hall* blew sparkling powder off a mirror.

Two years later, violence replaced slapstick. Dealers drove an armored van into Miami's Dadeland Mall, used sixty rounds of automatic weapon fire to execute a rival, then sprayed the parking lot with more gunfire to cover their escape. In New York, the growing number of Colombian homicides included the slaughter of a family driving on a highway. National attention was drawn to this grimmer aspect of cocaine: the intramural carnival of violence among the importers, distributors and longshoremen of the drug trade. They routinely ended disputes over profit or turf with machine gun fire. Demonstrations of force majeure that during Prohibition were reserved for an occasion as special as the St. Valentine's Day Massacre became all too common.

In New York, in the years after crack was crowned king of the illicit drugs, drug violence expanded to the shooting of law officers. This too was funded by the same otherwise law-abiding citizens who in town meetings and newspaper editorials called for more cops, more agents, more action while they sold the drug lords they publicly deplored property, stocks and the right to cross our borders.

"When is it going to stop, Bobby?" my wife, Lee, asked as she watched the violence grow. More and more, the telephone by our bed rang and the voice reported an agent or police officer was shot, stabbed or assaulted.

"Bruce Travers has been shot, it's pretty bad," the dispatcher said when I answered the telephone one September night in 1988.

The shooting took place right across the George Washington Bridge, a fast half-hour drive at night from my suburban home. It occurred on the edge of the crack-and-powdered-cocaine market of Washington Heights, a neighborhood that I and every other cop knew well. I pulled up to the shooting scene. The apartment building sported white turn-of-the-century globes, lighting the front. The slum-crowded, noise-crazed streets at the edge of Harlem were like another America. They were filled with the reverberations of sirens, radios, voices. It all sounded like broken glass. At 11 P.M. on the first day after Labor Day weekend, it should have been quieter, I thought, but what did I know? I had grown up in Providence, Rhode Island.

The shooting took place inside a third-floor apartment. Seventy rounds had been fired in the exchange between agents and the gunman. Bullet holes were everywhere and a pool of Bruce Travers's blood was drying in the hallway.

The guy who shot him had hidden in a hallway closet, and when Travers opened the door he opened fire. The slug from a .357 Magnum struck Travers in the face, knocking him down.

Somehow he was still alive.

I rushed to the nearby hospital. Travers lay in bed, alert, but unable to talk. The bullet had shattered most of the facial bones. He had just returned to work from a long, last summer weekend with his parents on Cape Cod and had gone straight on the raid. He was a kid from a New England family whose life now included a bullet from a Dominican illegal alien pushing coke for the Colombians.

"Hey pal, we're all really proud of what you've done. You are the best of what we stand for," I told Travers. It was the best I could do. It barely expressed the confused mix of pain and pride I felt.

Much later, after recovering his ability to talk, Travers said he wanted to go back on the job as soon as he was able. Full recovery took almost two years, but he went back. His description of the shooting and its aftermath still leaves me shaking.

"It was supposed to be a simple knockoff," he said. "It had been raining that day a bit, the streets were still a little damp. It was a nice night, a lot of people roaming around.

"The confidential informants and the two defendants went into the apartment building. The CIs, pretending they were buyers, had put the word out that they were looking for coke. Of course, these informants are working for us. They're good, they come from the neighborhood, everyone believes they're dealers, but they tell us everything they do. The defendants had met them the day before. The CIs thought they could get us a case with three or four kilos. They go in, make the buy. Then we go in and make the bust. They're in the building and we sit outside for about twenty minutes, waiting, which is normal. We get a signal. We get into the building as fast as we can, as quietly as we can. We don't know where they are in the building. We don't know who is with them. Obviously they don't tell us where beforehand to protect themselves from getting their drugs ripped off.

"I call out, 'We got the signal, let's go.' One team of two agents goes in front of me. Myself and my partner go in directly after that. Two guys behind us. The other two wait outside.

"The CIs are still inside the apartment. We're on the second floor. Two of our guys are in front of me on the third floor. And right then you could hear one informant talking loudly. Being good, and trained and whatnot, he's trying to let us hear his voice. It's dirty, not atrociously dirty, but your basic uptown apartment building. Nothing fancy. Nothing grotesque. The door opens. The CI is right there. And there's two bad guys with him. Two of our guys are right there. They immediately grab the guys. One of the guys had the defendants up against the wall.

"'Police! Nobody move,' I shout. I grabbed a guy who's against the wall. I pin him to the ground, give him a quick frisk. In the meantime the other defendant ran down the hallway.

"I can see this. I'm watching kind of out of the corner of my eye. I'm still on the third-floor landing.

"I hand this guy off to the agents coming up from behind.

"'Take him,' I tell the agents. Cause the guy is running into the apartment. Two of the agents have taken off after him. So I go in.

"I hear our guys yelling, 'Police, you're under arrest.'

"I see one of the agents standing in the hallway with his gun ready. If something ugly was really happening, he would have been in the midst of it too. But he was kind of sitting back.

"Well, at this point everyone has run by this closet. I'm pretty confident now that things are relatively safe down the end of the hall. I had a Berretta nine millimeter and my five-shot on my ankle; I carry it just for the sake of having it. I had my pistol in my left hand. My badge is on a chain around my neck.

"And I'm in the hallway facing the closet door directly in front of me. I grab the door with my right hand. It was just a closet door, a regular door. But you don't know what's behind there. That's the threat.

"So I open the door about halfway. I don't see anything. Just blackness. Mentally I know it's a closet, but for all I know it could be a room. So I peek in. I back away. That's the way we are taught. You back away to get out of harm's way. Then I start peeking in again.

"And I start reaching in with my right hand. I make out something like clothes hanging in the closet.

"And the second it hits me that it's a person, the bullet was fired. It's not like, 'Is that a person and then boom.' It's like: PERSONBOOM.

"I saw the flash. I heard the bang and I backed out of the closet and fell down in the hallway with my head facing down toward where the other agents were. I did like a pushup and tried to get up on my knees.

"And then I can see all the blood gushing out of the side of my face. You know, people ask you, 'Did you think you were going to die?' You say you were lying there bleeding all over the place, you didn't pass out. 'Didn't you think you were going to die?' Well, the thought of dying never entered my mind. It really didn't.

"My eye orbit was fractured in three places, it pulled my eye over. My entire cheekbone was shattered and removed. The doctors took all the pieces out.

"They brought bone up from my hip and put in three metal plates, one above my eye, one below my eye and one across my nose. The hole in my palate was initially the size of a fifty-cent piece. And I lost about a half inch off the length of my tongue. Then it knocked out about a third of my teeth and shattered my lower jaw, cracked it and fractured it in nine places. I have a metal jaw that's going to remain forever. The whole front of my mouth, the gum and all, was blown away. So now I wear a retainer. I put it in and it has a plug that plugs up that hole.

"After it happened, I couldn't get out of bed for a couple of days. The nurses wouldn't bring me any mirrors. I tried telling them, 'If I see a mirror I'm not going to have an attack.' Of course, they were worried because it was my face and if you have even a blemish on your face you think everybody in the world sees it.

"Finally, one day, I convinced one of the nurses to let me up to go to the bathroom by myself. Well, the bathroom was one way and I went the other way, I knew there was a mirror there. And I went and looked in the mirror. It wasn't pretty, but it was what I expected.

"The whole thing is, not to praise myself, but my physical appearance hasn't been that much of a big deal. I was never vain to begin with. I'm pretty happy about who I am and what I am. So I have a scar on my face. There's hockey players that look a lot worse. The whole ordeal is an occupational hazard.

"In the hospital President Reagan called me, he said:

"'No one knows better than you the plight that agents face and the scourge of drugs. Illicit drugs can't go on the way they are. You, standing up and fighting the battle in the front lines, are making a difference. And Nancy and I pray for you and we're indebted to you forever.'

"Politicians are politicians and they do what it takes to get the job done and they go for the best interest and whatnot. But when President Reagan can call me and President Bush, he was vice president then, can send me a letter, that means a lot to me.

"I've tried figuring it out. I've had more time to think in the last six months than I had in my life. It's more than a job because there's no glory in this. There's no great money in it. There's no great benefit. You might travel a little bit, but for the most part the low points are already the high points. Long hours, lots of driving, the headaches, the hassles. You do a good case and you get it thrown back at you by a defense attorney who tries to make you look like a liar and a criminal.

"I think I do it out of patriotism. I love the way America is. Sure it's got a lot of headaches, problems, things that are wrong. But it's like nowhere else in the world. I'm going back. When it's all squared away, I'm working again. This, obviously, what happened to me is the most affected by drugs anyone in my family has ever been."

To the casual onlooker, crack was the blame and the violence was urban. To my agents, the blame and the problem ran deeper. From their vantage point, the oft-expressed cry of middle-class users who insisted they harmed no one, and the even greater arrogance of the brokers and airline employees who knew they aided the cocaine cartels yet felt safe from the violent effects, seemed nothing short of despicable. Violence trapped the soul as surely as drugs captured the body.

Special Agent Uli Delgado finished removing the farmhouse window. He quietly rested it against the side of the house and slipped through the open frame. Inside, he stayed in a crouch until he was certain no one was home. Then he stretched, sniffed the air and followed his nose. Delgado quickly found what he was looking for: vats of sickly smelly green chemical broth, drying tables and ledgers. Smugglers had returned to German Flats, a perfectly idyllic and secluded section of the Mohawk Valley and a perfect location for a refinery.

Albany, the first port of call for the United Fruit Company's boats out of Central and South America, while a full day upriver from New York harbor, was only seventy miles east of this farm. The 150 banana boats that regularly docked were perfect vehicles to smuggle in drugs to be refined. The Great Lakes region and the St. Lawrence River to the north and northwest were other natural routes for cocaine arriving through the Midwest and Canada. Drugs could also be flown in or driven overland from Florida, where the raw cocaine was off-loaded and shipped north to be refined in order to avoid detection in the more heavily patrolled south Florida region.

The state police of New York's north country, the Canadian Mounties and the DEA were no strangers to the smugglers. Corsican heroin dealers had made good use of the region, and before them, bootleggers of alcohol and cigarettes. Smugglers had routinely outwitted the handful of law officers who patrolled it. The rugged region became the perfect place to manufacture cocaine once our own enforcement efforts forced the drug barons to cut back on refinery operations in South America.

In 1984, in an effort to reduce cocaine production in

Colombia, the State Department convinced South American governments to limit the importation of ether, acetone and any substitute needed to turn the raw product drawn from the leaves of the coca shrub into cocaine. The ban on imports pushed the Colombian price of ether from $1,400 to $10,000 a fifty-five-gallon drum. In the United States, the same fifty-five-gallon drum cost $250.

It became easier to buy farmhouses than ether. The B&V farm, located on the quaintly named Johnnycake Road, was a perfect example. Uli Delgado's look-see was the end of one phase of an investigation that had begun with a tip from an informer working at Kennedy Airport, and included real estate checks, telephone checks and manpower from task forces across the region, until finally the farm was identified.

Delgado was the perfect agent for the case. Cuban-born and Spanish speaking, he had spent much of his career in upstate New York, working as a narcotics cop in this same county before joining the DEA. He could understand the suspects and defuse the local suspicion of federal authorities.

He would now have to wait for a raid. The difficulty with cocaine labs, he knew, was they might cook cocaine twenty-four hours a day for a week or two, producing 2,000 pounds in the process, and then stop for a year. Other batches would be turned out at other farms to reduce the risk of detection. He also knew that if the DEA struck now it would not seize the drugs, chemicals and the operators needed to back up in court all the paper details of a conspiracy he had already gathered. The refinery was between batches. The agent summoned his patience and went back to his paper case, watching utility records and regularly driving by the farm searching for signs of activity.

While the farm had been purchased by a hospital maintenance man in Queens, a check of telephone records uncovered a number of calls to known drug distributors. An arrest in Miami of a known cocaine converter was also tied to the farm. Interviews with local residents drew out other tidbits. The dairy farm had no herd and there were no signs the land was used as a recreational getaway. As the case developed, the hospital worker put a deposit down on another farm. Ricardo

Villegas, a $17,000-a-year hospital employee, was clearly a front man.

The farm's lab was actually controlled by the upper management of one of the Colombian cartels, Delgado's paper chase determined. The farm was a factory for the distribution center in Queens that supplied the black, Puerto Rican and Dominican dealers of crack as well as the low-level Italian-American hoods who specialized in selling powdered cocaine to the middle class.

Delgado noticed the hospital worker's sick day record often coincided with the spikes in the use of electricity at the farm. In July 1987, Villegas began calling in sick at the hospital, giving Delgado and his team the tip they needed. They watched Villegas come up to the farm more frequently and stay longer. Cars came and went regularly. One day, a van pulled its back doors up to the basement doors. Chemicals and drugs appeared to be arriving.

Wiretaps were installed on the farm's telephones. Other taps were hooked to frequently called telephone numbers. Villegas was tailed on his trips from New York to the farm. During one 3 A.M. stakeout, Delgado, peering through his night-vision glasses, saw people in the driveway dumping heavy vats of chemicals. The odor of ether, not usually associated with a dairy farm, filled the air. Cooking had begun. Now was the time to strike. But was there enough evidence to get a warrant for a raid?

The agents discussed the issue, took it to a prosecutor who agreed that based on their knowledge of the drug-producing process and their observation of the unloading in the driveway, they had probable cause. A judge concurred and signed the warrant. Plans for a raid on the property were carefully drawn up by Fred Marano, the team's tactical expert. It took the entire complement of agents for the region, assisted by a task force of state police, FBI agents and county cops.

By the next day, the raiders lay outside the house and waited for Villegas. He arrived in a small car filled with ten bags of groceries. Once Villegas was inside, the raiders struck.

Delgado and Marano were the first in the door. They spotted Villegas and a woman, passed them to the troopers to be handcuffed and kept moving. In the basement, two men covered from head to foot in charcoal soot were standing at the bottom of the stairs. Delgado and Marano handcuffed them and noted the scales, charcoal-filled strainers and chemicals used to draw the finished cocaine out of the base. Drying beds, chemical drums and other manufacturing by-products were also seized. On the other side of the basement, six more men were spotted. Delgado shouted in Spanish for them to freeze, but they began edging toward a door. Just then, a backup team burst in and grabbed the six men.

It was 7 P.M. Agents had been staking out the house around the clock since the unloading was spotted in the driveway. Delgado and Marano were tired after the raid but they knew it was best to immediately begin the next phase. They knew they needed to analyze the charcoal for cocaine residue, search every room of the farm, review its ledgers and debrief everyone arrested. It seemed pointless to return to the office, so they went to sleep in their car for a few hours. When they awoke, Marano looked at Delgado and said, "Well, if we need to stay really long, we've got plenty of charcoal for a barbecue."

It would have been a costly one. The two agents would soon discover that the charcoal held all the cocaine. As a disguise during shipment from Colombia, the drug barons had impregnated the charcoal with raw liquid cocaine. The porous charcoal could absorb a great deal of the liquified drug—up to $25 million worth in the last batch produced, Delgado's analysis of records showed.

Eleven defendants went to trial in the case. All were convicted. That Delgado expected. But what surprised him, as it surprised me, was the assistance they had nationwide along the way; it was not just real estate brokers but corrupt chemical manufacturers, car phone installers who dealt drugs, and many others, who could never be charged, that had helped the conspiracy function. They were just regular citizens, in a cross-country chain of silence.

By the time the case was ready for trial, Uli Delgado determined that one of the key conspirators, Heriberto Torres, had used a RegalWare office in Miami as one business front, and had set up other offices in Chicago, Atlanta, Houston and San Francisco. Torres also set up an international finance company to launder the money the refinery operation generated and sent payment to bosses in Colombia. Some of the firms he set up are still doing business. The employees still claim Torres was, to them, an ordinary businessman, albeit one who generated an awful lot of cash.

Torres was sentenced to twenty-five years in jail, Villegas to twenty. The other defendants also received stiff sentences. None had been willing to cooperate with the investigation.

As Uli Delgado was putting together his case, Special Agent Billy Klein, Port Authority Detective Mike Molina, informant Ivory Hobson and a team of five more investigators patiently delved through their own mountain of allegations, phone records and airline computer jargon. Hobson, a one-time Pam Am employee, had explained the smuggling operation; now investigators were gathering the proof that would be needed in court.

When they were done, the investigation had unraveled a tapestry of greed that became known as the Air Cocaine conspiracy. It took them a year once Hobson began to help. Without him, it might have taken forever.

The case had been dormant since a 1983 bomb scare on a Varig Airlines flight prompted a check of the passenger list. Aart Vanwort's name popped up. Why, investigators wondered, did an employee with free travel on Pan Am choose to fly Varig? Ruled out as a suspect in the bomb scare, Vanwort became a suspected smuggler when the investigator's curiosity was supplemented by a few bits of airport gossip, that Vanwort lived well and seemed to travel an awful lot for a guy on a modest salary.

But there was no informant to get investigators inside the ring that somehow had rebuffed all other methods of attack—until January 1986. Then Hobson, who had the looks of a male model and the smooth patter of a disc jockey, was arrested in Chicago on federal drug charges. He wasted no time in trying to talk his way out of his sudden legal difficulty.

I can put you into a smuggling ring that moves tons of cocaine through Kennedy Airport using the passenger service representatives, the booking computers and the baggage handlers, Hobson promised. I know, I was a courier. Hobson's information was the missing piece that brought all the scraps of suspicion and airport gossip about Aart Vanwort sharply into focus. Hobson was placed in protective custody and became a federal witness instead of a drug suspect.

As detailed by Hobson, the smuggling operation Vanwort designed made cocaine-laden passengers, known on the street as mules, and luggage disappear without a trace. To make passengers vanish took but a little manipulating of the airline's computer. In a few keystrokes, there was no trace of the mule; instead, records showed the flight had carried one fewer passenger. Once at the airport, Vanwort's accomplices would help the ghost rider avoid any customs check, escorting him or her through a supposedly safe-from-infiltration set of employee corridors before removing the drugs and sending the mule on his way. When larger loads of cocaine, or marijuana, were delivered, the smuggling operation switched from using human mules to luggage. For that Vanwort developed a baggage carousel scheme. It required cooperation at both ends of the route—a caller who would telephone ahead the claim check number, and a baggage handler who would remove drug-laden suitcases before any search could take place. The handler could also substitute identical, but drug-free luggage in time for a check of luggage tags. The drugs, once again moved through the airport's high-security "Sterile Corridors," were later smuggled out of the airport by employees.

It was a perfect operation until Hobson confessed and the details checked out. The next year was spent with Hobson, the undercovers and prosecutors flying back and forth between Rio, the Netherlands, Miami and New York as they gathered the pieces that would tie together all the elements of the conspiracy and all of its members. This was aided by the covert recording of telephone calls and conversations between Hobson and the ring members. Then some time was spent sorting out the logistics of simultaneously arresting people who traveled with ease from Brazil, through Miami International and Kennedy Airport to the Netherlands, where there was no extradition agreement with the United States. Brazilian officials who cooperated with the investigation opted to prosecute their Mafiosi at home.

The majority of the arrests were ordered on a March day a little over a week after Aart Vanwort was quietly grabbed at his New York hotel. They went smoothly with hundreds of Port Authority police, local police and DEA agents grabbing employees at two U.S. airports.

By then Aart Vanwort was already talking. In some ways it seemed he had never stopped talking since the moment agents arrived at his suite at the Westbury Hotel and found him with his brother Chris snorting from a half ounce of cocaine.

"Remember us, Chris?" Molina and Klein asked. That Chris Vanwort was there was a bonus the investigators had not counted on.

"Yeah," he answered, "I was on vacation with you guys in Brazil." The brothers had just completed a shopping spree at Brooks Brothers and Barneys. The Vanworts must have tired of shopping. Aart still had $80,000 in his pocket when arrested. Bank records indicated that he had made somewhere around $10 million from his smuggling, $395,000 of which was found in a Long Island safe-deposit box.

In the aftermath of the raid and the arrests, many of Aart Vanwort's conspirators also decided to cooperate. They were middle-class people and, blind to the violence caused by the drugs they imported, they did not even consider themselves criminals. They would talk and talk to avoid jail at any cost, unlike the Colombians who know that to talk means death. Many of those arrested were let go, as they had played minor parts in the conspiracy and it seemed unlikely that they would cross into lawlessness again. A trial in Brooklyn federal court of six key co-conspirators ended with all of them found guilty on cocaine and conspiracy charges. Aart and Chris Vanwort pled guilty without trial, as did several others. Seven Brazilian members of the conspiracy were listed as fugitives. Seized computer disks indicated that the Brazilian Mafioso for whom Aart Vanwort smuggled had several other smuggling and distribution conspiracies going—wheels within wheels were turning. That was often the case in an operation where one conspirator was just a spoke of the wheel. Often he did not even know the other spokes on his own wheel. In this case, from the hub of Aart Vanwort the axle stretched across an ocean to the lab owners, who had several other axles stretching out to the United States and Europe.

Special Agent Robert Strang and Special Agent Dean Kiernan sat in the Wall Street bar, sipping cocktails and listening to the after-work chatter of brokers. The two boyish agents, with their tasseled shoes, button-down collars and stylish briefcases, had learned to plug right into the high-energy climate of the Stock Exchange bar where cocaine was spread with the same hushed respect as inside information.

They had already identified low-level dealers inside the stock clearing house of Depository Trust. They had identified dealers inside Brooks. They had even developed their own dealer who sold them ounces and gossiped about who else was buying on Wall Street.

The two agents had begun the case back in 1983 with occasional undercover forays into the financial district. The past year had been spent full-time undercover on Wall Street, posing as import-export brokers with their own real estate holding company in offices uptown on Madison Avenue. The magnitude of the dealing they discovered opened our eyes to the severity of the drug abuse problem and its impact on the world of very high finance. Strang, Kiernan and Special Agent Tom Pascarello had developed several conspiracy cases in the financial district. They had a small library of videotapes of brokers offering them cocaine at their Madison Avenue suite where a hidden camera had carefully been installed. Through tailing their own dealer, whose trust they had won with thousands of dollars in cocaine purchases, they had, early in the case, also worked their way back to a house in Bensonhurst, Brooklyn, where a vast quantity of drugs appeared to be available. They had developed a great deal of the paperwork in each of their conspiracies.

The agents had arrested the dealer and turned her into

an informant. It was now time to slip an undercover agent into Brooks, where the drug problem seemed centered, a part of the fabric of doing business that was condoned by top management.

They were talking to a secretary and some brokers at Brooks they had befriended when Terry Van Tassel walked in accompanied by their informant. Strang and Kiernan feigned surprise at seeing her. Van Tassel told the other undercovers that she was in the financial district looking for work. She sat down with the brokers and the two other agents, and soon after she did the brokers began wooing.

"We think we can get you a job where we work," one said. "If you're interested, I'm looking for somebody."

Van Tassel told him, yes, she was interested, and she had worked part-time at a brokerage house once before, but as a secretary, not a broker's assistant. The broker assured her it would work out fine. Once Terry Van Tassel began work at Brooks, the final pieces of that case came together within six weeks.

Earning $240 in untaxed dollars each week, she learned not only the extent of the cocaine use at Brooks, but the intricacies of how the firm violated security regulations. She learned to set up phony accounts in which discounted stocks could be purchased at the initial public offering, then sold when the security was released to the larger market, usually at a much higher price.

"Anything they could do, they were doing," Van Tassel later recalled. Each time she presented these apparent crimes to a U.S. Attorney she was coached on fresh aspects of criminal or civil code with which drug agents are not normally familiar. The brokers at Brooks were breaking every white-collar crime statute on the books.

"My whole picture of Wall Street went right down the tubes," Van Tassel said. "They were calling people who would trust their entire life savings to them, Mrs. Smith down in Oklahoma City, just to make a buck. And they didn't care about their own families either. If they were going to make a buck on Dad, they'd make a buck on Dad. 'We'll make him money next month, but this month Joe needs to buy such-and-such and he's got a customer that's willing to buy it at such-and-such price, and Dad's the only one that's got it.'" Dad, whether he liked it or not, would be selling that security.

When the closing bell sounded on April 16, 1987, sixteen stockbrokers were arrested, eight of them from Brooks. Financial records dating to 1984, the year the firm opened its doors, were seized for later civil actions. The police meanwhile announced that in the two weeks before the raid they had arrested, in coordination with the DEA investigation, 114 low-level dealers and buyers. These, at lunchtime and after work, transacted their illicit Wall Street business at curbside, hawking their offerings in much the same way as brokers from an earlier era.

Once again, most of the people arrested thought they did little to contribute to violent crime. They saw the wooing of clients with drugs as the normal course of doing business—no worse, ethically, than a three-martini lunch. They did not see themselves or their jobs, or the jobs of the small-time dealers they employed, as spinoffs of the lucrative cocaine economy. But that brownstone in Bensonhurst that warehoused a good portion of the drugs they consumed was at the center of that economy and the violence it spawned. When it was raided, ledgers were discovered that could link the money spent on Wall Street to a reign of terror in Staten Island and South Brooklyn. The house, its weapons and its drug wares were the mainstays of a loosely knit set of Italian-American criminals that included the man who killed Everett Hatcher.

FOUR

Aftermath

FIFTEEN

The Hunt for
Gus Farace

The murder took place on Tuesday night, February 28, 1989. At 10:02 P.M., Special Agent Everett Hatcher was caught by surprise and gunned down as he sat behind the wheel of his idling car in an empty intersection on Staten Island. His own gun, a semiautomatic pistol, stayed out of reach in the glove compartment. Thirteen minutes later, Special Agent Larry Hornstein found Hatcher's body and the hunt for the man who fired the four shots into him began.

Hornstein searched the shrubby area around Hatcher's Buick and began to feed urgent information to the DEA dispatchers. But by then, the killer, Costabile "Gus" Farace, had dropped his steel-barreled revolver onto his lap and sped off into the night in a tan van driven by his cousin, Dominick Farace. Though the cousins had only a short head start, the initial search for them was useless.

In the early stages, police officers hearing the alarm broadcast over their portable radios learned only the sketchiest information—Costabile "Gus" Farace's misspelled name and a description of the dark brown 1987 Lincoln Town Car he usually drove. Of the five agents in Hatcher's backup team, only two had caught shadowy glimpses of the cousins. The team could not provide a description of their clothing or appearance. The two who had seen the cousins, FBI man Dan Miller and DEA agent Claudia Pietras, also knew they drove a van, not the Lincoln Gus was expected to drive. But they had not mentioned this. Attempts to block Staten Island's roads to dark-colored late-model Lincolns with Florida license plates were futile.

When Miller and Pietras, still numbed by death, spoke up over an hour later, descriptions of the van, Dominick Farace's Corvette, and a mention of a second suspect, possibly Dominick, were added to the broadcasts. From Miller's notebook now came the addresses for the Faraces, the locations of bars, gyms and restaurants they frequented, and names of their associates. These had not been used during the backup team's hour-long search for Hatcher.

It was almost 11:30 P.M. Kevin Gallagher, my chief of operations and the man who took charge of the hunt, had organized dozens of agents, detectives and uniformed officers into teams. He handed out the few available pictures of Gus Farace and one of Hatcher taken from his wallet ID. Then he sent the teams around the quiet island, knocking on doors. Other agents and officers paired off to drive each side street looking for the van as well as for Gus's Lincoln and Dominick's Corvette. The blockade of the island was now as tight as could be managed.

One of the first raids was on the house of mobster Gerry Chilli, the capo who had befriended Farace during a stay in state prison. When agents pointed their guns at the door to 61 Sommer Avenue, Farace, gripping a AK-47 assault rifle with a thirty-round clip, watched the backs of the raiders from the safety of the apartment of Barbara Sarnelli, almost directly across the street. Chilli, who had been in New York for a wedding, had returned earlier in the day to Florida. Sarnelli was away in Florida for six weeks. Chilli's daughter, Margaret "Babe" Scarpa, had secreted Gus in the empty Sarnelli apartment. At age thirty-eight, Babe was a widow. Her husband, Alfred, had been killed in 1988 in a mob execution staged in a Manhattan bar. She had fallen for the twice-married Farace. He took advantage and had run to the capo's daughter for help. By doing so, he violated his second old-world mob law in one night: He had involved a woman in his crimes.

The first violation was killing an agent. Not really a surprise considering the world Farace came from. But Hatcher and his colleagues on the case were more accustomed to the ground rules laid down by Chilli's older generation of mobsters, a world in which professional gangsters did not shoot professional law officers. A new team of investigators, called into the case by Gallagher, would soon provide a chronicle of violence attributable to Farace's peers that made clear they were not old-world professionals.

That team, headed by State Police Senior Investigator Robert F. Donovan, over a period of five years had compiled a thick docket on this loosely linked network of young thugs, who called themselves the Wimpy Boys. The first clues to their network were all contained in the ledgers found in 1983 in the double-width brownstone in Bensonhurst, the one that supplied the drugs to Wall Street and was owned by a family named Fama.

Dozens of drug cases followed. The clan's father, Joseph Fama, was sentenced to thirty years to life in prison in one of the first. His wife, Toni Ann, their daughter, Barbara, and their sons, Gary, Danny, and Joseph Jr., were also convicted. One son, offered a reduced sentence in exchange for cooperation, told the prosecution, "My mother can do her time, I can do my fucking time." A fourth son was not prosecuted because of his youth. The first clues to the violence began two years after the ledgers were found.

"It all began with a fifty-watt radio station," Donovan explained, using the dry humor that earned him the nickname "Sunshine." For Donovan's investigators, the violence began with the murder of a low-watt hoodlum, Albert Nacha, in 1985, which showed that the marijuana business on Staten Island was more than the small-time peddling of dope by college kids. Donovan talked as he moved across his seventeenth-floor office at the DEA's New York headquarters. Then he slipped his slim, dungaree-clad legs beneath his desk and sat staring across the room. He wore a black T-shirt, his white hair pouring down toward his shoulders. His only decoration was the zircon stud set into his left ear. He had hard eyes.

Vintage rock music by the Doors drummed out of twin speakers he had perched on the sill of his picture window to spoil the bottom of his view of the Hudson River. A kicked and scraped waist-high refrigerator full of Rolling Rock beer was set against a wall decorated with his police and military memorabilia. His U.S. Marine Corps flag flew proudly over the refrigerator.

Above a low-slung, soft-sprung couch pushed against the far wall and facing his desk, an eight-by-ten-inch photographic icon of the heroin addict, long-spared by death of his need to score drugs, stared back at Donovan. He had been dubbed "Gloves" because his hands were swollen to the size of boxing mitts. Donovan liked to recall the maggots that thrived in Gloves's abscessed and bloated arms. A death Buddha for Donovan to contemplate while recounting the world of the Wimpy Boys.

Shot three times in the head and once in the chest at close range, Nacha's body had been found in 1985 sprawled face-up on the grass of Clove Lakes Park in Staten Island. A $5 bag of marijuana was pressed into one extended hand. The bag was a message carried by the corpse for anyone who sought to interfere with the Wimpy Boys' lucrative marijuana business.

The investigation into Nacha's death went nowhere for a while. Then an enforcer for Wimpy Boy chief Greg Scarpa, Jr., broke the arms of Eric Leon, a young drug dealer who had been late paying the fee on his street corner franchise. Detective Richie Puntillo visited Eric Leon in the hospital several times. Finally Leon agreed to help the government.

"It wasn't right," he told the detective. "It just was not right to beat me. I would have made up what I owed even though I thought it was unfair, I would have made it up, I would have just done twice as much business. They didn't have to beat me. That was ridiculous." The next time Leon visited the Wimpy Boys at their clubhouse, resting inside the cast that surrounded one of his damaged arms was a compact tape recorder.

By the time the Wimpy Boys DEA case file was complete

it listed their major accomplishments as the biting of a police officer's ear, the beating of another officer, baseball bat beatings of craven associates, hatred of "niggers," extortion from neighborhood store owners and fourteen mob homicides. Their criminal deeds were often performed for one of the region's five La Cosa Nostra crime families. They wanted to be made members, and their rap sheets were the scouting reports. Donovan said that if the crews had not been so deadly, their members would have been "nothing more than amoral caricatures" of gangsters, young wannabe hoodlums who seemed to have learned how to act by watching videotapes of the *Godfather* movies.

By the time Farace killed Hatcher, the Donovan team had prosecuted interconnected marijuana, heroin and cocaine organizations run by the Fama family, who were distributors; the Fortunato brothers, bulk marijuana suppliers; Teddy Persico, Jr., who was the nephew of Colombo crime family boss, Carmine Persico; and Gregory Scarpa, Jr.

Gus Farace, it seemed, had ties to them all, most notably acting capo Gregory Scarpa, Jr., head not only of the Wimpy Boys but heir to his father's powerful faction of the Persico-run Colombo organized crime. Scarpa, who was now known to be a relative of Babe Scarpa's dead husband, was a cousin of Farace's.

From his base in the Wimpy Boys Athletic Club, in Brooklyn, Scarpa had controlled a lucrative network of drug outlets in Brooklyn candy stores and on a Staten Island college campus. By June 3, 1988, when Farace was paroled from Arthur Kill Correctional after serving a manslaughter sentence begun on September 11, 1980, that business was a shambles and most of the ring's members were in prison.

Muscles pumped hard and augmented with steroids, Farace stepped from prison ready to inherit Scarpa's world and its marijuana, heroin and cocaine trade. Divorced from his first wife, he quickly married again and began to prepare for what he felt was rightfully his—a top spot in the drug trade and a dream that had languished for almost eight years of imprisonment: membership in the mob. With connections to both the Colombo crime family of his cousin, Scarpa, and the Bonanno crime family, whose capo, Gerard Chilli, befriended him in prison, Farace saw little to stand in his way. The government, suspecting this ambition and aware of Farace's ties to Chilli, began laying the groundwork for the drug case that we thought ultimately would lead to Farace's and Chilli's arrest. In early February, the case went sour.

The Wimpy Boy network sent word out from Arthur Kill prison that Farace should be wary of Hatcher. In the prison's shadow, Farace killed Hatcher, turning the first nine days of March a blur of grief and anger for the New York office of the DEA. Between making arrangements for Hatcher's funeral, conducting the manhunt for his killer, preparing for a presidential visit and catering to the media's need for explanations and updates on the whereabouts of Hatcher's killer, there was barely time for any of the 500 cops and agents to sleep.

For two days after the murder, raiders interrogated every Wimpy Boy connected with Farace, every mob associate who lived on Staten Island, employees of every business where Farace had spent any time, including the Narrow Bar & Grill, which was owned by his childhood friend Joseph Scalfani, and every relative of Farace's. A federal grand jury, empaneled immediately after the execution, took testimony from many of those questioned.

The task force set up to hunt down Farace was headquartered at the Staten Island detectives' office on Hylan Boulevard. "It's slow going," confessed Inspector Bill Wallace, the commander of those detectives. Gallagher, after forty-eight hours, countless questioning sessions and at least eighteen raids on mob-connected drug locations, also knew the manhunt would be long. Some of the grand jury witnesses lied, others genuinely knew nothing of the murder. Farace, wherever he was hiding, seemed well protected.

On Friday, the Lincoln and then the tan van were found. The Lincoln was registered to Chilli, and carried his Florida plates. The van came back through the computer as registered to Ralph Pollio, a neighbor of Gus and Dominick's who ran a small construction company out of his home. When questioned, he talked.

He confirmed that after the murder Farace had driven

the van, Dominick had followed him in the Lincoln, and the two had dropped off the keys sometime around 11:30. He said that Farace had laughed as he heard the keys clank against the bottom of the mailbox.

It was decided that for now Dominick would not be arrested, but he would be tailed closely. It was obvious that he had lied to a federal grand jury on Wednesday when he stated he was unaware of the events connected with the death of Hatcher.

By the start of the weekend, all telephones connected to Farace's associates were placed under electronic surveillance. Incoming and outgoing numbers were checked and the callers visited. A review was begun of telephone and beeper calls to, or from, those numbers in the hours before and after Hatcher's death. On Saturday, March 4, Hatcher was buried. On Sunday, ballistic tests showed that the gun used was a .357 Ruger with a stainless steel barrel. The bullets were probably Winchester. Right after the murder, Farace had handed the Ruger to Dominick, saying, "It's a shame to get rid of it." So he left that task to Dominick. After picking up Gus's Lincoln, the cousins returned the van. Gus drove off after dropping Dominick at his father's house. There, Dominick climbed into his Corvette and drove to his girlfriend, Doreen Perito, a bond broker who earned $113,000 a year. She was in bed. He began to undress and climb in.

"I hope you weren't with Gus," she said. A police friend of her family had phoned to say that Gus was involved in killing a cop.

Dominick panicked. He asked Doreen for the keys to her sister's yellow Mustang, parked in front of the apartment at 11 Kathy Place. Doreen refused. He slapped her, grabbed the keys, drove to the bridge over Fresh Kills and threw the murder weapon, underhanded, into the creek. He returned to Doreen's apartment in time to see her about to pull away in his Corvette. He stopped her. They went inside. Then Dominick realized he should also get rid of his own .45 caliber pistol. He asked Doreen to take it to another friend's house. Again, she refused. Again, he slapped her. She put the gun in her purse and carried it to Frankie Vigilante's home nearby. Dominick climbed into his Corvette, and as he sped off he called Vigilante on the car telephone to alert him of Doreen's arrival.

Stopping for a traffic light, Dominick spotted Gus in his Lincoln. He motioned for Gus to pull over, and behind the Burger King in the Staten Island Mall the cousins talked. Dominick told Gus he was certain that Hatcher, or the Colonel as they knew him, was a cop. "We're dead men, Gus, the feds will kill us."

"Calm down," Gus told him, "I'm gonna go low." He began laying the plans for his escape by getting rid of the Lincoln. With Dominick following, he parked behind some nearby condominiums. Then Gus climbed into the Corvette and had Dominick drop him at Gerard Chilli's house. Babe answered the door and let Farace in. She had been waiting for him patiently. She had not heard from him since she sent her telephone number to his pager at 9:42 and 10:05 P.M. Dominick followed Gus into the house about five minutes later and saw Gus and Babe sitting on the couch. At 9:42 Gus had been too busy debating whether to kill Hatcher to return her call. At 10:05, he was fleeing the scene. Babe was shaking her head in what Dominick thought was disbelief.

"I'm leaving," Dominick told Gus. Since Dominick had no dealings with Hatcher, he knew the feds had nothing on him. But before he left, Dominick gave his cousin all the money in his pockets—between $200 and $300—and said goodbye. It was the last time Dominick saw his cousin or had firsthand knowledge of his whereabouts. Dominick drove home and began a series of telephone calls aimed at covering his tracks. One of the first was to the owner of the Marina Cafe, Anthony Graziano.

"You know the place where you eat," Dominick said, in a cryptic reference to the cafe.

"Yeah, yeah," said Graziano.

"You know the kid who's always smiling? He was never there," Dominick said.

"What are you talking about? These phones are always screwed up," Graziano said. Dominick assumed he got the message but was acting dumb in case the phone was already bugged. Not one employee would ever admit to recalling the

visit by Hatcher, Gus and Dominick. Gallagher had anticipated this type of reluctance and throughout the first days of
the hunt bore down with relentless pressure on organized
crime in an effort to break the silence around Farace. The first
fissures were quick to show.

By Sunday, Gregory Scarpa, Sr., told David Krajicek of
the *Daily News* that the families of Farace and Scarpa were no
longer close. Although his first wife was Constabile Farace,
Sr.'s sister, Scarpa Sr. was seeking to distance his clan from
that of Farace. He pointed out that no one from his family
had gone to Gus's wedding a few months earlier to Toni
Acierno. He feared that a strong connection would send his
convicted drug dealer son, Greg Jr., to a federal prison too far
away to visit. The father was ailing, his power almost gone; his
son's influence limited by a jail cell.

"I feel that this type of thing shouldn't be," the old-time
mobster told Krajicek. "Once you start killing law enforcement
people, it'll be like a jungle out there...We need law and
order, bottom line."

The younger wiseguys, made brash by the successful
defiance that reputed Gambino crime lord John Gotti showed
when he defeated the feds in court and then conducted his
daily rounds despite their surveillance, felt no such allegiance
to law and order. Dominick heard on the street that the word
from these wiser wiseguys was, "If you can't stand the heat
from the feds and the cops then you shouldn't be wiseguys." It
seemed that at least the Gambino organized crime family felt it
could withstand the pressure brought by Gallagher. But against
the Lucheses, the Bonannos and the Colombos, whose ranks
were most seriously depleted and which relied heavily on easy
targets of official pressure—bookmaking, numbers—the crackdown would bear dividends. Each day the agents clamped
down a little harder on vice. My intention was clear: I wanted
Farace driven into the hands of my agents or thrust into the
hands of an angry member of the mob. If he could sign my
agent's death warrant, I was willing to sign his.

Dominick, in early March, and with permission from
parole, took a trip to the Cayman Islands. We thought he
might be headed for a meeting with Gus. Undercover agents

sat beside him on the plane. Another undercover agent was behind the wheel of the cab that picked him up when he arrived. At the hotel, his room was bugged and a team of agents occupied the adjoining suite. Dominick never saw Gus and our agents returned disappointed.

On Thursday, March 10, George Bush arrived at the DEA's Manhattan headquarters, shared a few private moments with Mary Jane Hatcher, then spoke to a roomful of disarmed agents while standing behind an armor-plated lectern.

"It used to be unthinkable to shoot a cop," Bush said, sounding a lot like the old-time mobster. "No longer. Today, narcotics agents are sometimes the first ones shot." Then he promised to intensify efforts against the drug dealers. "We've got to deliver some bad news for the bad guys—hunting season is over. The rules on our side have changed too." The 300 agents stood and applauded.

Within a few weeks eavesdropping devices were installed in a pizza parlor where Dominick worked. But investigators were too late to hear Babe Scarpa tell Dominick, two weeks after Hatcher's murder, where Gus was hiding. "He's across the street at Barbara's," Babe said. "What are we going to do?" Farace stayed in the safe house for most of the six weeks Sarnelli was in Florida. But by the time we raided the apartment, Gus had moved on. That would be the pattern throughout the manhunt. Leads would be found, surveillance set up, and always Farace would elude us. In the early days we were a few hours behind him. As the months wore on it seemed to Gallagher we were a steady week and a half late.

On April 5, the FBI helped us increase the pressure against Farace's mob associates. A racketeering indictment was unsealed against Gerard Chilli, his brother, Joseph John, Joseph John's son and several alleged accomplices, charging the ring with loansharking. The case had been sped up to help with the Farace investigation. In the indictment its members were alleged to have dunned the fishmongers of Manhattan's Fulton Fish Market—the wholesalers of seafood for most of the city—for 150 percent interest on loans. The loans ranged from $100 to $30,000. The case eventually put most of the ring behind bars.

It also served the purpose of cutting off a lucrative source of income. Nobody was going to be collecting debts once the indictment was unsealed.

A few days later we discovered that Dominick kept a hideaway apartment across the state line in New Jersey. He routinely commuted back and forth to it from his business on Staten Island, a technical violation of his 1987 parole.

On April 15, we decided to arrest Dominick and revoke his parole for this routine offense. Threatened with serving out the remainder of his prison sentence, Dominick Farace agreed to cooperate with investigators. His testimony was a major turning point in the case. He began by helping us reconstruct Hatcher's final hour, telling us the reason for the murder, and explaining how Gus Farace had purchased the murder weapon and his AR-15 assault rifle.

On April 20, based on Dominick Farace's information, Jeff Connelly, one of his Staten Island neighbors, was arrested and charged with illegally transporting guns. Federal prosecutor Charles Rose said that the government had learned Donnelly had supplied the murder weapon and AR-15 to Farace. During the course of questioning, Donnelly was routinely asked what he might know of the fugitive's whereabouts. "You can thank Gus for this," he was told before the questioning ended.

The same message was given to every parolee on Staten Island. Each one was pulled in for a hearing and told they faced the prospect of a parole revocation if they heard a word about Farace's whereabouts and failed to tell us.

"You can thank Gus for this," they were told, as were the dozens of mobsters whom our agents tailed as they attempted to complete their daily rounds. They were photographed going to a barber shop, their mistresses' beds, the corner store.

One racketeer, as he sat down for coffee, found an agent sitting across from him.

"You know how it goes," the agent said.

"Sure, you got a job to do," the racketeer said, as he sipped.

"Good, cause I'll be with you until he's caught or you guys kill him."

By May 13, neither had occurred. On a morning filled

with the warm promise of summer, I stood with Mary Jane Hatcher in a corner park in Boonton where her boys liked to play. I was there for the unveiling of a monument to her husband. When town officials pulled the blue tarp off, the monument was revealed as large rock with gentle edges. Set in a far corner of the grassy little plot, it was surrounded by a border of forty-eight red flowers and marked with a thick bronze plaque.

"Dedicated to the memory of Everett Emerson Hatcher, Special Agent, United States Drug Enforcement Administration. A resident of Boonton, New Jersey, who was killed in the line of duty, February 28, 1989, in the service of his country."

At midday we left the sunny park and walked to the nearby fire station for sandwiches, coffee, beer and soda. While Kevin Gallagher maintained a close relationship with Mary Jane Hatcher, I only saw her at ceremonial functions such as this. Her courage was compelling. A visitor to her house in the weeks after the ceremony told me he bit his lip as he sat in the kitchen and watched her little boy Joshua color a picture of a grassy scene. In the middle he made sure to place a great big rock.

On May 18, Dominick formalized his cooperation agreement and began giving formal statements that took twenty-three single-spaced legal-sized pages to record. These gave us another set of leads.

On May 24 we raided Gerard Chilli's house again, and this time he was home. Chilli greeted us in gold chains and a royal blue bathrobe with his name "Gerry" emblazoned across it in six-inch letters. His brother John Joseph pulled up in a Cadillac and, clad in a brown bathrobe emblazoned with his name, went to his side. Babe, wearing tinted sunglasses, was brought out of the house in handcuffs.

"Whatsa matter?" Gerry asked.

I leaned close to whisper in his ear, "You can thank the guy who fucks your daughter for this." The man who the morning after the murder had called Dominick to say, "Anything you need, remember I'm only a phone call or a plane ride away," was visibly unhappy. Through his involvement with Farace, Chilli now faced a racketeering indictment of his own and the arrest of his daughter on charges of harboring a fugitive. Fingerprints lifted from a simultaneous raid on Sarnelli's apartment across the street backed up Dominick's words that Babe Scarpa had harbored Gus Farace there.

Until now, Farace had enjoyed the protection of Chilli in his hiding. But the pressure had grown too strong. A few days after the raids we learned that the mobster had changed his mind. He put out the word in the underworld that he wanted Farace. Our strategy had succeeded, we thought, in cutting off Farace's avenues of escape. Fear of the Scarpas and the Chillis might drive Farace into the hands of the law.

In June, we had evidence that indicated otherwise. John Petrucelli, a mobster who had known Farace in jail, was executed at the Westchester County apartment of his girlfriend, Margaret Mary Murphy, the daughter of a retired cop. Once again, with a tip that Farace was being harbored by people who knew him since prison, we had begun to explore an avenue of investigation a little bit too late. The mob had arrived first.

After the Petrucelli murder, we could reconstruct another piece of Farace's travels. From Staten Island, he had gone to Brooklyn to find sanctuary for a short time with another set of friends and had set up the mail drops he needed to stay underground. From Brooklyn he traveled to the city's northern suburbs to connect with Petrucelli. Petrucelli, convicted of manslaughter in a mob-related Bronx bar slaying twenty-one years earlier, had served a long stretch in the tough confines of upstate Green Haven prison. Blamed for some infraction of the inmates' code, Petrucelli was about to be killed with a set of barbells in a weightroom brawl when Farace interceded, saving his life.

Petrucelli stashed Gus in a Bronx apartment for a time, then shipped him to Westchester. From there, sensing how hot a property Gus had become, Petrucelli moved him to a relative's cabin in Brewster, a secluded town outside of the city, in Putnam County. As Gus sat there in relative safety, Chilli, through sources of his own, had learned that Petrucelli was harboring the killer. "I want him found," Chilli had told his associates.

So did Toni Farace, who used the Brooklyn underground mail system to send her husband letters and money. "Life is so unfair," she wrote. "I don't know why God is doing this to us. Fate is cruel."

He wrote back in his own way. "I can't wait to get my hands on you," he told his pregnant wife. "I'm gonna rape you."

Chilli would soon begin to crack the mail system as well. But as a start, Chilli asked for a sitdown with Petrucelli. The younger man refused. "I don't want to meet without my boss," the recently made member of the Luchese family said. Mike Salerno, a Luchese capo, agreed to the sitdown and Chilli traveled to the Bronx.

"You took this guy, right," Chilli said to the two fellow mobsters. "We don't need a meeting to make this right. Get rid of the guy."

"I can't do that," Petrucelli said. "I owe this guy a lot."

By now, we had a team of surveillance agents in the Bronx. They saw Salerno walking down the street with two men. Later they would be identified from the surveillance photos as hitmen. The capos had reached a separate peace. The surveillance team was too small to cover all of the Bronx and Westchester, so the hitmen were unobserved when they arrived at Petrucelli's girl-friend's basement apartment in White Plains and opened fire.

Farace, learning of the hit, grabbed a weapon, fled his cabin and lived "Rambo style" in the woods upstate for several days, our informants told us.

The loss of Petrucelli was a serious blow to the Luchese family. He had done nothing wrong. He had stood by a friend and they had been forced to execute him because of Chilli's request. Then, as we put pressure on other associates through numbers obtained in a search of Petrucelli's apartment, one of them, Peter Damineo, cracked and killed himself.

This was a more serious problem for the mob—Damineo, like Petrucelli, was an earner, bringing in thousands a week from lucrative numbers spots. Farace was not worth this cost. By midsummer, Farace's mob ties were frayed and his prison network shattered. We felt Farace soon would have nowhere to run. So we tightened the vise another notch.

Even as we stepped up the pressure, we were running out of leads.

A $280,000 reward on Gus Farace's head had still not turned up any takers. Those loyal to Farace couldn't be swayed by money, mob violence or the threat of prison.

One ex-prisoner who had served time with Farace explained it for us: "I'm serving two lifetime paroles. I was a weightlifter inside, we all stood together in the can. We were all in for homicide—$280,000. I'd never do it for that. If I knew and I knew you knew I knew, and I might lose my parole, I might think about it for that, but I really don't think I'd do it. You don't understand. You never lived in that rough a place."

Still, each arrest, each questioning, each death, made it harder for Farace to survive.

Summer turned to fall and we arrested Toni Farace on a marijuana conspiracy charge that predated the Hatcher murder. It was a case that could have been brought anytime, I suppose, but having kept her under surveillance even as she gave birth and still finding no trace of her husband, we felt the arrest might help.

It didn't. October passed. It was time, I decided, to visit John Gotti, the reputed top mobster in America. My retirement was completely in order and in a desperate bid to bring Farace either to justice or into the hands of the mob I broke all the rules that bind a federal agent. I drove to Queens one day to knock on the door of the reputed boss of the Gambino organized crime family.

I had told no one of the visit. I wanted my agents held blameless should anything go wrong.

As I parked my silver Riviera a block and a half away from the crime lord's simple Howard Beach home, I scanned the quiet streets for signs of the FBI and police surveillance teams that routinely patrolled there, gathering videotape of Gotti's visitors. It was the last thing I needed. I saw none, took a deep breath and walked down the middle of the cool, empty pavement to the don's doorstep.

As the screen door opened soundlessly, I listened for Gotti's guard dog. I heard no growl, but caught a glimpse of Gotti's wife's raven hair as she peered from an upstairs window, a woman whose wrath was said to be as fearsome as the don's. Her young son, bicycling down the street, had been killed a few years earlier by a luckless motorist. The motorist, a neighbor who ignored warnings to move, who ignored the whisperings that Mrs. Gotti's grief had caused her to swear revenge, was soon seen struggling in the grip of two burly men who tossed him in the back of a van and drove off. He has not been seen since.

Gotti answered my knock clad in a beige bathrobe. His silvered hair was already swept back in a flawless mane.

"John, do you know who I am?" I asked.

He nodded. "Yes. How can I help?" he said.

"Our guy got whacked, I've been bringing pressure. You know how much it costs you in business. John, do what's right or the pressure isn't going to get easier."

He nodded, and keeping his hands in his bathrobe pockets said, "There is little I can say, but of course, I'm sorry."

"Farace whacked our guy. If you hear where he is, let us know. We want him."

He nodded, but this time said nothing as he stepped backward to close the door.

If Gotti started getting personal visits from the head of a federal agency, maybe he, like Chilli, would change his mind about Farace. Maybe this mob don would also decide Farace was better off dead. But later I heard through informants that the mob underbosses passed the word that Gotti told them privately that he didn't give a damn for the life of a federal agent and he didn't care if the heat didn't let up. "You wanna be wiseguys, you gotta take the heat. It's part of doing business," they reported Gotti said. We kept the heat on high.

We also returned to pressuring a small network of people very close to Gerry Chilli. "We want Gus," we told them. "Tell him his wife is facing jail time and won't be around to raise his kid."

Chilli also pressured them. "I want Gus," Chilli told one of them. "Tell him we have got to talk."

We went to Dominick Farace's father, Frank, and told him that word might get out that Dominick was cooperating. "If Dominick has a problem, you have a problem," we told him.

"I disowned him," the father replied.

"You try telling that to Chilli," we said. "A lot of other people have had problems because of Gus."

The last thing the mob capo would want was a witness

able to testify that he might have been connected to the case that led to Hatcher's death.

The vise was now as tight as it could go. Frank Farace reached out for Gus's mailman, Louis Tuzzio, and said he needed to meet Chilli right away. On November 8, Tuzzio flew to Florida and met with Chilli.

Tuzzio caved in and decided to deliver Farace to the mob. Tuzzio, through the months Farace had run, was the safety net, keeping him supplied and informed in each hideout. Tuzzio knew that with the pressure mounting he couldn't ask Farace to come to Brooklyn without Gus suspecting Chilli was behind the request. Instead, Joey Scalfani, a childhood friend of Gus's, told Farace there was mail waiting. He would accompany Gus. Scalfani had harmed no one, so his presence would keep Farace relaxed.

After the hit on Petrucelli, Farace had moved again, to Manhattan's Upper East Side. This time, a young woman he had once saved from assault, Donna Marie Nicastro, helped hide him. A real estate broker, she knew that Gus had killed a cop. But the man she sent him to, Julio Bofill, a small-time hustler, did not. All Bofill knew was that his new roommate would pay more than a fair share of the $800-a-month rent on a studio apartment at 305 East 85th Street.

But on November 18, the mailman summoned Farace. Gus watched the ending of *The Godfather,* and shut off the VCR and got dressed. With a .38 caliber revolver stuck in his waistband, Farace was driven to the meeting by Scalfani, who was also armed. Farace sat double-parked in front of Tuzzio's mother's apartment building on 81st Street in Bensonhurst and waited for Louis Tuzzio to arrive.

A blue van swung fast around the corner of 18th Avenue onto 81st Street and pulled abreast of the double-parked white Pontiac. The van was so close to the passenger door that there was no way for Gus Farace to open it. He rolled down the window to talk with the men in the van, men he knew, since one of them was Tuzzio. They responded with gunfire.

Scalfani, pressured or tricked into luring Farace to his death, had been promised he would be spared if he stayed calm. But Scalfani, who admired Farace, changed his mind at the last minute and tried to pull his gun and get out onto the sidewalk and safety.

Another gunman, waiting on the corner for just such an occurrence, stood up next to the park bench where he had sat patiently and opened fire with a .45. The range was long and the bullets merely creased the roof of a parked car, but they pinned Scalfani, enabling the gunmen in the van to successfully get a few rounds into him.

Scalfani crawled down the street, half collapsing in his own blood while the van sped off, its occupants having expended sixteen rounds from .380 caliber and nine millimeter pistols. Eleven rounds found their mark in Farace's face, chest, neck, spine, right arm, upper abdomen, pelvis and buttocks.

A young Bensonhurst woman, who was snapping gum when investigators found her later, rose from behind the car where she hid when she heard the gunfire break out. She had been walking down the street when the assassination took place. Now she did what any right-thinking Brooklyn woman would do. She got up and walked over to the scene of the carnage, decided the convulsing and dying Farace was beyond her wit and walked over to deliver her last rites to Scalfani.

"You must be some kind of fucking asshole to get yourself into a mess like this," she said, smiling down on the bleeding relative of one of Gotti's closest aides, Butch Corraro.

Scalfani smiled back as if he understood, and he would have laughed if he could, she told detectives. He survived the gunshots, but her words held true. Scalfani was indicted by the federal government. One by one, everyone in any way connected with Farace, his life on the run and his execution has been indicted by the government or wiped out by the mob. Tuzzio, the last, was killed three weeks after the Farace hit.

The next day, at the local precinct, where detectives who worked the Farace case now were hunting his killers, I performed my own last rites.

"He died the way he lived, in the gutter," I said at a press briefing. I tried not to smile. Federal agents are not supposed to applaud mob executions. But I was glad he was dead; he didn't deserve a trial. I turned my back on the war of drugs with that thought. It had taken the killers I had hunted to complete my final act in the war on drugs. Through them, I had killed a criminal, and I had discovered that I didn't mind at all.

INDEX